Galena
Bay
Odyssey

Ellen Schwartz

Galena Bay Odyssey

Reflections of a Hippie Homesteader

The author wishes to acknowledge that Galena Bay lies within the traditional territories of the Ktunaxa, Okanagan, and Secwépemc Peoples.

Heritage House Publishing Company Ltd.
heritagehouse.ca

Cataloguing information available from Library and Archives Canada

978-1-77203-445-5 (*paperback*)
978-1-77203-446-2 (*e-book*)

Edited by Jesse Marchand
Proofread by Renée Layberry
Cover and interior design Jacqui Thomas
Cover images by Ellen Schwartz and Jacqui Thomas

The interior of this book was produced on 100% post-consumer, acid-free paper, processed chlorine free, and printed with vegetable-based inks.

Heritage House gratefully acknowledges that the land on which we live and work is within the traditional territories of the Lkwungen (Esquimalt and Songhees), Malahat, Pacheedaht, Scia'new, T'Sou-ke, and W̱SÁNEĆ (Pauquachin, Tsartlip, Tsawout, Tseycum) Peoples.

We acknowledge the financial support of the Government of Canada through the Canada Book Fund (CBF) and the Canada Council for the Arts, and the Province of British Columbia through the British Columbia Arts Council and the Book Publishing Tax Credit.

27 26 25 24 23   1 2 3 4 5

Printed in Canada

We were naïve ...
but it was the kind of naïveté
the world needs.

—AN AMERICAN SOLDIER FIGHTING WITH THE
REPUBLICANS IN THE SPANISH CIVIL WAR

For Bill—
then and always

In memory of Michael Lesnik

Contents

Introduction

On June 20, 1972, my boyfriend, Bill, and I loaded the last box of provisions—homemade granola, wheat germ, brown rice, lentils, powdered milk—into our green Volkswagen Beetle, squishing it in beside our sleeping bags, tent, and duffel bags of clothes. Then we drove north from Pennsylvania to the Canadian border. We were part of a commune that was moving to British Columbia. We were leaving the United States, the country of our birth. We were going back to the land.

What was I, a nice Jewish girl raised in an affluent home in the suburbs of New York, thinking? Why was I doing such a thing?

Well, it was the 1970s. Vietnam. Watergate. Psychedelics. "Turn on, tune in, drop out," as Dr. Timothy Leary put it. All over North America, young people were rejecting the middle-class, corporate, establishment, militaristic values of their parents and governments, and were choosing a simpler, purer lifestyle. Along with my peers, I believed that by dropping out of the consumer society and becoming one with nature, I would change the world.

That was one reason. The other? I was in love. I was following my man.

A year earlier, after graduating from the University of Wisconsin with a bachelor's degree in special education, I had gone to visit a friend, Paul, who was living on a hippie commune in southeastern Pennsylvania. The members shared a ramshackle house on a large farm in Bucks County. Their goal was to pool their money, move to Canada, and buy land in the mountains of British Columbia.

I did not share these goals. My boyfriend of four years had just broken up with me. I was heartbroken and rootless, and Paul's invitation, to help out on the Farm for the summer, came as a lifeline because I had no idea what to do next. I figured I'd hang out for a couple of months, look for a teaching job, and mend my bruised heart.

But during that summer, I fell in love with Bill, one of the commune's founders. After a few months, I knew I couldn't live without him. Bill was moving to BC, so I faced a choice: I could either give him up or join the commune.

I joined the commune.

In the summer of 1972, five members left the States in our two jointly owned vehicles—Bill and I in the Beetle, the others in a newly purchased Chevy three-quarter-ton pickup truck.

I was terrified. I had no clear idea of what "going back to the land" entailed. I was a city girl. My interests were music and art, literature and dance. I had never gone camping, had done little hiking, had never wielded an axe, or a saw, or a shovel. The idea of moving across the continent to dwell in the wilderness, clear land, build a cabin, and possibly live without electricity or running water or an indoor toilet nearly paralyzed me with fear: *It's Canada—won't it be freezing cold? What about wild animals? Will I be strong enough to do the physical work? What about money? How will we live?*

I kept my fears to myself and pretended that I was just as enthused about going back to the land as everyone else in the commune.

Soon after we arrived in British Columbia, the commune split up over a disagreement about where to buy land. Bill, Paul, and I bought twenty acres of second-growth forest in a place called Galena Bay in the West Kootenay region of BC. Galena Bay was thirty-five miles from the nearest town to the north, and thirty miles from the nearest one to the south, on an unpaved road. There was no town there, no electricity, no stores, no services; it was simply a landing where a ferry crossed Upper Arrow Lake. When we bought the land, we became the ninth, tenth, and eleventh residents of the entire valley.

Paul soon realized that the homesteading lifestyle wasn't for him, and opted for life in town. But Bill and I lived in Galena Bay for eight years. Over that time, we built a cabin, sauna, root cellar, tool shed, woodshed, and outhouse; raised honeybees and chickens; grew amazingly productive gardens; learned to snowshoe and cross-country ski; became friends with our far-flung neighbours; and had encounters with bears, martens, skunks, deer, and cougars.

To my amazement, I loved the lifestyle. I found that I *could* do the physical work—in fact, I enjoyed it. I didn't mind the isolation. I loved learning about gardening and building and livestock-raising; about astronomy and ecology; about foraging for healing herbs and planting by the phases of the moon. I loved the slower pace of life. I loved knowing that every day was filled with productive activities, activities that fed us or kept us warm or expanded our notion of what it meant to live lightly on the earth.

Those years in Galena Bay brought Bill and me closer together. We left Galena Bay in 1980 for what was supposed to be a one-year hiatus. We never lived there again. We didn't change the world, but we did change ourselves. And we had a wonderful, meaningful, adventure-filled time along the way.

Beginnings

The 1960s

November 1963. I'm fourteen years old, in the ninth grade at Myles J. McManus Junior High School. On the morning of November 22, I'm in algebra class with Mr. Waldstein, a middle-aged, balding man with a big schnozz who resembles the entertainer Jimmy Durante. When Mr. Waldstein's back is turned, my classmates and I doff imaginary hats and wave around imaginary cigars, imitating Durante. Mr. Waldstein never notices.

"Consider this equation," Mr. Waldstein says, writing on the board $ax = b$. "How do we determine what x is?" He turns around, chalk dust speckling his lapels, surveying the class. "Ellen?"

I know the answer. Although I'm not a natural math student, preferring English and languages to math and science, I find algebra interesting and satisfying. In this case, I know that the solution is $x = b/a$.

As I'm walking to the board, a crackle comes over the loudspeaker. "Excuse the interruption. Something terrible has happened." The school secretary's voice shakes. "There has been a shooting in Dallas. President Kennedy has been shot. It is not known whether he will live." She gives a cry. "School is dismissed."

I stop, chalk in hand. Thirty students sit there, stunned. Silent.

What? Who? Where? The president—shot?

A sob draws me out of my stupor. It is Mr. Waldstein. Tears stream down his cheeks. He removes his glasses and buries his face in his hands. His shoulders shake.

I drop the chalk. Not bothering to empty my locker, not giving a thought to the half-finished lesson, I run out of school. I find my friends. Arms around one another, forming a tight circle on the sidewalk, we hug, weeping.

No one has any words of comfort. There *are* no words of comfort.

Letting go of one another, we stand there, silent except for our sobs. We turn in different directions and start walking home.

As I trudge down the street, images flash through my mind. JFK and Jackie at the inaugural ball—both impossibly gorgeous as they dance in each other's arms. Kennedy on the deck of his sailboat, his thick brown hair tousled by the wind. Robert Frost reciting "The Gift" on the steps of the Capitol—how cool is it that JFK had asked a *poet* to read at his inauguration? Caroline and John-John, the two most adorable children in the world, hand in hand with their dad.

After boring, staid Ike and Mamie Eisenhower, the Kennedys are a breeze of modernity. Young and glamorous, they represent everything exciting and sophisticated, everything I want America to be. Everything *I* want to be.

But my infatuation isn't only about the glitz. Jack and his brother Bobby, the Attorney General, have introduced civil rights legislation, promising to overturn two centuries of racial inequality. Kennedy has started the Peace Corps. And he has stood up to Nikita Khrushchev, that fat little blustering tyrant, forcing the Soviet leader to withdraw his nuclear missiles from Cuba. ("We will bury you!" Khrushchev had boasted, predicting the triumph of Communism over democracy. Oh, yeah? We'll show you—and we did.)

Tears streaming down my face, I remember the words Kennedy spoke at his inauguration: "Ask not what your country can do for you. Ask what you can do for your country." As I sat with my family watching the speech on our small black and white television set on that January night in 1961, I felt that the president was speaking to my generation. To *me*. I thrilled to those words, and I silently vowed that I would live up to them. I would join the Peace Corps, or I would work with poor people, or I would march to ban the bomb, or I would hop on a Freedom Bus and register Black voters down south.

I knew that, at fourteen, I couldn't do any of these things—yet. But I would. Someday.

Now, as I run into the house and throw myself on my bed, all of that hope, all of that idealism, is gone. Wiped out by a gunshot in Dallas.

When I look back, I can see a line from that moment on November 22 to my decision, nine years later, to leave the United States. It's not a direct line, and it's not the only reason. But the assassination of JFK was a turning point. It marked the beginning of my loss of faith in America, in the historical truths I had been taught to believe, in the sense of security and confidence and pride I had always had in my country.

For the first time, I began to question everything: *Who says we're the greatest country in the world? Why is America so violent? Why are we going to war in Vietnam? Why are we polluting our environment? Why is everyone so obsessed with making more money and having more things?*

Of course, it doesn't take a national cataclysm to evoke disillusionment in teenagers. It's a normal part of growing up. And, to be sure, through the rest of my high-school years, I wasn't obsessed with these questions. I had a normal life: boys and school, dance classes and friends, rock 'n' roll and hours-long gossip sessions on the telephone.

But underneath, I was questioning, questioning.

Family life

Born in 1949, I grew up in Linden, New Jersey, a suburb of New York located about twenty miles from Manhattan. My parents, Ruth and Bernard Rosenberg, were well educated and prosperous. My father, initially an internist, later specialized as a cardiologist. My mother briefly taught high-school French before becoming a stay-at-home mom to me, my younger sister Audrey, and my little brother David.

We lived in a large, new, split-level house with my father's medical office downstairs. Reproductions of paintings by Renoir and Cézanne hung on the walls, French colonial-style furniture graced the living room, and classical music wafted from the stereo.

There was nothing remarkable in that. In the post-war period, white families like mine were flocking to the suburbs, moving into new housing developments, and experiencing upward mobility. What *was* remarkable was the speed with which this prosperity had been achieved.

My ancestors, impoverished Jewish immigrants who had fled the hardships and pogroms of Lithuania and Poland, could not have imagined such affluence when they sailed past the Statue of Liberty in the early 1900s. They squeezed into already overcrowded tenements in the Lower East Side, where life itself had the bittersweet inflections of the Yiddish language they spoke.

From the garment sweatshop and the soup kitchen, they slowly moved upward. By the 1930s, my mother's father had taught himself the plumbing trade, started a small company, worked hard, saved, and moved the family to New Jersey. Although my father's father, a furrier in a department store, remained poor and died young, he too gave his family a better life than they would have had in Poland.

When my parents married, my father was still in medical school. They had very little money, and it was only through the generosity of my mother's parents, who bought them a car, allowed them to live rent-free in their home in Linden, and helped finance my father's first office, that my parents were finally able to build the split-level house in Sunnyside, a newer, nicer neighbourhood across town.

My father's medical practice prospered, and our family became, if not wealthy, comfortable. My father drove a Chrysler New Yorker. My parents had seasons' tickets to the New York Philharmonic and the Metropolitan Opera. Every fall my mother took me to Saks Fifth Avenue to buy school clothes. I had piano lessons (which I hated) and dance lessons (which I loved). Audrey and I attended a summer arts camp on Martha's Vineyard Island, Massachusetts. I went with my parents (happily) to art museums and (unhappily) to classical music concerts. We dined in good restaurants. I ate steak and lobster.

All through my childhood, I accepted my family's affluence without question. I vaguely understood that other people had less, had to work harder, struggled more, but it didn't mean much to me. When my brother David was born (Audrey was four and I was eight), my mother hired a "nurse" (read: maid) to help out. Bertha, a light-skinned African American woman with stiff, curler-set waves, arrived every morning in a white uniform and sensible shoes. I never knew her last name, or what her home life was like, or how she felt about coming up to Sunnyside to look after my brother. I never thought to ask.

Bertha seemed genuinely fond of David, and of Audrey and me, and often I found her in the kitchen enjoying a cup of coffee with my mother. *It's good of Mom to sit down with her like that*, I thought.

But, of course, Bertha didn't sit much. She fed David his bottles, changed his diapers, washed and dried and folded our laundry, helped my mother get supper ready. At the end of the day, she left to catch the bus and return to her home on the other side of town, where, presumably (although it never occurred to me at the time) she repeated all the same tasks for her family.

Seeing Bertha work so hard while my mother snuggled with David, or talked on the phone, or took a nap pricked in me a vague feeling of unease.

"Does Bertha mind working for us?" I asked my mother.

Looking surprised, she shook her head. "She's happy to have the job."

"How come we have so much and Bertha doesn't?"

My mother smoothed my hair behind my ear. "That's just the way it is."

"It's not fair, is it?"

"No, you're right, Ellen, it's not. But that's life."

The feeling of unease didn't entirely go away, but I soon forgot about it. We were lucky. Other people weren't. That was life. Meanwhile, I enjoyed the clothes, the summer camps, the pride (and snobbery) that came with being Dr. Rosenberg's daughter. When I grew up, I imagined, I would marry someone handsome and successful and continue my comfortable life.

At school, I was a model student. Bright and curious, I was a voracious reader from an early age. A good little American girl, I believed everything my teachers taught me. The United States was the greatest country in the world. The Soviet Union was our evil enemy. (I had no idea that the USSR had been our ally a mere decade earlier.) The Soviets wanted to take over the world and force Communism down everyone's throats.

I had no clear idea of what Communism was, but I knew it was bad, something to be feared and resisted. When I imagined the unlikely but horrifying scenario of the Communists conquering America, I pictured soldiers herding us into concentration camps, like in the Holocaust pictures I had seen from World War II.

If Nikita Krushchev was the enemy, then John F. Kennedy was our hero. I was eleven in 1960, the year JFK was elected, and to me he was the emblem of America: handsome, brave, young, and modern. He would lead us into the glorious future—until that fateful day in 1963.

Now, everything about my parents irritated me. Their lifestyle, which had always seemed so full and satisfying, appeared empty. What was life all about, anyway? Two cars in the garage? The mink coat in the closet?

"How can you kill all those baby minks?" I railed at my mother when she snuggled into the coat, on her way to a New York soirée. "It's just a snob thing to wear a mink coat anyway."

"You're right. It *is* snobby. It's also warm and cozy on a cold night."

"Hmphf." I didn't want to hear any rational reasons for wearing fur. I just wanted to be right.

I switched arguments. "I'll never go to the beauty parlour like you!"

"Never say never, Ellen."

"I won't! It's such a waste of time. All those ladies just sitting around and gossiping. There are more important things to do."

"Just a minute now. I volunteer for Audrey's Girl Scout troop."

"Girl Scouts!" I said disdainfully.

"And I help out at the synagogue fundraisers."

"Synagogue!" Everyone knew religion was just brainwashing.

My mother rolled her eyes. "Well, what would you have me do?"

There was the rub. I didn't know. Something. Anything. March for civil rights. Sign a ban-the-bomb petition. Shun the beauty parlour and have ugly hair as a political protest.

I began to listen to the news. Everything horrified me. Infuriated me. Confused me.

The US was sending "advisors" to Vietnam. Then troops. The government said that we had to shore up South Vietnam because if we let the

Chinese-backed North Vietnamese overrun the South, the domino effect would result in country after country falling to Communism, and then Communism would take over the world.

At first, I believed this. But stories began to trickle out, first on the radio, then in horrifying images on television, of American planes bombing Vietnamese villages, compounds going up in flames, women and children and old people running for their lives, falling, burned or shot.

We didn't look like the good guys.

Then it became personal. My junior-year boyfriend, Norm, who was a few years older than I, received his draft notice. I became hysterical, imagining his body blown to bits, the American flag draped over his casket. (In fact, Norm was in no danger of getting drafted, since he helped to support his widowed mother. But that didn't quell my angst. Secretly, I was the tiniest bit disappointed when he received his deferment. There went my chance to be a martyr.) Still, the war had become real in a way it hadn't been before, and I began to wonder: *Do we have to be there? Why aren't we winning? Is it possible that our government is lying to us?*

When Bob Dylan—my favourite songwriter—castigated warmongers and arms dealers in "Masters of War," I chanted along righteously. By the time I was fifteen, I had changed my position.

"The domino theory is a crock," I announced to my parents. "The government just wants to make war."

"So we shouldn't defend South Vietnam?" my father said. "We should just let the Communists take over?"

I didn't have a good argument for that. It was true that the North Vietnamese looked just as ruthless as we did. The ambiguity made me uncomfortable. I wanted black and white.

Civil rights gave me Black and white—pun intended.

When four little girls were killed in the firebombing of the 16th Street Baptist Church in Birmingham, Alabama, I cried for days. "How could this happen? What kind of terrible country is this?" I sang "Birmingham Sunday" along with Joan Baez and vowed that I would do something to change things. I just didn't know what.

Young people, both Black and white, began to ride "freedom buses" down south to register Black voters. *Yes! That's what I can do.* I imagined sitting on a bus full of righteous northerners, singing "We Shall Overcome."

Then three civil rights workers were murdered in Mississippi. *Oh my God.* This wasn't just protest; this was peril. I didn't go.

Thankfully, I still had my comfortable fallback: dumping on my parents.

Linden was a typical Eastern Seaboard town, evenly divided among low-income Black families who lived, literally, on the other side of the tracks; white, blue-collar families who worked in New Jersey's many industrial plants; and upper-middle-class, professional families like mine. My parents had no Black friends. In fact, they had no contact with Black people other than the series of maids who came in to clean our house once a week.

Thinking about that reminded me of Bertha. She was long gone from our lives, but I squirmed as I remembered how blithely I had taken for granted her role in our family. One night at dinner when I was about sixteen, I threw my liberal-minded Democratic parents who supported civil rights a withering look.

"It was terrible, the way we treated Bertha."

"Who?" my father said.

"Bertha. David's nurse. Remember?"

"Sure, I remember, but what about her?" my mother said, confused.

"She came up here to work for us, and you probably didn't pay her much, and then she had to go home to the other side of the tracks, and I'm sure her house wasn't nearly as nice as ours, and it's not fair!"

"I paid her a fair wage," my mother said. "I pay all our maids a fair wage."

"It's not fair that they have to be maids in the first place!"

"You're right," my mother said. "But let's face it, Ellen, most of these women don't have much education. They don't qualify for other work. Don't you think it's good that they have this job?"

When she put it that way ...

I switched topics. "You would hate it if a Black family moved into our neighbourhood!"

My mother raised her eyebrows. "Where did that come from?"

"It's true, isn't it? You talk about equality, but you'd freak out if Black people actually lived next door."

"It's not likely to happen," my father said drily. "Most Black families in Linden couldn't afford a house in our neighbourhood."

"But if they could—"

"We wouldn't mind," my mother said, "but I don't think it would be much fun for them, being the only ones. Most people want to live with others like them."

"See? You're prejudiced!" I shouted, triumphant.

In my last two years of high school, my righteous ardour cooled. I put my guitar away and stashed my folk music albums at the back of the closet. I listened to The Beatles, Motown, the Stones, the Doors. Had boyfriends. Went to dances. Wore heavy black eye makeup and pale lipstick, like Twiggy. Wore my hair in a teased, curled flip. Read *Seventeen* magazine.

In short, I became exactly the sort of shallow, popularity-seeking person I had disdained only months before. Well, not entirely. I still had ideals.

Still wanted to fight for a better world—only, someday, in the future. Not right now. Now was for having fun.

Love and education

In 1967, I started college at the University of Chicago. Oh, the freedom! Away from my family, away from boring Linden, away from the rules, the restrictions, the expectations: don't raise your voice; don't speak your mind; don't be disrespectful; excel at all you do. Now I was free to do whatever I wanted—whatever I could get away with.

The first day in my dorm, I met Kate Julin, a short, funny, athletic blond from Seattle. Kate had a sarcastic sense of humour, like me, and we quickly became best friends. She was the perfect partner because she was more daring than I was. If I hesitated, Kate said, "Come on, let's try it." Fearfully, I would try it, and course it—whatever it was—was great fun. Every Friday night, we paid upperclassmen to buy us vodka (the drinking age was twenty-one in Illinois), mixed screwdrivers, and danced on our desks. (And then threw up side by side in the bathroom down the hall.)

Three important things happened to me that first semester. I began to think—*really think*—for the first time ever. I fell in love. And I began to get high.

The university had just introduced a multi-disciplinary course for freshmen that combined literature, social sciences, philosophy, and history. I had enrolled in it, and so had Kate. We ended up in the same section. At our first class we were discussing Thucydides' *History of the Peloponnesian War*. I had read the assigned fifty pages—or, rather, my eyes had scanned the words—but I had no idea what they were about. The author detailed battles and cited generals and troop movements, but what was he saying? What was I missing?

"Thucydides is a political realist," said a tall, bespectacled student, leaning back in his seat with his long legs stretched into the aisle. "Without pandering to emotion, he brilliantly analyzes the power politics behind events on the battlefield."

"He's saying that the relations between states are a construct of national self-interest," said a girl with frizzy hair.

The professor nodded. Other students nodded.

I darted a panicked glance at Kate. *What the hell are they talking about?* I mouthed.

She shrugged.

For the first time, I worried about my academic performance. I had achieved nearly straight A's all the way through high school. I was a National

Merit Scholar. But now I realized that I had succeeded only by regurgitating the right bits of information, not by thinking in any rigorous way. That was not going to cut it here. My professors were not content with *what, where* and *when*; they wanted to know *how* and *why*. How does modern social science relate to the formation of gangs? Why is the Peloponnesian war relevant today?

For our end-of-year assignment, we had to choose a topic and write a paper. I decided to analyze the role of the Fool in *King Lear*. As I pored over the text, wracking my brain to come up with something intelligent to say, I began to see that the Fool was actually wise—wiser, in many ways, than the master he served. The Fool spoke the truth. The Fool saw beneath the surface. He pointed out Lear's failings and foibles. And that was why the king kept him close: because the Fool was the only one, aside from Cordelia, whom the king could trust to be honest, painful as those truths were to hear.

Somehow, thirty pages poured out of me. I sat at my new Olivetti electric typewriter—with a correction ribbon!—and wrote and wrote. I received an A on the paper, and from then on, I couldn't learn enough. I discovered Greek philosophy, plunged into the histories of Western and Eastern civilizations, devoured French literature. I fell in love with ideas, with the thrill—the goosebumps, the surge of energy, the catching of breath—that came at the moment of understanding.

"Do you know what I learned in Western Civ today?" I said to Kate one day as we sat in a campus coffee shop. "During the Industrial Revolution, the French peasants didn't want machines to come in because they would take away their jobs. So they threw their wooden shoes—their *sabots*—into the gears, to make the machines break down. And that's where we get the word *sabotage!*"

"Far out," Kate said, brushing back her hair as a handsome student (or maybe a teaching assistant) entered the café. "And get a load of this. The water cycle wouldn't work without gravity to pull the precipitation back down to earth. So biology and ecology and physics are all interconnected."

"Heavy," I said. I paused, then squeezed her arm as a new thought struck me. "Kate, it's all one."

We gazed at each other, wonderstruck.

Ned Levine (pronounced Le-VINE) was a fellow freshman, from Milwaukee, Wisconsin. I met him just before Christmas vacation when a dorm-mate hung a branch of mistletoe over her doorway. Ned and I kissed. Sparks flew.

Ned was incredibly handsome, with blue eyes over a prominent nose. He wrote poetry, loved the Doors and Cream (as did I), played touch football, and was a great kisser.

I felt sexual longing when he touched me, and I yearned to feel the real thing. I knew that some of my new girlfriends were having sex, and I wanted to be in that club, too.

With ridiculous ease, I obtained a prescription for the Pill, then a relatively new contraceptive.

The first time Ned and I made love, it hurt only a little. It felt wonderful—not the actual penetration, which felt weird, like an overlarge, questing tampon—but the closeness, body to body, skin to skin. *So this is love!* I thought. I didn't reach orgasm the first few times, but I felt mild pleasure and, more important, knew I had pleased Ned. So brainwashed was I that that was what I thought my goal should be.

Now I was sexually active. Experienced. I walked around campus with a knowing thrill. *Look at me. Can you tell? I'm a woman!*

Soon I did find real pleasure, and began to understand that sex wasn't just about pleasing the man. Sometimes, in class, just thinking about Ned, I tingled, and couldn't wait to meet up with him, hoping that one of our roommates would be out.

I figured Ned was The One. I imagined that we'd go through our four years together and eventually marry.

Back home in Seattle during Christmas vacation, Kate smoked pot. She came back to Chicago a convert. No more alcohol. Booze was passé. Getting high was better.

As usual, I was hesitant. *Will it feel weird?* Or, more important, *What if I don't feel anything?*

She convinced me to try it. One night, Kate, our friend Chase, and I closeted ourselves in Kate's dorm room and passed a joint. I smoked cigarettes at the time, so the act of inhaling was familiar, although this smoke was sharper, more acrid. Copying the others, I held it in as long as I could, then released it in a cloud.

I thought I felt a mild buzz, though clearly I didn't feel as much as Kate and Chase, who were cracking up over the look on each other's faces as they held in the smoke. It was pleasant enough. I thought Jimi Hendrix's "The Wind Cries Mary" sounded slightly strange, more *there*, somehow.

The second time I got high, I was with Ned. The frozen shoreline of Lake Michigan became a moonscape, and it was only his pulling me back that stopped me from walking out onto the lunar dust. And, yes, "The Wind Cries Mary" definitely sounded different. There were whisperings and echoes, layers of sound I had never heard in a piece of music before.

It was wonderful. It was a revelation. So this was what the beat poets were talking about. This was what The Beatles were singing about on

Sergeant Pepper's Lonely Hearts Club Band. Time moved in a different rhythm. Ice cream tasted more delicious. Everything was funnier. Or sadder. Just *more*.

Soon my friends and I were getting high several nights a week. We'd sit in a circle, Kate, Ned, Chase, Ned's best friend, Terry. As the joint came around, we held our breath with the one who was inhaling, smiled at the smile that crossed that person's face. I was convinced that no group of friends had ever been so in tune with one another. *My tribe.*

Early in our sophomore year, Kate dropped acid.

"How was it?" I asked.

"Amazing. Fun. Mind-blowing."

"Not too weird?" My mind was filled with recent newspaper reports of hallucinating kids jumping off buildings, believing they could fly.

"Weird, but in a good way."

"Like pot?"

"No. Sharper. Clearer. More mysterious." When I hesitated, she said, "Come on. You'll love it, I promise."

Ned, Kate, Terry, and I gathered in Kate's room. She held out her palm. Four tiny white pills nestled there. Exchanging a look, we each took one and swallowed it down.

Then we waited. And waited. After half an hour, when I hadn't felt a thing, I said, disappointed, "I guess this isn't going to work for me."

"Whoa," Ned said. "Did you see that?" Pointing to a Cream "Disraeli Gears" album poster on the wall. "Those flowers just bloomed."

"No way—" I began. Then the hot pink and red and orange flowers surrounding the faces of the band members moved. They wiggled ever so slightly. They spread out as if opening to the sun. "Oh my God."

I looked at Terry. His blue sweatshirt turned purple. Then back to blue. He pointed at my shirt. I supposed he was seeing the same thing on me. We grinned at one another, then burst out laughing. We rolled on the floor, holding our stomachs.

"Let's go outside," Ned said, and, in a moment, we had run out to the middle of campus and were turning somersaults on the lawn.

"There! The wiggly orange lines! Did you see them?" Kate shouted.

"I saw a shooting star!" I said. "Or did I really see it? Was it just in my mind?"

"It doesn't matter," Ned said.

"You're right!" I said. It didn't matter. All that mattered were the colours and the light and the air and the grass and these friends. I pulled them into a group hug. "I love you guys!"

Later, we went back to the apartment that Ned and Terry had moved into, where we'd painted the living room walls in iridescent turquoise and yellow designs. Sprawled on cushions on the floor, we listened to music: first, loud, driving Led Zeppelin; then bluesy Super Session; then, to help us come down, mellow Donovan.

As the psychedelic wore off and our fingers twitched from the amphetamine, we smoked a joint to smooth the edge, and talked. And talked and talked. What was the purpose of life? What could we, as individuals, do to improve the condition of the world? Did art matter? Was spirituality relevant anymore?

Then, philosophy exhausted, we jumped up, laughing. Without a word, we fetched the paints and started embellishing the colours on the wall, adding flowers, vines, swirls, blobs, spirals.

We stood back to admire our work, then sank back onto to the cushions and resumed our conversation as if we had never left off, sometimes flinging our arms around one another, feeling almost that our souls were touching.

"You were right," I said to Kate as we sat at the window, watching the sun rise. "That was mind-blowing. And don't even think of saying it—"

"I wouldn't dream of saying I told you so."

We laughed and hugged.

My friends and I smoked pot and hash, and did acid, MDA, psilocybin, and other hallucinogenic drugs throughout our college years. I know that some young people ran into trouble with drugs, but for me they were never a problem. I never felt overwhelmed or paranoid or had a bad trip. On the contrary, drugs, especially hallucinogens, showed me deeper levels of life. They made me think but, perhaps more important, they enabled me to perceive the beauty and mystery of the world *without* thinking. To simply be in awe of everything around me.

And they were a hell of a lot of fun.

The late 1960s were a time of political turmoil on American college campuses. The 1968 Democratic convention in Chicago, at which young people protesting the war in Vietnam were beaten and arrested by the police, made students see themselves as a cohesive group united in opposition to The System. (I wasn't in Chicago that summer but wished I had been there to feel the camaraderie and suffer for the cause. How glorious a broken arm would have been!) Across the nation, students were marching, sitting in, burning draft cards, and sometimes rioting in the streets.

In 1969, four students were shot and killed by National Guardsmen during an anti-Vietnam protest at Kent State University. The image of a young woman cradling her friend's dead body, splashed across newspapers and television screens, brought back the Kennedy assassination for me, and I wept, feeling despair and anger.

Along with my friends, I attended a march through the University of Chicago campus, where students with megaphones made speeches denouncing Nixon and the National Guard and the war and the police and political parties and everything else.

"Off the pigs!" someone shouted, and several people took up the chant.

"No!" I said. "You can't fight violence with violence!" But no one listened.

"Give peace a chance!" someone else yelled, and people started singing the Lennon song.

I joined in, but once again, as I had in high school, I felt impotent and frustrated. Killing police officers wasn't the answer. Neither was singing protest songs, or signing petitions, or staging sit-ins. How did you get the government to listen? How did you stop a war?

In 1969, I transferred to the University of Wisconsin. (My purpose was to be a dance major, but, after working at a summer camp for who were then called "brain-damaged children," I switched to special education.) That summer, in protest of the university's ties to the Dow Chemical Company— which manufactured the napalm the US was dropping on Vietnamese villages—radicals tossed a bomb into the chemistry building, killing a graduate student. His death tormented me. Didn't the protesters realize that their tactics, however nobly inspired, were despicable?

In the fall, anti-Vietnam protests turned into riots. Students broke store windows and overturned cars on the streets of Madison. To me, the protesters were just as bad as those they condemned, and I stayed away from the demonstrations. Yet I was torn. American society had to change, and I suspected that the radicals were correct when they argued that the necessary changes would never come about through the gradual democratic process. But I preferred civil disobedience to violence; I saw myself as siding with Martin Luther King rather than with Malcolm X. From my apartment in Madison, I heard the shouts of the students and smelled the tear gas. I closed the windows. I was ashamed not to be out there with them, yet turned off by their approach. Once again, I felt like a hypocrite.

Although Ned transferred with me to the University of Wisconsin in 1969, our relationship began to fall apart soon after we left Chicago. I knew that he felt hemmed in, pinned down; that he wanted more freedom. I wanted more commitment. I suspected that he was cheating on me with one of our housemates. But I didn't confront him, didn't ask.

I was too afraid to hear the answer. What would I do if he told me the truth?

I was jealous—but felt guilty. It wasn't cool to be jealous, not in the liberated ethos of free love. I echoed the correct sentiments—"Love is selfless. Love is not possessive"—but I didn't mean it. Ned and I separated for short periods, usually at his suggestion. Just as I was getting used to being on my own, he came back with tender, erotic poems, and we started all over again.

I found some comfort with a new friend, Paul Galewitz. A frizzy-haired, bearded fellow, Paul was a guitar whiz whose playing reminded me of that of John Fahey—mellow, meandering, virtuosic. His smile revealed a chipped front tooth that gave him a vulnerable, endearing expression. When he looked at me, the warmth in his eyes beamed through his wire-rimmed glasses.

Paul was shy, especially with women. Perhaps because he had met Ned and me together and knew I was "taken," he and I were able to avoid romantic innuendoes and quickly become friends. He called me Ellie, an endearment I loved.

Paul came from a well-to-do New York family. Like me, he was some-what embarrassed about his parents' affluence and considered their lifestyle excessively materialistic. We often talked about our desire to live differently, to contribute to a change in global consciousness. Neither of us knew how to achieve this. But somehow, when he played his guitar, hugging it close to him, an inward-facing look in his eyes, I heard hope in the chords. Sometimes, after playing a particularly beautiful passage, he looked at me, and a communication passed between us, an unspoken shar-ing of our deepest goals.

All this meant that I found it easy to talk to Paul. I discovered that, beneath his reserve, he had a dry sense of humour. He was an inveterate punster: "This is a great bird sanctuary. Toucan just tell." "I used to work at a knife factory, but it got dull." "I'm reading a book about anti-gravity. It's impossible to put down."

I was the only one in our crowd who laughed at Paul's jokes. I don't know why they tickled me. They were, without fail, groaners. I loved his quiet delivery, the way his eyes sparkled behind his glasses while he waited for the punchline to hit.

Paul graduated in 1970, a year ahead of me. He moved out to Oregon, where he became friends with a guy named Michael Lesnik, who was living in Oregon with his wife and young son. When Michael and his wife split up, and Michael moved back to his home state of Pennsylvania and started a commune in Bucks County with his best friend, Paul fol-lowed. He and I wrote letters back and forth. He told me about his travels, and I told him about my studies, carefully skirting my failing relationship with Ned.

On a sweltering day in June 1971, along with thousands of other students, I sat on a folding chair on a football field in Madison, sweating under my cap and gown at my graduation ceremony. I duly went up and received my bachelor's degree in special education.

Inside I was in despair. Two weeks before, Ned and I had broken up for good. He had told me that he didn't want to be with me anymore. He wanted to travel, to bum around the West. He wanted to be free. I was devastated. In spite of all the signs, I had held on to the hope that we would work it out, find jobs in Wisconsin, and eventually marry. Now what? There was nothing to keep me in Wisconsin. But where would I go? What would I do?

Certainly, I was *not* going back to live in my parents' house in Linden. For one thing, where would I get high? For another, I couldn't stand the scrutiny. And for another, Linden was too boring, too suburban. But what else could I do?

The day after graduation, as I packed up to leave, a letter arrived from Paul. I tore it open.

Dear Ellie,

I'm living on a commune in Newtown, Pennsylvania. There are six of us here. We're renting the old tenant farmers' house on a 100-acre farm. The owners of the farm live in the original "masters'" stone house up the hill.

The owners don't work the land, so we have planted several acres with asparagus, peppers, melons, and corn, and are selling the produce at a roadside stand. Most of us work at jobs outside the farm. Only one member, Jon, works on the farm full time.

We are living communally, pooling our money, sharing the house and farm chores. We have decided to move as a group to British Columbia, Canada, as soon as we have enough money saved—probably by next summer. Officially, to live here in the house, you have to be a member of the commune and be committed to moving to BC. But Jon needs help working the crops, so if you wanted to be a farmhand, we would make an exception for you, and you could stay here for the summer. The house is pretty ramshackle, but we could fit you in if you didn't mind sleeping in a little alcove next to the bathroom.

What do you think?

What did I think? I thought that this sounded like salvation. Like a life-line. That it gave me somewhere to go, something to do, at least for the short term.

So when my parents asked me, "What are you going to do next?" I said, "I'm going to visit Paul and work on a farm for the summer. After that, we'll see."

In early July 1971, on a hot, humid, hazy morning, I arrived at the Farm.

The Farm

Welcome to the Farm

In July 1971, Paul picked me up in Newtown, Pennsylvania. As I slid into the passenger seat of a beat-up grey Corvair, I spied the road through a hole in the floor.

"Nice car," I said, and Paul laughed.

"Yeah, this was a hand-me-down from Michael's parents," he said. "We're getting rid of it. Buying a truck."

Dust swirled up through the hole as we drove past fields of shoulder-high corn. Paul turned down a long, straight driveway lined on both sides with silver-green poplar trees whose branches pointed skyward like ballerinas' arms. We stepped out of the car beside a red barn. Crickets sang in the afternoon heat. In the distance, I heard the rumble of a tractor; nearby, the whinny of a horse.

Paul held out his arm. "Welcome to the Farm, Ellie," he said, smiling over his granny glasses. There was his chipped front tooth, peeking at me like an old friend.

I looked around. On the downhill side of the driveway lay a field of low green bushes that Paul said were soybeans; on the uphill side, knee-high meadow grass rippled as a gust of air stirred it. From the barn, a path led to a large, stately stone house.

"Is that where you live?" I asked.

Paul chuckled. "Not quite. That's the manor house, where the owners live." He took my suitcase, and I shouldered my rucksack. "We rent the tenant house, down at the bottom of the hill. It's ... well, you'll see."

He led me over a corral fence and across a downhill-sloping pasture. Two caramel-coloured horses trotted over, sniffed at us, then ambled away. At the lower end of the pasture, he held apart two strands of barbed wire while I squeezed through, and then I did the same for him. We walked across another field, past thickets of wild blackberry vines and oak trees measuring nearly three feet through the trunk. Beside the soybean field was a large stand of corn, and, beyond that, an expanse of hardwood forest. From somewhere in the woods, I heard the sound of rushing water.

Another house came into view. This one was old and worn-looking, its boards the brownish-grey hue of weathered wood. Tall and thin, it looked like a dowdy centenarian with its collar buttoned up tight. Several gables jutted out at odd angles, like eyes peering in different directions.

Paul opened a door on the lowest level, and we entered the kitchen, which was partly dug into the hill. Our shoes rang on a slate floor. The enamel sink was chipped, and gallon jars of beans, rice, lentils, and granola stood on open shelves.

"Odd to have the kitchen in the basement, isn't it?"

Paul motioned toward a fireplace. "It's from when meals were cooked over the fire."

"Wow, this place must be really old."

"Yeah, from the early 1800s."

I noticed a bead curtain that separated a small alcove from the rest of the kitchen. "What's that?"

"Bill's room."

I pushed apart two strands. The entire floor space was taken up by a double mattress. A lamp, candle, roach clip, incense holder, and a few books filled a small shelf beside the bed. Psychedelic posters adorned the walls: Janis Joplin with swirling bands of colour emanating from her head. Jefferson Airplane, with Grace Slick got up like an Egyptian goddess in a long red gown. Monstrously large and misshapen magic mushrooms.

"Not much privacy," I said.

"True," Paul agreed, shrugging. "That's how it is in a commune."

Great, I thought, wondering what it would be like to make love while someone fixed a grilled cheese sandwich on the other side of the beads.

Paul led me up a steep, winding staircase into a large living room on the main floor. Beat-up couch, couple of easy chairs with protruding stuffing, several guitar cases, books, stereo, at least a hundred records. On the wall, a picture of Jimi Hendrix with electric hair, and a poster of Meher Baba with shoulder-length curls and the most beatific smile I'd ever seen, over the caption DON'T WORRY, BE HAPPY.

Off the living room was another small alcove, empty, and past that, the bathroom. The bathroom walls were purple and green, and the toilet was black. I looked at Paul questioningly. "Well, we did this acid a few months ago ..."

We both laughed.

We went up another winding staircase to the top floor. There were two bedrooms. "This one's mine," Paul said. I peeked in. There was a mattress on the floor with a rumpled sheet on top. Beside it, a wooden crate held books, songbooks, guitar picks, tissues, and a few water glasses. Clothes were strewn on the floor.

"I see you've become a neatnik," I teased. Paul had always been a slob, careless of everything except his guitar.

"Yeah, well, deftly changing the subject ..." Paul pulled me out of his room and pointed to a door at the end of the hall. "That's Michael and Vivianne's room."

I mentally counted. "I thought there were two other people here."

"Yeah, Jon and Aileen. They're part of the commune, but they don't live here. Not enough room. They rent a house in Buckingham—that's about half an hour away—and Jon comes over every day to work in the fields."

"Uh ... Paul?" I said.

"Yeah?"

"I notice everybody's got their own bedroom. Is it—I mean, I know it's a commune and all ..."

Paul smiled. "Not anymore. When I first came, there were more people here. We decided to try this open-sex thing, like in *Stranger in a Strange Land*. You know, no attachments, no jealousy, sleep with whoever you like."

"And?"

"Well, it was fun, especially for single people like me." He shook his head. "But it didn't work. People *did* get jealous. So we went back to couples."

Whew, I thought. In theory, I supported the idea of open relationships. But the thought of doing it in real life made me squeamish. If I had a boyfriend, I'd want him to myself. I knew it was unhip to be so traditional, but that was how I felt.

Paul led me outside, to where a multi-coloured hammock hung between two oak trees. "Bill made this," he said, pulling out the edge of the hammock so I could climb in. "In Mexico."

"Really?" I was impressed. The hammock was large enough for three adults, and woven in an intricate pattern of pink, yellow, purple, and green fibres. *This Bill must be an interesting guy.*

Paul climbed in and lay facing me. Pulling a rope, he made the hammock rock like a cradle. It was shady and cool under the oaks. The creek hummed, and birds warbled. I decided the Farm was going to be a nice place to live.

As we rocked, I said, "So how did this place get started?"

"Well, it was really Michael and Bill," Paul said. "They were childhood friends. All through college, they wrote letters back and forth about getting a group of people together and going back to the land—somewhere outside the US."

"Why? Vietnam?"

"Yeah, that and other things. Pollution. Corruption. Materialism. Just the general screwed-up state of American society."

"I can dig that."

Paul nodded. "About a year ago, they found this house and moved in. I came a few months later. At first it was more of a crash pad than a true commune. Dozens of people came and went. But this past winter, Bill and Michael decided it was time to get serious. If you wanted to live at the Farm, you had to commit—contribute your money and possessions, and be prepared to leave the US."

"Don't tell me—a whole bunch of people split in a hurry."

Paul chuckled. "Yup. It came down to the six of us: Michael and Vivianne, Jon and Aileen, Bill, and me."

Paul told me that the commune members then discussed where to move to. Most leaned toward Canada, although Bill was in favour of Central or South America, arguing that living in a foreign culture would force the members to rely on each other more and bring them closer together. In the end, though, Canada prevailed, mainly because it was closer and culturally similar to the US.

"So we did a bunch of research and decided on British Columbia," Paul said. "It's beautiful, it's got mountains, and land is available."

As we continued to rock in the hammock, Paul told me that the Farm was a true commune. Members took turns cooking, cleaning, and doing laundry. Major possessions such as cars and stereos became common property. Everyone's savings and earnings went into a joint bank account, and all expenses were paid for from that account.

And everyone contributed. Paul worked in the post office. Michael and Bill were youth development counsellors in a reform school. Vivianne was substitute teaching and holding down two waitressing jobs, in a restaurant and a bar. Aileen earned a little money performing as a folksinger in coffee shops. Only Jon didn't have a paying job. He worked on the Farm, practising gardening for the time when the commune would rely on what it could grow itself.

"So far we've saved $15,000," Paul said. "When we've got $30,000, we'll pack up and leave. We figure we'll reach that in a year—in the summer of '72. Then it's goodbye, US of A, and hello, Canada. We'll buy land and start a new life. And change the world."

He gave a self-mocking smile as he said these last words, but I saw the seriousness in his eyes. I considered what he had told me. Moving to Canada and buying land sounded heroic, and it was a good way to make a statement about American society. Into my mind floated the image of myself in denim overalls, scattering grain to a flock of chickens. Quickly, it floated out again. Intriguing, but not my style.

I lit a cigarette (in those days, I smoked a pack a day). Just as I exhaled the first puff, I heard footsteps. A man loomed over the hammock. He was of medium height, heavy-set, with broad shoulders and a thick chest. He was wearing a sweat-soaked Grateful Dead T-shirt over faded jeans with an American flag embroidered on one knee. Scruffy sneakers. Shoulder-length brown hair, thinning on top. Stubbly chin. Large, hooked nose. Almond-shaped, hazel eyes.

"You're not allowed to smoke in the house, you know!" he snapped.

"I know!" I said (though I didn't).

"This is Bill," Paul said sheepishly. "My friend Ellen."

Bill just glared at me. I glared back. *What a jerk*, I thought.

Dinner was lentil stew over brown rice. We ate on our laps in the living room, since there wasn't enough space in the basement kitchen for a table.

"So you're the new farmhand," Michael said with a friendly smile. He was very good-looking, with wavy black hair, a black beard, dark eyes, and a finely chiselled nose.

I laughed. "I don't know the first thing about gardening. I hope Paul told you that."

"That's okay. It's basically weeding, hoeing, and fertilizing, nothing tricky. Right, Jon?"

A tall, handsome guy with a thick head of curls nodded. He turned blue eyes on me. "I'll give you the tour tomorrow. The asparagus is done, but the peppers and cantaloupes need weeding. And the corn needs thinning."

His girlfriend, Aileen, scooted her chair closer to his. "Don't forget you have to take me to that audition in the afternoon." She had a corona of frizzy brown hair. Her voice was deep and husky. Sexy.

I remembered what Paul had told me. "You're a singer?"

"Yeah. I'm trying out for a gig at the Singing Onion."

"Cool."

She gave me a half-smile, putting her hand on Jon's arm.

Yeah, I get it, I thought. *I'm not after your man.* Though he *was* very cute.

I felt eyes on me and turned. Bill was looking at me with frank curiosity. "So you and Paul know each other from Wisconsin?"

"Yeah, Paul was friends with my ... my ex-boyfriend ... and we stayed in touch after he graduated, and, well, here I am."

"You're a special case," Bill said. "We made an exception to let you live here—just for the summer." His tone seemed to say, *And you'd better hold up your end or you'll be out.*

"I know," I said defensively.

Vivianne fished in her pocket and pulled out a wad of cash. "Oh, I forgot. Look at the tips I got today!"

Michael whistled. "Hey, keep it up with the mini-skirt."

Everyone laughed. Vivianne was beautiful and curvy, with straight, platinum-blond hair, delicate features, and a rosy complexion. And her short black denim skirt was showing a lot of leg.

Bill pointed. "Straight into the cookie jar."

I turned and saw a ceramic lidded jar sitting on a buffet in the corner. I gave Paul a quizzical look.

He explained, "Necessities, like groceries and gas, come out of our bank account. But every week, on top of that, we take out thirty-five dollars and put it in the cookie jar. That's for extras: movies, records, the odd meal in a restaurant ..."

"What if you run out?"

"Then we do without," Bill said. "It's the whole idea of a commune. If you take more than you need, you're taking away from the others. So we don't."

I was impressed. These people seemed to be making a communal system work. I wondered if I could be so selfless.

After dinner, Bill rolled joints. The grass was strong—Panama Red, Paul told me—and I was soon very stoned. Bill, Paul, and Michael took out guitars.

Paul started finger-picking softly. He had gentle hands with long, slim fingers—musician's hands. He held the guitar not in the aggressive way some men do, as if their guitars are weapons, but lovingly, sheltering it in the curve of his chest.

Everyone joined in on Joni Mitchell's "Woodstock," but Aileen's voice stood out. Like her speaking voice, it was raspy and warm. Vivianne chimed in with a light, high soprano. I could hear Michael singing off-key, and Paul, head down as always, singing quietly as if addressing his guitar.

I had always been embarrassed by my singing voice. It wavered above and below the note, never hitting it spot-on. But these people, even those who didn't have good voices, sang without self-consciousness. Just singing for the joy of it, singing *together*. I wanted to join in, but, inhibited, just listened.

Paul improvised along the melody line while Bill and Michael strummed along. I noticed that Bill's sense of rhythm was faulty. He seemed always to be a fraction behind the beat. But no one seemed to care. Either that, I thought, or they were too stoned to notice.

There was a moment of silence at the end of the song. Then Paul started strumming harder, tapping his foot, and everyone bellowed the words to "You Can't Always Get What You Want."

I couldn't hold back any longer. Flat or sharp, I didn't care. I belted out the words with the others.

Cheers greeted the last chord. Then Paul finger-picked a familiar introduction. When he started singing "Here Comes the Sun," everyone stayed silent. This, I remembered from Wisconsin, was *his* song.

Paul didn't have a great voice, but, like him, it was quiet and true. The melody, the words, and the guitar-playing meshed harmoniously. When he finished, everyone smiled at him.

"Okay, time for our theme song," Paul said, and launched into a boogie-woogie rhythm. Everybody sang along to "Goin' Up the Country." When it came to the line about leaving the USA, they fist-pumped and hollered out the words.

I sang along, even though I wasn't going to leave the USA. For a moment, I felt envious of their closeness, of the shared goal that pulled them together.

Paul, Bill, and Michael put away their guitars. Jon and Aileen said good-night and headed out into the night. Bill went downstairs. Michael and Vivianne went upstairs.

I picked up my suitcase and rucksack. "Uh ... Paul?"

"Yeah?"

"Where do I sleep?"

There was a pause. "Well, there's this little alcove." He led me over to the small space next to the bathroom. "We could fit a mattress in here. Or ... you could sleep with me."

His face was red. I felt my cheeks grow warm. This was something I had been wondering about ever since he had written to me. Was he inviting me to be *with him*, or was he just inviting me as a friend? The answer he'd just given me suggested the former, though his offhand manner made me unsure. Nor was I sure that I wanted a relationship. My heart was still broken from Ned's rejection. I wanted to be *wanted*—but not necessarily *involved*.

"Um ... okay," I said.

Paul took my suitcase and climbed upstairs. I followed with my rucksack. While he went to the bathroom, I debated how to dress—or undress. Go naked? Keep my underwear on? In the end, I put on a long T-shirt and got into bed.

Paul turned off the light and lay down beside me. We turned toward each other and started kissing. His lips were soft and sweet. But his kisses were without passion. I sensed that he was going through the motions, and I knew I was. It was as if we knew we were *supposed* to have sex but neither of us really wanted to.

After a few minutes, we pulled apart. We lay on our backs, staring at the ceiling in the dark. Through the open window, the crickets sang in the summer night. Finally, Paul said, "Goodnight, Ellie. I'm glad you're here."

"Goodnight."

He rolled over and went to sleep.

I lay there for a while. Part of me was hurt. Mostly I was relieved. We'd gotten that out of the way. We loved each other, but there was no spark. Now we could go back to being friends.

My life settled into a routine. In the morning I gardened with Jon. There were two large gardens: a three-acre patch of mixed vegetables and a six-acre field of corn. Jon often used the property owner's tractor to cultivate the corn. (I learned that that meant turning over the soil between rows and between plants to eliminate weeds and aerate the soil.) While he drove around, I weeded the vegetables: peppers, eggplants, tomatoes, zucchinis, and green beans, plus cantaloupes and watermelons. At first, red-faced, I had to ask Jon what were weeds and what were vegetables. He was kind enough not to laugh as he pointed out the pigweed and chickweed. Bending over and pulling unwanted plants was tiring and tedious, but as each row emerged from its camouflage of weeds, I was proud of my efforts.

During the hottest part of the day, I helped clean the house, or took a shift at the roadside stand where we sold our sweet corn (there was almost no traffic on the country road, and thus very few sales, but it was nice to sit in the shade and read), or walked into town and bought groceries, or lay in the hammock and talked to whomever happened to be home.

Although I was closest with Paul, I soon developed relationships with the others. Jon was open and friendly, and we had an easy rapport from working together on the land. Aileen was often away from the Farm, practising or performing her music. She seemed to be the least involved in the commune, but we were cordial with one another. Bill, nicknamed "Coach" because he tended to take charge, seemed to tolerate me, now that I had shown that I was earning my keep, though his manner could still be brusque. Michael, nicknamed "Scar" because of a scar on his forehead, was easy to talk to. He was interested in my plans to teach special education, I was interested in his childhood as the son of former Trotskyists and labour organizers, and we had long, rambling talks.

Vivianne was pleasant to me, but I sensed some coolness there. Both of us liked to cook, and we collaborated on Sunday brunches, Vivianne baking spicy coffee cakes while I cooked omelettes. On those occasions, we chatted amiably, complaining about "the boys" and their sloppy habits, the condition of the farmhouse, the muddy fields.

But Vivianne didn't seem interested in me. For one thing, with her three jobs, she was rarely home. Even when she was around, she didn't ask me about myself: my past, my goals. It was clear that she was madly in love with Michael and appeared to be wholly focused on him, to the exclusion of everyone and everything else. I couldn't tell if she was keeping me at a distance or if she was just busy and distracted. At times, I wondered if I imagined it. I didn't ask.

Every Sunday evening, Michael or Bill stood in the living room and yelled, "Let's rap!" That was the signal that a Farm meeting was about to begin. At those meetings, the members discussed their finances, shared information they'd gathered about British Columbia, and debated whether to buy a truck now or later.

I was excluded from these meetings, but, lying on my bed in the alcove between the living room and the bathroom, I couldn't help but overhear the discussions. (The alcove still didn't have a door, but I had put up a curtain, which afforded a modicum of privacy.) I felt the members' cohesion and wished I had that sense of belonging in my life. Sometimes I fantasized about joining them (not that anyone had invited me). Living in the woods, building a house, hiking and fishing and chopping wood. Ellen, the Mountain Woman.

Then I'd think, *Yeah, right.* Ellen, the Mountain Woman? Me, hauling water and chopping wood? No way.

Bill

As the summer days went by, I found myself spending time with Bill. Often his shift at the reform school ended in the early afternoon when I was taking a break from the garden. We walked along the creek or swung in the hammock or went for rides in his (now the Farm's) blue Dodge Dart. I told him about my desire to teach learning-disabled children. He told me about the kids under his care at the reform school, who were court-remanded gang youths from the ghettos of Philadelphia.

One day when Bill and I were swinging in the hammock, he began to talk about Reggie, one of the boys in his group. Reggie was bright, and right away Bill had sensed that he could make something of his life if he could break out of the street scene. Bill had helped him with his studies and taught him sports skills. Finally, Reggie had served his time and was ready to be discharged. Bill re-enrolled him in school.

"A few days ago, I was taking one of the other boys on a home visit, and I saw Reggie on the street," Bill said.

"What happened?"

"He found out he had cancer."

"Oh, no."

"He quit school and is back in the gang. Looked like he was back on drugs again, too."

Bill's eyes were soft with misery. I was filled with admiration for him. He cared. He wanted to make a difference. He *was* making a difference. I felt confused. This wasn't the jerk I had met on my first day.

We grew friendlier. We discovered that we both had a passion for Chicago blues and coffee ice cream. We both had a sarcastic sense of humour. We both loved the novels of Hermann Hesse and Jack Kerouac. I told him he had a lousy sense of rhythm, and he told me I had an awful voice.

One evening in early August, Bill and I were walking in the shade beside the blackberry thicket. A red-winged blackbird called, then flew out of the brush and up into the sky. We leaned our heads back to follow its flight. Bill turned to me. "You know what? We're going to fall in love."

I burst out laughing. "No way."

He smiled. "It's going to grow, little by little. You'll see."

"Bill, I hate to hurt your feelings, but you're wrong. That's not how love works."

"How does it work?"

"It hits you over the head. You look at the person and there's sparks. Right away. That didn't happen with us." I knew what I was talking about. That's how it had been with Ned and me.

"That's one way," he agreed. "But it can happen slowly, too."

I shook my head. "You're talking about friendship, not love."

He smiled. "You'll see."

One Sunday night a few weeks later, in early August, the commune was having its weekly meeting in the living room. I was in my little alcove, trying to sleep. Normally I could tune out the voices, but for some reason on this night I couldn't. After covering my head with a pillow, to no avail, I decided to move. I figured I'd go downstairs and read in Bill's bed until the meeting was over.

I fell asleep. No doubt Bill was surprised and delighted to find me in his bed when he came downstairs. In the morning, he gave me a quizzical look. "I couldn't sleep," I said, but I knew it was more than that. We made love. He was tender and gentle, and it was wonderful.

"It's only sex," I told myself.

We continued sleeping together. One morning about a week later, I jolted upright in Bill's bed. Like a cartoon character, a lightbulb flashed on over my head.

"Oh my God!" I whispered to myself. The bastard was right. It had happened. "I'm in love!"

Whole days passed while we lived on spine-melting kisses and infatuated stares. We rushed downstairs to the beaded alcove several times a day, and if anyone was making a grilled cheese sandwich on the other side of the beads, I didn't notice. I gazed into Bill's hazel eyes. "I love you," I said. "I can't believe it, but I do. How did you know?"

He shrugged, smiling. "I just did."

All of his love, which he had guarded so patiently, now burst forth. He looked like a child who had just opened the most wonderful birthday present in the world. I too was elated. This was better than anything I'd ever known. It was more than romance. It was friendship and respect as well.

"This is Bill," I said with a bright smile. We had just arrived at my parents' house.

Bill stuck out his hand. "Hi. Ruth and Bernie, right?"

My parents looked stunned, first at Bill's presumption to call them by their first names, then at his clothes. He had dressed for the occasion in a Cream T-shirt, scuffed sneakers, and his worn jeans with the upside-down American flag patch on the knee. His long, stringy hair hung down his neck.

"How do you do?" my father said, shaking Bill's hand gingerly.

We sat down at the kitchen table. My mother served coffee and rugelach, delicious pastries filled with cinnamon, raisins, and nuts. While I nibbled on one, Bill stuffed one in his mouth and grabbed another. My mother looked away.

"How's the farming going?" my father asked.

"Good," I said. "I'm learning how to thin crops."

"We're working her to the bone," Bill said. My mother looked alarmed until Bill said, "Just kidding."

"What do you do, Bill?" my mother asked.

"Work in a reform school with gang youth."

"That must be tough."

"Yeah, the kids are pretty screwed up. But then, what can you expect, given where they come from? The ghetto is filled with crime. The kids just reflect their environment."

There was a silence.

"Ellen tells us you are part of a group that's moving to Canada," my father said.

Bill nodded. "The sooner we get out of this country, the better."

Oh God.

Ever reasonable, my father said, "Why do you say that?"

"Well, let's start with Vietnam—"

"Are you in danger of getting drafted?"

"No, I got a deferment." (Thankfully, Bill didn't explain how. He'd gone to the Quaker Resistance movement, which was active in Pennsylvania. They had referred him to a sympathetic psychiatrist, who had asked him, "Do you spend all your time thinking about, procuring, and using drugs?" "Yes." "Fine. You're unfit to serve.") He went on, "But it's a totally unjustified war, an act of aggression by a warlike government. And then there's all the pollution. Acid rain. Polluted water and soil. And Americans are so materialistic. There's more to life—"

"Is there *anything* you like about the US?"

Bill thought for a minute. "Music. Sports. Beautiful places. But the country is so f—, I mean, screwed up, it's beyond saving. I mean, look at how big business calls the shots. And they rape the earth—"

"More coffee, anyone?" my mother said brightly.

In the car on the way home, Bill said, "Your parents are pretty uptight, aren't they?"

"Yeah, but you really pushed them," I said defensively.

"I did?"

I looked at him. Did he really not know? Apparently not, judging from the bland look on his face.

I wanted to say: *You came dressed like a slob. You criticized everything about the US. You challenged all their values. What did you expect?*

But I didn't. Because that wasn't how I was raised. And because Bill's and my love was new. I was reluctant to confront him.

Your parents are uptight, Bill had said. *So am I,* I thought, half ashamed and half angry.

"They're proper," I said. "Polite. We don't talk like that in my house."

"Wait till you meet my family, then," Bill said with a grin.

Uh-oh, I thought.

A week later, we drove to Levittown. Bill explained that it was one of the first planned communities in the United States, built after the Second World War to provide standardized, affordable houses for veterans and their families. The development was divided into sections, each with a name, and all the streets within each section began with the same letter.

We passed a sign that said Snowball Gate. "That's where Michael grew up," Bill said. "Their houses were a little bigger and a little nicer than mine. My section was pretty much blue collar."

A little farther on, we came to Cobalt Ridge, where Jon had grown up. Bill turned into a section called Juniper Hill. The streets curved in circular patterns. Every house followed the same design; the only difference between them was the colour and whether the garage was on the left or right.

"And I thought Linden was boring," I said as we turned onto Jasmine Road.

Bill laughed. "No kidding. Ultimate suburbia. Now you know why we're so hot on getting out of here."

I nodded.

Bill went on, "But the great thing is that there were a million kids to play with, and parks and creeks and woods. It may have been cookie-cutter, but it was a fun place to grow up."

Bill pulled up at a pale green house. A black and white Thunderbird convertible was parked in the driveway.

A woman with bouffant hair and a cigarette dangling from her lip met us at the door. She had broad shoulders and slim hips, and I saw Bill's build in her body. She wore a leopard-print blouse over pale yellow slacks. "What took you so damn long?" she said in a raspy voice. Then, to Bill, "Your hair's too long. You should get a haircut."

"Hello to you, too," Bill said, giving her a kiss on the cheek. "This is my mom, Maxine Sacks. Ellen Rosenberg."

"How do you do?" I said.

"You're awfully young," she said without removing the cigarette. An inch of ash fell onto her bosom. "How old are you anyway?"

"Twenty-two."

"No shit! Well, come on in and take a load off." Bill and I followed her inside. She yelled down the hallway, "Leon, they're here!"

"Just a minute. Hold your horses," a voice answered.

"He's a pain in my ass," Maxine said, though she said it in a matter-of-fact tone, without animosity.

A moment later, Bill's stepfather (his parents had divorced when he was young), a short, slim man wearing an obvious toupee, came into the living room. Unbidden, the nursery rhyme "Jack Sprat could eat no fat, his wife could eat no lean" popped into my mind. Not that Maxine was fat, but she was taller and heftier than her husband. She looked as if she could hurl him across the room.

Bill and I sat down on an orange couch with plastic covers over the cushions. Beside the couch stood a fake orange tree with stuffed toy monkeys perched in its branches. I stifled a laugh.

"When are you going to get some decent clothes?" Maxine asked Bill, pointing to his patched jeans.

"When you do," Bill replied, indicating her shirt.

"Oh, shut up," Maxine said.

I jerked. *Shut up* was never uttered in my parents' house.

Maxine went to the bottom of the stairs and hollered, "Julie! Get down here!"

"I'm busy," came a youthful voice.

"Now!"

Several minutes went by. Then a beautiful young teenager pounded down the stairs. She had long, straight, light brown hair and her father's thin nose, in her case sprinkled with freckles.

"Hey, Billy."

"Hey, Jule."

I was introduced to Bill's half-sister, and we sat at the dining room table. Maxine set out platters of cold cuts and rye bread, along with potato salad, pickles, and coleslaw.

"I don't want this," Julie said, pouting. "Why don't you ever cook anything?"

"Because I'm too tired. And I don't feel like it. Fix your own food."

"Screw this," Julie muttered. She went into the kitchen and clattered about, making herself a peanut butter and jelly sandwich.

"Still not eating meat?" Maxine said to Bill. When he shook his head, she said to me, "Did you know that when he was little, the only thing he would eat was hamburger and mashed potatoes?"

I had to smile. "Really?" Not exactly the vegetarian boyfriend I knew now.

Leon lifted a jar of mustard. "You know I hate this kind of mustard. Why can't you buy the kind I like?"

"Shut up, Leon, and eat what's there."

"Damn annoying woman."

And so it went. Everyone yelled at one another, swore at one another, called one another names, criticized one another. At times the shouting seemed playful; at other times it felt truly hostile. I sat there, terrified.

On the way back to the Farm, I said to Bill, "Is it always like that?"

"Always like what?"

At first, I thought he was kidding. But he looked at me curiously. "The yelling. The swearing. The insults."

Bill shrugged. "Yeah. That's my family. Now you know why I'm moving across the continent."

But even as he said it, I reflected that he had seemed comfortable in there. He had bantered and traded insults with ease. I pondered the differences between our families. Mine, so polite and restrained. His, so in-your-face and rude. Was this gulf too wide to bridge? I thought back to the first words Bill had said to me: "You can't smoke in the house, you know!" That pushiness made me uncomfortable, but at the same time it was one of the things I loved about him. His honesty. The lack of pretense.

I love him anyway, I thought. And when he turned his hazel eyes on me, I melted. *We'll make it work.*

Decisions

One day at the end of August, when I came in from the garden, Paul, Michael, and Vivianne were waiting for me in the living room. Bill took my hand and led me into the circle.

Paul cleared his throat. "This is really hard. I hate to be the one to say it."

"I will, then," Vivianne said. "You know the rule, Ellen. Unless you commit yourself to the land thing, you can't live here anymore."

"I know," I said, amazed at how composed I sounded. I'd known this was coming. I'd dreaded it. Secretly, I'd been hoping that the others would understand how Bill and I felt about each other, and make an exception to let me stay.

Nope.

"It's nothing personal," Paul said. "It's just the rule."

"Of course, if you want to join us ..." Michael began.

I didn't answer.

"I'm really sorry, Ellie," Paul said. He, Vivianne, and Michael left the room.

Bill and I rushed into each other's arms. "I'm not ready to commit," I said into his chest.

"I know," he said, stroking my hair. "I wouldn't want you to say so if you didn't mean it."

Suddenly I thought, *What if I persuaded him to leave the commune and stay with me? He loves me enough that he probably would.*

In the next instant, I abandoned the idea. It wouldn't be right. What would a relationship built on such selfishness be worth? And in a strange way, Bill's acceptance of the rule, despite the pain it brought him, made me respect him even more. It was the act of a person who stuck to his ideals. That was the kind of partner I wanted. It was just ironic that his noble idealism brought me heartache.

At the beginning of September, I moved into a house with some new friends in the nearby village of Richboro. Although I thought the separation from Bill would be miserable, it wasn't. I got along well with my house-mates, and we had fun cooking together and hanging out. Bill and I saw each other almost every day, alternating sleepovers at his place or mine. With a loan from my parents, I bought a forest-green Volkswagen Beetle, and when it was my turn to go to the Farm, I zipped along the country roads, filled with the delicious agony of anticipation.

And whatever energy of mine wasn't consumed by love was taken up by teaching. My ten students (nine boys and one girl, a common ratio in special education) ranged in age from five to ten, and in ability from near-genius to significantly impaired. Some could read above their grade level but couldn't write. Some could perfectly copy printing off the blackboard but had no idea what they were copying. Some were math whizzes but hopeless spellers.

In university, I had been trained in different methods of remediating learning disabilities. Now I applied them, designing individual learning programs for each child in reading, spelling, perceptual ability, math, and writing: 250 different lessons per week. I arrived at school at 8:00 each morning and left at 8:00 each evening.

I awaited improvement. It didn't come. Michael, for example, reversed *b* and *d*, *g* and *p*, and so read *dog* as *bog*, *did* as *bib*. I had him do a series of exercises in which he matched shapes. He worked at these diligently, and his reading improved. But only briefly. Soon he was reversing again, and neither he nor I knew why. He vented his frustration by beating up smaller children on the playground.

Then there was Bobby. He was the most beautiful child I had ever seen, with sandy hair fringing his forehead, big brown eyes, and an upturned nose. I should have realized that there was rage inside him by the way he wrote: he gripped the pencil so tightly and pressed so hard that he tore the paper. For weeks or even months he was peaceful, pleasant, even-tempered. Then, for no reason I could discern, he exploded. He flailed his arm and legs, screaming, "Go away, I hate you, shit, shit, shit!" The next day he'd once again be angelic, saying, "Yes, Miss Rosenberg," and giving me his dazzling smile.

I was baffled by the lack of progress in my students. No one had told me what to do when my methods didn't work. All I knew was that I was failing. I didn't know enough, or I didn't care enough, or I wasn't working hard enough. So I worked harder. I read education journals. I went to workshops and semi-nars. I stayed at school until 8:30, 9:00 at night, and became friendly with the custodian.

Now, in hindsight, I realize that my expectations were unrealistic. Special education is a bumpy road, littered with setbacks. Even an experi-enced, competent teacher couldn't succeed with every student all the time.

But I didn't know that. I wouldn't accept failure. I became a workaholic, desperately trying to find the key that would unlock each child's learning problems.

Worse, my dedication began to affect my relationship with Bill. To be sure, he was incredibly supportive. I told him all my worries, the many defeats and the few victories. He told me I was doing my best, doing a good job—the phrases I needed to hear. But he was also frustrated. "Couldn't you come home early tonight for a change?" he'd ask.

I was torn, wanting to be with him, yet needing even more to prove myself as a teacher. I'd shake my head. "I can't. I've got all the spelling lessons to do for the week, and piles of marking, and I need to do some research to find something that'll work for Howard."

Bill would nod, but I knew what he was thinking: *You care more about those kids than you do about me.*

No! I wanted to tell him. *I love you more than anything.* But I knew that he was partly right. The children had meshed with my definition of who I was. If I was worth anything, I had to show it through them.

Many years later, I asked Bill if he had felt neglected.

"At times," he said.

"Were you angry?"

"At times." He paused. "I knew you loved me. I knew it didn't mean you loved me less."

"I didn't."

He nodded. "But I was getting mixed messages. You were always choosing schoolwork over spending time with me. I guess I was more confused than angry."

"You seemed awfully patient. How'd you manage that?"

Grinning, he said, "Well, being madly in love with you helped. Even if you were an infuriating perfectionist. And still are."

"Hey!" I laughed. But there was an edge to my laughter. Not everyone would have put up with being neglected like that in the early stages of love—or at any stage. I was lucky Bill had.

For a while, travelling back and forth between the Farm and my house in Richboro was fun for Bill and me. Our first kisses when we rushed into each other's arms were sweetened by anticipation. We enjoyed filling each other in on what we had been doing since we'd last been together.

But our love began to grow deeper. What we had initially *thought* was right, we now *knew* was right. With surprise and delight, I suspected that I had met the love of my life. Being apart began to lose its appeal. We wanted to be together all the time.

There was only one option: I would have to join the commune as an official member.

This idea appealed in many ways, apart from the obvious one of being with Bill. The Farm members' goal resonated with me more and more. As the Vietnam War dragged on, as the environment became more polluted, as the West drowned in materialism, as racial inequality continued, I began to feel that there was no point in trying to change American society from within. No, I thought, the only answer was to do something radical: drop out of established society and try an alternative lifestyle, one that would be purer and closer to nature. The Farm had shown me that communalism could work, and that it was a better way to live than with each person striving for him or herself.

But to leave the US! Move three thousand miles away! Live in the wilderness with no electricity, doing brutal physical labour, enduring extreme cold and blizzards and other, unidentified hazards! All of this terrified me. Despite my avowed love of the natural life, I was a city girl. My interests were music and art, literature and dance. I had no outdoors skills. I had never gone camping, had done little hiking, had never wielded an axe or a saw. In the past, when I imagined trying an alternative lifestyle, I pictured myself tending a garden in some quaint little New England town, maybe learning to weave or make ceramics, surrounded by like-minded, artsy people, bookstores, and a good coffee shop. What the Farm proposed was way too extreme: *Won't it be freezing cold? And what about wild animals? How do you survive?*

Even though I championed the idea of communal living in theory, secretly I shied away from it. I liked the people at the Farm. I just didn't want to live with them in such close proximity. I was—and am—an introvert, a private person. I wanted time and space to be alone with my thoughts. I wanted not to have to be "on" with the group. Mostly, I wanted time alone with Bill. Time to grow as a couple, not as part of a social experiment.

But how else could I be with the man I loved?

One day in November, about three months after I'd moved out of the Farm, Bill and I were walking into town. A cold wind blew against us and rattled the few dry oak leaves that still clung to the trees.

"Have you been thinking about moving back in?" he said, looking at the road ahead of his feet.

"I think about it all the time," I said.

"And?"

"Oh, Bill, I don't know." I wiped my eyes that were streaming from the wind. "I go back and forth. I love the idea, but how can I know if it's for me?"

There was a pause. "What would you rather do?"

"Well, I want to keep teaching ..."

"Marry some rich Jewish doctor—"

"Bill!"

He laughed. "Just kidding."

"There's no one else I want to be with, you know that," I said. "It's just ... sometimes this land thing is so overwhelming, it crushes me."

We walked in silence.

"We're leaving in June," Bill said. "In seven months. We decided that at the last meeting."

So there was an ultimatum. I took a deep breath. "What if I can't commit myself? What if I don't come?"

We were walking across a stone bridge that crossed the creek upstream from the Farm. The water rushed beneath our feet. Bill turned to me. His eyes were moist, whether from wind or emotion, I couldn't tell. "Don't ask me to choose, Ell, because I couldn't. You know how I feel about you. But this land thing—Michael and I have been talking about it since high school. I've been committed for so long, I couldn't give it up."

Don't ask you *to choose*, I thought. *But I have to.*

Bill took my hands. "I want you to come with me. I want to do this with you." We kissed, long and sweet, on the stone bridge. Then we continued walking into the wind.

I went on vacillating. The pros and cons of joining became a mantra that I chanted silently all the time. But the final point of every mental debate was the unalterable fact that I couldn't live without Bill. When school let out for Christmas vacation, I made up my mind.

At the next Farm meeting, I sat quietly as routine business was discussed. Then Paul turned to me. His face was friendly but guarded, as if he was not going to let our closeness influence the process. "So you want to join the commune? Why?"

"Because I believe in what you guys are doing," I said, not untruthfully. "I want to try the lifestyle."

"How do you feel about living communally?" Michael asked.

I feel hemmed in by it, I thought, but of course I didn't say that. "I believe in the principle," I said. "I like your guys' energy."

"You're ready to pool your money?" Vivianne said.

"Sure." That was the easy part, signing over the material things, my salary, my car.

"And leave the US?" Jon asked.

"I have to admit that feels a little weird," I said. "But this place is so screwed up, I don't see any hope for it. So, yeah, Canada looks good."

"What about the lifestyle?" Paul said. "We don't know what it's going to be like, but chances are it'll be pretty rough at first. Are you up for that?"

"I think I can handle it." *Liar.*

Michael looked at me. "Do you really want to go to British Columbia, or do you just want to be with Bill?"

I hesitated. The truth was: both. "I want to make a difference," I said. "I want to come with you guys."

Paul spoke up. "I say we let Ellen in. I've known her longer than any of you. If she says she's committed, she is. She'll be a great addition to our group."

Michael smiled. "Okay, then. You're in."

"Same here," the others echoed.

I looked at Bill. He had an almost shy smile that said, *I don't want to make a big deal out of this, but I'm ecstatic.*

We all stood and hugged in a group embrace.

Michael whooped. "Let's celebrate. Got a j, Billy?"

Bill pulled a joint from his shirt pocket and stuck it between Michael's teeth. When Paul took out his guitar and began to strum "Goin' Up the Country," I sang along, belting out the line about leaving the USA.

On New Year's Eve 1971, I did two momentous things. I quit smoking cigarettes forever (partly motivated by pity for Bill, partly for my own sake). And I moved back into the Farm.

Together again. No more driving back and forth, your place or mine, oh shit I forgot my toothbrush. Bill moved his bed upstairs into the living room (the basement was too cold and damp in the winter). Vivianne and I went shopping and found some brown fabric with a pattern of black triangles, truly hideous but cheap (I've held on to a small piece of that fabric out of nostalgia), and rigged up a curtain to partition off a space around the bed. Of course, the location en route to the bathroom didn't afford much privacy. Many times, while Bill and I were making love, someone tiptoed past the curtain. I stiffened, trying to stop panting, trying to tell from the tread who it was—not that it mattered, but I couldn't help it. After the flush and the reverse footsteps, Bill and I resumed, our passion somewhat cooled.

Though I was now a member of the commune, I felt guilty about being there under false pretenses. I kept waiting for Paul, Michael, Vivianne, Jon, or Aileen to unmask me. There were times when I wanted to yell, *Wait a minute, I've been lying, I don't want to go to BC, let me out!* But I didn't. I couldn't. I kept my ambivalence a secret, even from Bill. When it entered my thoughts, I fought down the feeling of panic by reminding myself how beautiful it was going to be, how good it would feel to leave the corrupt, materialistic US, how wonderful it would be to be with Bill. I almost kept it a secret from myself.

At the same time, I found myself growing more excited about the goal. Lots of people talked about going back to the land, but, damn it, we seven were the only ones among all our friends who were actually going to do it. I remembered sitting in my little alcove early in the summer, listening to the group's weekly meeting and wishing I could be part of something bigger— and now I was. More and more, instead of mostly dread and fear, I felt excitement at the idea of going out west with these people. I imagined us digging and hoeing the soil, carrying baskets of carrots and potatoes, climbing mountains, hammering boards into a house. I saw Bill and me walking hand in hand, sitting on a boulder by a creek, watching the water rush by, kissing in dappled sunlight. Shivers went up my back and I thought: *Maybe. Yes. Yes.*

One night in April, Jon called a special Farm meeting. We gathered in the living room. Jon looked uneasy. Aileen huddled close to him.

"What's up?" Michael said.

Jon hesitated. "I don't know how to say this . . . well . . . Aileen and I are pulling out. We're not going to BC with you."

There was a silence. "Why?" Bill said, then, trying to lighten the mood, "Is it something we said?"

Jon managed a smile. "It's not you guys. It's . . . well, it's just not for us. We don't want to homestead in the wilderness. We want to travel—"

"And I want to pursue my singing," Aileen said.

More silence. I was shocked—and yet not surprised. Over the last few months, I had noticed that Jon and Aileen seemed increasingly unhappy. They often went off by themselves to talk. When we had group discussions about the move, they sat holding hands, saying little.

"We're really sorry," Jon said. "I feel like a shithead—"

"That's 'cause you are," Bill said. Then, when Jon turned a startled look at him, "Kidding!"

Everyone laughed nervously.

Paul rose. He wrapped his arms around Jon. "I'll miss you, brother."

That did it. Jon started crying, and then Vivianne and Aileen were hugging, sobbing, and then the rest of us stood and hugged and cried.

"No hard feelings," Michael said. "We still love you."

"We still love you, too," Jon said.

After he and Aileen had left, the rest of us sat in a circle in the living room.

"I could see that coming," Bill said. "I knew Aileen didn't want to do it. I think she's been working on Jon for a while."

"I think so, too," Paul said. "But it still hurts."

Michael looked around. "Well, guys? Are we still in? Are we still going to do this? Can we make it work with five?"

"Of course," Bill said.

"I'm in," Paul said.

"Me too," said Vivianne.

"Yes," I said, and I meant it. These guys were counting on me, and I didn't want to let them down. I loved them and felt close to them.

"All right!" Michael said. "To us!" He raised his fist in the air.

"To us!" we cried, hugging. "To us!"

"Here you go," Michael said, handing each of us a yellow pamphlet. It was the spring of 1972, a few weeks after Jon and Aileen had left the group, and the five of us were gathered in the living room.

Earlier, Michael and Bill had sent away to the government of British Columbia for information. What came back was a bundle of pamphlets, each one focusing on a different region. The pamphlets listed such data as the size of the region, the annual rainfall and snowfall, the population, the key industries and types of employment, the average cost of land, the principal cities and towns, and so on.

Leafing through them, we quickly eliminated the North Coast (too rainy), the Northwest and the Northeast (too cold), the Central Interior (too short a growing season), the South Okanagan (too dry), and the Southwest Coast (too populated).

I picked up another booklet, this one about the Shuswap – North Okanagan region, located in the south-central part of the province.

"They only get about twenty-two inches of precipitation a year," I said, "and the growing season is 160 days."

"That's pretty good," Bill said. He read over my shoulder. "You can grow corn and tomatoes and squashes there, so it must be good and hot in the summer."

I turned the page. "The average price of land over the last five years was from one-thousand to three-thousand dollars an acre."

"That's a bit steep," Michael said. "In the West Kootenays it ranges from five-hundred to two-thousand an acre. And the growing season is about 140 days."

"So the West Kootenays is more affordable, but the Shuswap–North Okanagan has a better climate," Paul said.

"Looks like the West Kootenays and the Shuswap–North Okanagan are our best bets," Bill said. "So that's where we'll start looking." With his finger, he drew circles around the two chosen regions.

We grinned at one another. We had our destinations. The place names were already sounding familiar: Salmon Arm, Armstrong, Enderby, Revelstoke, Kaslo, Nelson. Shuswap Lake, Slocan Lake, the Columbia River.

It was becoming real.

In May, we bought a three-quarter-ton, four-wheel-drive Chevy pickup truck—a mountain machine. Parked at the barn, it became the king of the lot, lording over my Volkswagen Beetle and Bill's Dodge Dart. Michael and his father built a camper on the back, complete with fold-out storage compartments for the trip. When it was finished, we walked around it, admiring the deep green of the body against the gleaming white of the camper. It looked so ... Canadian. It looked like an ad in *Field and Stream*: "Rough. Rugged. Discover Adventure with Chevrolet."

Paul, Vivianne, Bill, and I lay side by side in the back while Michael drove around the Farm. We bounced from hillock to hillock, felt the power of the engine as it pulled the machine across a muddy pasture. Michael put it in four-wheel-drive, just for the hell of it, and the truck rolled effortlessly up the hill toward the manor house. At the top, he honked the horn, three short blasts, and we howled like coyotes.

June 20: A red circle appeared around that date on every calendar in the house. Departure Day. Bill and I would travel in the Volkswagen across Canada and check out the Shuswap – North Okanagan. Michael, Vivianne, and Paul would load up the truck with the commune's possessions, drive across the US, and explore the West Kootenays.

When are we gonna meet? July 14, how's that? Fine. Where? Someplace in between. Get a map. What's this little town? Needles. Great. Meet you in Needles on July 14.

Feeling both regret and elation, I handed in my resignation to the school district. Despite my twelve-hour days, most of my students had made minimal progress. None was ready to rejoin a regular class. Some had advanced only one grade level in their reading when the gap was three or four years. Others, when the forward and backward steps were balanced out, had not improved at all.

Part of me wanted to stay and try again, to find the breakthroughs that had eluded me. But mostly I felt relieved. I couldn't wait to clean out my desk and walk out of the classroom for the last time.

About a week before the commune was to leave the United States, Bill and I drove up to Linden one last time, to say goodbye to my family.

My parents hosted a barbecue in their back yard. My grandparents were ensconced in webbed lawn chairs in the shade of an oak tree. My father, grim-faced, presided over the grill. He hated anything to do with the outdoors and, I knew, would rather be reading medical journals than squirting starter fluid onto charcoal briquettes and spearing slabs of meat. My sister Audrey, eighteen at the time, made sure our grandparents' glasses of ginger ale stayed full. My mother carried platters of potato salad, pickles, coleslaw, potato chips, hamburger and hot dog buns to the picnic table, covered by a flowered paper tablecloth. Only my brother David, fourteen, showed high spirits. He bounded around the back yard, shooting a basketball at a hoop on the garage, pausing to kid my grandmother about the fact that her feet didn't reach the ground, giving my mother a kiss on the cheek, grabbing the basketball again. David, the baby, the charmer.

While Bill and David shot hoops, Bill easily knocking the ball out of David's skinny arms but letting him sink the occasional shot, I made the rounds.

First, my grandfather, Joe. I adored this man. Quiet and unassuming, he had immigrated from a Jewish *shtetl* in Lithuania as a teenager, leading his three younger siblings overseas. He had "made good" in America, first becoming a plumber and eventually owning his own plumbing company. Now he had Parkinson's disease and emphysema (the latter, no doubt, from a lifetime of smoking; he used to bum cigarettes from me, and even though I knew my mother would have killed me if she found out, I never could say no to him).

I sat on the grass beside his chair. "Huh-huh-he's a good boy," he said, nodding at Bill, who was pretending to have difficulty taking the basketball away from David.

My eyes filled at these kind words. "I know, Papa."

"You're going far away."

"Yes."

There was a silence. I wondered if he was remembering his own leave-taking all those decades ago.

"Stay in touch. Don't let us worry."

"I will. I promise."

He beckoned me closer. "Get married."

I burst out laughing. What a relief to laugh. "I will, Papa."

"All right, all right." He waved a hand. That was his refrain when he was satisfied: "All right, all right," and then the slight wave, as if to say *I understand. I approve. Everything's okay.*

My grandmother, Gussie, turned toward us. "What're you talkin', Joe?"

"Always the *yenta*, Gram," I teased.

She fixed me with her grey eyes. "Tell me."

"Papa's giving me romantic advice."

"What does he know?" Then, in an apparent reversal, "Listen to him. He knows."

I scooched over to sit beside her.

"Where are you going again?" she asked. "British Canada?"

"British Columbia, Gram. It's a province in Canada."

"They don't have states there?"

"Provinces are just like states," I said.

She waved her hand, as if this information were irrelevant. "I don't understand why you're going."

"It's an adventure," I said, trying to keep my voice light.

"You couldn't have an adventure in New Jersey?"

I laughed. "Not this kind. We want to be in the mountains."

"Mountains," she said dismissively. Then, taking my hand, "Will I see you again?"

"Of course! I'll come visit."

She nodded. "You listen to me, Ellenka. It all sounds crazy. But you know what you want. You just make sure you're happy, that's all."

I hugged her.

My mother filled a platter with hamburgers and hot dogs at the grill and set it down on the picnic table. "Food's ready."

My father gratefully shut off the grill and went to sit in the shade.

David, eternally hungry as only teenage boys can be, scurried over to the table. "Fish—yuck."

"That's for Ellen and Bill," my mother said.

"Thanks, Mom," I said. Bill and I hadn't even wanted to eat fish, but, given that I could hardly expect my mother to make lentil burgers for us, we were prepared to make the best of it.

Audrey and I fixed plates for our grandparents. Then she got her own hamburger, I made myself a fish burger, and we sat on the grass.

She took a bite. "You don't know what you're missing."

"Ugh, no thanks."

Silence fell. I didn't know what to say to my sister. I hadn't seen much of her over the past year. When we did talk, I got conflicting reactions. I knew Audrey was getting high, and she was tuned into the hippie ethos. Today she wore an embroidered peasant blouse over cut-off shorts, her hair long and loose, dangly earrings with little blue stones.

At one point, earlier in the year, when I'd talked to her about going back to the land, she'd said, "Far out," and I'd thought I had an ally.

But then another time she'd said, "I get what you're trying to do, but do you have to go so far away to do it?"

And another time: "Mom and Dad are really freaked out. I heard Mom crying."

What about you? Are you freaked out? I'd wanted to ask. But I'd been too afraid to.

Now, Audrey put her bun down. "I don't want to be the oldest one."

I gave a strangled laugh. This was a long-standing issue in our family: Audrey having grown up as the second daughter, always in my shadow. Apparently, when she was little, she had asked our parents, "When do *I* get to be the oldest one?"

"Hey, I'm not dying, just moving out west," I said.

"But who knows how often you'll be back. Or *if* you'll be back."

"I'll definitely visit."

"You know what I mean."

I did. When I moved away, she would have to be the one to come home for the holidays, to look out for our grandparents, to comfort our parents. When I'd made my decision, I'd had no intention of inflicting this burden on Audrey. But I had done it anyway.

"And what about you and me?" Audrey said. "I'll hardly ever see you, Ell."

I swallowed down tears. "Just because I'm far away doesn't mean we can't be close," I said, but even I knew that was probably untrue.

"I hope so," Audrey said in a low voice.

I couldn't sit there. On the pretext of stacking my plate, I went over to Bill and David.

David leaned against me, just like when he was little and I read him stories. *Stuart Little* was his favourite. He always claimed, wrongly, that we'd never finished it, just to get me to promise that I'd come home and read him the final chapter.

"Are you going to build your own house, Ell?"

"Yup."

"And chop down trees?"

"Yup."

"But won't it be cold and snowy?"

"Probably." I didn't add that that terrified me.

David regarded Bill with a stern look. "You better be good to my sister."

Bill grabbed him in a headlock. "And if I'm not? What're you going to do about it, punk?"

They wrestled, David laughing and flailing ineffectually as Bill pinned him to the ground.

I was grateful that David was too young to really understand. I knew that he was unhappy that I was leaving, but I had lived away from home from the time he was ten, so he was used to my absence. And for him this probably sounded like a wild-west caper: chopping down trees and encountering bears and, who knows, wading into an icy river and grabbing a fish with our bare hands. I could imagine how he would embellish my actions to his friends: "And she shot a grizzly with a bow and arrow!"

Finally, after the dishes had been washed and the food had been put away, Bill and I sat down at the kitchen table with my parents. I clung to his hand.

My mother's face was stone. I could tell she was using all her willpower not to break down.

My father looked at me. "Are you sure you want to do this?"

"Yes. I want to go back to the land. I want to make a difference."

"But how will you live? What will you do for money?" my mother asked.

"We plan to grow our own food," Bill said.

"And get jobs if we have to," I said.

"It's awfully far away," my mother said in a low voice.

"I know." My throat felt thick. "I wish it wasn't so far. But I love Bill—"

My father reached across the table and put his hand on mine. "We know you do, Ell."

"And we know you love her," my mother said to Bill.

"You better believe I do," Bill said, and my mother managed a smile.

She looked at me. "He has a good heart. I know he'll take good care of you."

"I will," Bill said. "I promise."

"And you take care of him," my father said. "Be good to him. Every day—" His voice wobbled.

That did it. I burst into tears. I sobbed on their shoulders. *I'm sorry,* I wanted to say, but instead choked out, "I'll write. I'll call when I can. I promise."

I grabbed Bill's hand and pulled him from the house. As I ran down the back steps, I heard my mother's hoarse sob. "Oh, Bern . . ."

I cried halfway back to Newtown, a welter of mixed emotions. Gratitude to my parents for their graciousness. Grief, as the finality of the move sank in. Guilt, most of all, at hurting them, at tearing my family apart.

In the last week, the five of us cleaned out closets and packed and labelled boxes. We had a rummage sale, took a truckload of stuff to the Salvation Army, and received almost as much back from friends and relatives eager to give us useful things for our journey. (To this day I have a long-handled spatula that someone—I have no idea who—gave us before we left.)

Then there was one last party, a colossal goodbye bash that lasted all weekend, with hundreds of friends and relatives gathering to send us off with good wishes (some of them looking at us wistfully and saying, "Gee, you guys are really doing it, let me know how it is out there, maybe I'll ..."), and non-stop music, electric and acoustic, and rented Port-a-Johns dotting the fields, and one terrifying, hilarious moment when a demonic-looking black Nubian goat belonging to the property owners escaped from its pen and made its way up the stairs of the tenant house and burst into the living room, where it thrust its snout into Bill's stepmother's face, and she leaped up and shouted, "Oh my God, what is it?" and then, realizing it was only a goat—*only a goat in the living room*—joined the rest of us in whooping laughter, and a seemingly endless supply of joints and hash pipes and pills, and more food than a small village could eat, and tears, and volleyball and frisbee, and then—

Goodbye, families. Goodbye, friends. Goodbye, jobs. Goodbye, America. We're off!

Buying Land

The search

Up through Pennsylvania in the small green Volkswagen, Bill at the wheel, map spread out on my knees. Alone together at last, three weeks of delicious privacy ahead of us.

New York State. Cups of burned coffee and styrofoam food at one Howard Johnson's after another. The road wound through the Adirondacks and the trees changed from mostly deciduous to mostly coniferous, darkening to match the afternoon shadows.

Just before Watertown, Bill and I smoked our last joint, threw the roach out the window, and rehearsed our story. Not knowing the regulations, we didn't want to say we were moving to Canada, so decided to tell the officials we were just visiting.

Then the border: Welcome. *Bienvenue.* Citizenship? American. Purpose of visit? Vacation. Thought we'd do a little camping. Length of stay? Three weeks. Money? About $200. (And $30,000 more to follow.)

Out of earshot, we whooped. They didn't even hassle us. *Bienvenue,* all right. And am I just imagining it, or does the air smell sweeter up here?

To see some of eastern Canada before pushing westward, and to practice our camping routine, we spent three days in Gatineau Park in Québec. This was my first camping trip: first time putting up a tent, first time building a fire, first time cooking in soot-blackened pots.

"Where does this pole go?" I asked Bill.

"Right here, in this bracket," he said, showing me the hole at the top of the tent entrance.

As soon as he pointed it out, I saw that that was the only logical place for the pole. As I wiggled it into place, I caught a smirk on Bill's face. "Don't laugh at me!"

"I wasn't."

"You were so." Sounding like a three-year-old, and hating it. I tried not to ask, but finally gave in. "What do I do with this rope?"

Rain leaking through the canvas tent walls, soggy flannel sleeping bags, cold seeping up from the ground through my bones, sputtering fire, half-cooked rice. By the third day, I was ready to turn around and go home, or at least check into a motel. My clumsiness at hammering tent pegs and my sore muscles, cramped from huddled sleep, confirmed what I'd dreaded to learn: that I hated the outdoors. I refused to make love on the cold, damp tent floor. Mixing powdered milk into granola and then stirring in water, I glowered at Bill as if the weather and my discomfort were his fault. My only salvation was the *tasse de café* I wrapped my fingers around in a warm, dry restaurant each morning.

Through Québec on back roads. Churches everywhere. Mixed farms, with the occasional team of horses pulling a cultivator or a plow. When we stopped in small villages to fill up the car or buy snacks, I tried to use my high-school French. "*Combien coûte cette barre de crème glacée?*" "Fifty-tree cent." I didn't know if it was my American accent or a natural antipathy to outsiders, but no one answered me in French. And, certainly, I couldn't understand *their* nasal-sounding French, so unlike anything I had learned from Mlle Molinaro in eighth grade: *Voici la fenêtre. La fenêtre est ouverte.*

In Ontario, the landscape was dark: deep green evergreens, darker shadows between them, brightened by the occasional silver glint of a waterfall. We had a succession of flat tires and argued about whose fault it was. Bill accused me of losing the map. I sulked. I found the map in his rucksack. I gloated. He sulked. We made up with sweet kisses.

Lake Superior looked like the sea, waves crashing like ocean breakers. I stood on the shore, pulling my jacket around me in a gusty breeze that had the chill of autumn in it. (*Autumn in June: what the hell?*) Looking at tugboats pulling freighters in the distance, moving so slowly that they barely seemed to move at all, it occurred to me that Canada *was* geography, land rather than people. Such vast distances, so many trees, so much water, wildlife, terrain. I felt swallowed up.

Bill and I took a detour into Minnesota to visit my college friend Terry, who had grown up in Grand Marais on Lake Superior. Terry had recently had a spiritual epiphany and was living a hermit's life in a small cabin in the woods, reading the Bible, meditating, foraging, going for long walks. When we told him about our plans to go back to the land, he smiled warmly and said, "Good for you guys. What a noble thing to do." I felt righteous, as if I and my commune-mates were on the cutting edge of something important. Terry took us canoeing on a string of lakes, my first-ever time paddling. He manouevred the canoe as if he had been born in it. I developed blisters. But it was lovely to paddle from one secluded cove to the next, pulling onto a sandy beach to bask in the sun for a while and pick wild berries, then paddle on.

Manitoba. I had never been on the prairies before. People had told me they were dull and flat, but they were neither. The land rose and fell in swellings and depressions, and the divisions reminded me of a Mondrian painting: the fences were the thick black lines, and the fields were rectangular blocks of green, brown, and tan.

And the sky! It was like a vast, curving movie screen where a succession of scenes constantly played. First, unbroken blue. Then long wisps of cirrus clouds brushed like watercolour strokes across the ceiling of a dome. Then huge grey nimbus clouds that gathered in mere moments and pelted us with fat drops of rain or chunks of hail that rat-a-tatted on the car roof like machine-gun fire.

The prairies uplifted me. I wanted to stand on top of the car and stretch my arms toward either horizon. I drove fast, glancing at Bill dozing in the passenger seat, admired his Jewish profile, fell in love with him all over again. I sang Motown hits, pounding the steering wheel in rhythm.

Saskatchewan. That name! It sounded like a children's chant, and I whispered it to myself. On either side of the highway lay fields of brilliant yellow canola. I wondered if the farmers took all this golden beauty for granted, or marvelled at it daily, as I did.

Every evening Bill and I unpacked the car, set up the tent, rolled out the sleeping bags, removed the food for that night's meal. Every morning we repacked everything in the precise reverse order. The Beetle was so crammed that each item had to go into its specific place, or we couldn't fit it all in. More than once we were left holding a box for which there was absolutely no room; then we had to unload down to the level of the mistake and repack.

"Why'd you put the duffel bag there? You know the tent has to go in first."

"I didn't, you did."

"I did not. I always put the tent in first. I've been doing it since the day we left."

But as the miles sped past, a change was happening in me: I was gaining competence in outdoor skills. In Gatineau Park, I hadn't known how to put up the tent. By Manitoba, I could do it in ten minutes flat. In Ontario, when I'd gathered sticks for kindling, they'd been punky. Two provinces later, I could not only collect the right kind of kindling, I could start the fire, feed it, and could cook passable meals in camping pots that rested on a blackened grate. My sleeping bag began to feel as comfortable as a quilt. I started to see myself as moderately competent. Not a frontierswoman, to be sure, but not a helpless urbanite either. *I might actually be able to do this.*

By the time we arrived in Banff National Park, it was July 1, which turned out to be Dominion Day, Canada's national holiday of independence. Of course, having grown up in the US, we knew nothing of our neighbour to the north, least of all that Canada had a national holiday and that it was on July 1. *You mean they don't celebrate Independence Day on July 4?*

What this meant was that all the campgrounds were full. We kept driving farther and farther north, from Banff National Park into Jasper National Park. Finally, we found a campsite at the Columbia Icefield campground. Located at an elevation of some six thousand feet next to a large glacier, it was freezing there—literally. There were no dirt tent sites, but rather raised wooden platforms. Bill and I had no idea how to erect a tent on one of those, but we did our best, futilely trying to push the tent pegs into the hard-packed gravel beneath the platform.

In the middle of the night, we were awakened when the tent collapsed on us. Crawling outside, we discovered why: the tent was covered with three inches of snow. On July 1! We were so cold and wet that all we could do was laugh hysterically. Deep down, though, I had serious doubts about this frozen country.

But the next day, the sun shone and the snow disappeared. We went on a hike in Banff National Park. Me—Ellen Rosenberg—in new boots with Vibram soles, hiking up a mountainside! Huffing, certainly. Feeling jabs of pain in my side, frequently. But still, I was hiking, enjoying the muscle-weary feeling, and even keeping up with Bill. And the feeling when we reached the top of the trail: all my straight-A report cards were nothing compared to this. I'd never imagined a colour as beautiful as the milky turquoise of the glacial lake that spread out below. It is still my favourite colour.

Even better, the park naturalist who led the hike taught us a great trick: warm up a large rock in your campfire, wrap it in a towel, and stick the towel in the bottom of your sleeping bag. From then on, I had toasty feet.

British Columbia! Crossing the border, we honked the horn, laughing at the stares of passing motorists. The air felt fresher in our lungs, the sun shone brighter, the sky looked bluer. The little green car, dwarfed by the mountains, rolled around treacherous switchbacks, through gloomy snow sheds, up hills in second gear, down, into the next curve, following the railroad tracks westward, westward.

Bill's and my land search began in the Shuswap Lake area. The area was beautiful, with the enormous lake framed by tree-covered mountains, and, here and there, prosperous-looking farms with horses, cows, and silver-roofed barns.

We contacted real estate agents who specialized in rural property, or sometimes just drove down back roads searching out FOR SALE signs. There was land available, in parcels ranging from a few acres to hundreds. But the prices were in the $15,000 to $20,000 range, rather than the $10,000 to $15,000 we'd expected. And most of the places we looked at had second-growth timber, sandy soil, and carelessly logged hillsides, with stumps and slash piles and bulldozer tracks embedded in the mud. I was astonished, and dismayed, that people didn't take better care of the land. *How can they live in such a beautiful place,* I wondered, *and leave these eyesores behind?*

Here and there we met hippies living in school buses while they built their A-frames, geodesic domes, or log cabins. They gave us herbal tea, shared their home-grown grass, and told us that the Shuswap was a groovy place to live, lots of freaks scattered about, good growing season, and that yes, land prices were going up, better buy soon.

When they said that, an anxious current passed between Bill and me. That was all we seemed to hear: more hippies are moving to BC, demand for land is high, better buy soon. Bill and I discussed whether our expectations were out of line. A few places we had seen were okay. You'd have to dig up rocks or clear trees to get sunlight or have the road graded, but all of those things were possible. So even if the places weren't ideal, and even if they seemed overpriced, maybe we should go for it anyway, while there were still properties available.

But in the end, neither the Shuswap nor the North Okanagan grabbed us. They didn't feel like home. They didn't say *"Here!"*

On July 13, in Armstrong, we pulled out a map of BC to figure out the best way to get to Needles. We were to meet Michael, Paul, and Vivianne there the next day.

Needles wasn't on the map.

Come on, it's got to be there. It's not. But it's supposed to be on Arrow Lake, across from Fauquier. Well, it's not. What the hell happened to Needles?

We asked at a gas station. The attendant burst out laughing.

"What's so funny?"

"Needles no longer exists."

"*What?*"

"Several years ago, the government built a bunch of dams on the Columbia River. Needles is now under twenty feet of water."

Bill and I looked at each other.

"How are we going to find them?" I said.

"I have no idea."

"This province is so big, we could wander around forever, never meeting up." A thought crossed my mind. *If we never find them, I can have Bill to myself.* But I had to admit that I didn't want him to myself under these circumstances.

We sat in silence. Then Bill said, "Wait a minute. I just remembered something. Michael has a college friend up here. He's picking fruit in a place called Naramata. Maybe they'll go there."

"Okay. What's his name?"

"Matthew."

"Matthew what?"

"I don't know. I only met him once, about five years ago."

I cocked my head. "Bill, how are we going to find a guy named Matthew in a town we've never been to?"

"I don't know. It's the only idea I've got."

We drove down the Okanagan Valley. In Naramata, population one thousand, after making dozens of inquiries, we narrowed the search to a cherry orchard on a hillside outside of town. When we pulled up the driveway, a tall, lanky guy with a dark beard and a Detroit Tigers baseball cap came out of a small, whitewashed cabin. He looked at us curiously.

"Matthew? From Michigan State?" Bill said.

"Yeah."

Bill and I shot each other a smile, and the guy looked even more confused. Bill stuck out his hand. "Bill Schwartz. Michael Lesnik's friend."

Matthew shook Bill's hand. "Hey, how you doing? I thought you looked familiar, but I couldn't place you." He paused. "What are you doing here?"

We explained. Matthew laughed. "That's quite a story. Well, come on in. We'll see if they have the same idea."

We followed him into the cabin. Several hours later, the Chevy truck, now dusty and mud-spattered, pulled up the driveway. Bill and I ran outside.

"You came!"

"*You* came!"

"Unbelievable!"

We smooshed together in a group hug.

"How'd you know to come here?" Bill asked.

Michael waggled his fingers. "Just felt the vibes."

"Right, Scar," Bill said, rolling his eyes. "Into the mystic."

I laughed. "You heard about Needles?"

"Poor old Needles," Paul said, and everyone laughed.

Standing in the front yard, I was surprised at the strength of my love for the others. It actually brought tears to my eyes. This was my new family, and I was genuinely glad to see them. At the same time, I felt a pang, realizing that Bill's and my privacy was over.

While Matthew gardened, the five of us lay in the tall, tickly grass, ate juicy, purple-red cherries, passed a joint, and swapped stories of our travels, comparing thunderstorms in Kansas and Saskatchewan, the Rockies in Alberta and Colorado, funny and frightening moments.

"What'd you find?" Michael asked.

Bill and I told them about the places we'd seen. "It's a pretty region," Bill said, "but it's a bit overdeveloped."

"And the prices are high," I added.

Michael nodded. "We saw some great areas all the way from Revelstoke to Nelson. Big mountains, lakes, rivers, most of it unspoiled."

"Affordable," Paul said.

"Lots of hippies," Vivianne said.

We decided to focus on the West Kootenays. The next day we'd go in convoy and explore.

Castlegar, Nakusp, the Slocan River valley. The five of us looked at farms, undeveloped mountainsides, the remains of logging operations, once-prosperous homesteads reverting to bracken and scrubby pine. We found ourselves on a first-name basis with real estate agents, most of whom looked at us disparagingly (oh Lord, another goddamn bunch of longhairs), until we mentioned we were ready to pay cash (oh yes, I see, well now, I've got a couple of terrific places, why don't we talk business?).

Every night we gathered around the fire in whatever spot we were camping in, discussed what we'd seen, and debated. Should we pay more for a developed place with cleared land and a building or two, or pay less for raw bush and develop it ourselves? Should we go for electricity or not? What was more important, growing season or good view? Creek or well? Near a town or more isolated? Blow our whole wad or keep a safety margin in the bank?

No one had any answers to these questions. In hindsight, I realize that there *are* no clear answers: it's a matter of making choices and living with the consequences. But at the time, it seemed urgent to answer them, and we couldn't. We were confused, unable to decide anything. And always, shadowing us, was the worry that land prices were going up, going up fast, and we had to buy soon.

At a site near Kaslo, the owner, Wilf Ziegler, met us at the bottom of a hill. A slim man in his forties with Johnny-Cash-style slicked-back hair, cowboy boots, and a cigarette dangling from his mouth, he shouted, "Hey, good to meet you!"

He *had* to shout to be heard over the roar of the water. We were standing beside the South Fork of Keen Creek, about four miles west of town. All I could think was that "creek" was a misnomer. This was no creek. It was a river, a rushing, pounding river with sofa-sized boulders in the middle and spray showering up as the water crashed into them. Overhanging willows and cedars glistened with moisture.

I caught the look on Michael's face. He was transfixed.

"Pretty amazing, eh?" Wilf yelled. "The property includes a short stretch of creek frontage and goes uphill."

The five of us climbed into the back of Wilf's pickup truck. He started driving up a logging road. Vertically. The road rose steeply, and we had to hold onto the sides of the bed to avoid being thrown out the back. The truck alternately plunged into potholes and groaned as it crawled over boulders sticking out of the dirt. We jostled from side to side.

The land on either side of the road was a logged-over mess. Stumps dotted the hillside, piles of bark and branches lay everywhere, and deep ruts from logging machinery were gouged into the clay-like soil.

The truck reached a flat bench about a hundred feet up from the creek. Wilf idled the truck, but didn't turn it off. "This landing is part of the place," he hollered. "More up on the second bench. Hold on!"

Up another impossibly steep section of road. More potholes. More boulders. More logging slash. After another hundred feet, Wilf pulled onto a landing. When he turned off the motor, the silence was startling. The creek was out of sight, but we could hear its steady hum.

"This is the top of the property," Wilf said, sweeping out his arm. "Just under twenty acres. A couple of cleared landings, a road, the rest undeveloped. How do you like the view?"

"Magnificent," Vivianne said. She and Michael were holding hands, gazing into the distance, their faces full of wonder.

I couldn't argue. Across the valley, to the north and east, the peaks of the Kokanee Mountains thrust into the sky, still, in July, capped with snow. I could almost imagine taking a giant leap onto one of those peaks.

Wilf walked us around the property. On each of the two landings, the land was logged. On the steepest places between the landings, clumps of forest remained. He paused at a spot at the eastern end of the bench. "This would make a great building site, and you could put in a garden at the front edge of the cliff. That way you wouldn't have to clear that many trees, and you'd get morning sun. It's perfect for a little homestead."

Huh? I exchanged a look with Bill. Nothing was going to grow on this denuded land. The logging operation had scraped off all the topsoil.

"Speaking of sun," Bill said, "we're facing northeast, right?"

Wilf nodded.

"The valley is pretty narrow," Bill went on. "Does this place get any sun in winter?"

Wilf lit another cigarette. "Well, not direct sunlight. But you only lose the sun for a few months."

"Which months?"

"November to February."

I gasped. *No direct sunlight for four months?*

"What's the price?" Paul said.

"Ten thousand."

Five hundred an acre, I thought. That was reasonable compared with other places we'd seen in the Kootenays, but, considering the condition of the land, it seemed excessive.

There was a brief silence. Wilf started walking back to the truck, and we followed. "I know the land looks messy—"

Understatement of the year, I thought.

"—but that's just temporary. It's got lots of potential. You get a Cat up here to pull the stumps, burn the slash, cut a few trees to make a clearing, plant a cover crop to build up the soil, say rye or clover, and you're in business."

"Could you raise horses up here?" Vivianne asked. I knew this was a long-standing wish of hers.

"Absolutely. Nothing easier. In fact, you get a couple of draft horses, and they can pull the logs for your house for you."

As we piled into the back of the truck, Michael's and Vivianne's heads were together. I couldn't hear what they were saying, but from the looks on their faces, I could tell that they were smitten.

I glanced at Paul. His face was grim, as if the ugliness of the logging devastation pained him. I felt the same way, and I knew Bill did, too.

A few days later, a real estate agent in Revelstoke told us about a place called Galena Bay where twenty acres of bush were for sale. We spread out our map, traced the Columbia River down past Revelstoke, thirty-five miles southward to where it widened to become Upper Arrow Lake (the same lake whose expansion had been the demise of Needles).

The ferry was called the MV *Galena*, and it held about forty vehicles, most of them empty logging trucks, waiting to be refilled on the eastern side of the lake. The five of us stood at the railing. To the northeast, the lake scooped out a curve from the shore: Galena Bay. Poking up beyond the bay, a finger of water pointed to the northeast, toward Beaton. The

Selkirk Mountains framed the bay on the east. On the west, the massive Monashee Mountains towered over the lake, rising to glaciers that thrust into a cobalt sky.

The ferry landed. Past the landing, a gravel road stretched south to Nakusp, thirty miles away, and north and east to Trout Lake, eighteen miles away. No town, no stores, no gas stations, no electricity, no campsite.

I looked at Bill. His face said, *Hey, I like this place. I'm not committing myself now, but this might be okay.*

I smiled at him. I'd fallen in love with the ferry.

We drove north for a few miles, turned onto a dirt driveway, parked, and followed the sound of hammering to a small clearing in the woods. A large, newly built house, still sheathed in plywood, stood at the end of the trail. A man and a woman, both forty-ish, were nailing slabs of cedar siding to the house. He was on a ladder, she on the ground. A small boy, maybe three or four, was playing with sticks beside her, and a chubby baby slept in an infant seat.

The man and woman turned. He was tall and husky, with big, strong-looking hands and a crewcut. She was short and slight. Close-cropped hair framed a tired expression. Flickers of surprise ran over their faces at the sight of us, long hair streaming down our shoulders, Grateful Dead T-shirts, patched jeans, smock dresses, dirty feet.

"Hi there," Bill said. "You've got some land for sale?"

"Oh," the man said, and smiled. "The real estate agent sent you?"

"Yeah."

"Well, then, welcome."

"I'm Pat Harrington," the woman said. "This is Bob." Indicating her husband. "Nelson." The child. "And Christopher." The baby.

We introduced ourselves. Bob came down from the ladder. "We have an eighty-acre spread. We're looking to sell the northern twenty acres. Come, I'll show you around."

Bob didn't mention that this land, indeed all of the Kootenays, had been inhabited and cared for by Indigenous Peoples since time immemorial, particularly the Ktunaxa people, from whom the word "Kootenay" was derived. Nor did we think to ask. At that point, we did not realize that the land we were considering buying had been Indigenous land. It was only later that we learned about Canada's treatment of Indigenous Peoples and the movements for land back and reconciliation.

Bob led us back toward the gravel road, where we had parked. "The land forms a long, thin rectangle. The eastern end starts here." Across the road loomed eight-thousand-foot mountains, their forested slopes rising to bare granite peaks.

Bob turned back and plunged westward into the woods. A short distance from the road, a spring burbled out of the ground. "Good water," Bob said. "Best there is. Straight off the mountain. You could put an intake in here and have gravity feed all the way down to the other end of the land, if you wanted to build down there."

I exchanged a look with Bill. That was a good start.

The spring fed into a two-acre swamp. Mosquitoes buzzed around my head, and I constantly had to wave my hand to drive them away. I felt a sting on my arm, slapped, and found a smear of squashed insect and blood.

Bob grimaced. "Where there's still water, there're mosquitoes. And Galena Bay has a lot of still water."

Strike one, I thought, remembering that there had been almost no mosquitoes on the Kaslo land.

The swamp gave way to forest that gradually sloped down toward the lake. Here and there were enormous Douglas firs, three feet across, as well as slim cedars, wild blueberry bushes, orange fungi on rotting logs, clumps of tiny white flowers. The forest was lush and gentle. *What a contrast to the other place,* I thought.

The western end of the land bordered on a winding, rutted dirt road that Bob told us was called Dedosenco Road, after some early settlers.

"I have to warn you," Bob said, "this back road is full of mud holes in wet weather, and it's not plowed in the winter. So if you built down here, you'd have to snowshoe in and out."

Who cares? I thought, looking at the strip of wild chamomile that grew down the middle of the road. A birch tree curved overhead, its crown forming a green arch. I could imagine walking on this road, passing under the arch, creating paths through the woods that would become more familiar than any city streets.

"What's the winter like?" Paul asked.

Bob laughed. "Well, I hope you like snow. We're in the Revelstoke snow belt. We get about twelve feet of snowfall here. Starts falling in early December and doesn't disappear till April."

"Holy shit," I said. I couldn't imagine that much snow.

"Yup," Bob said. "But there's always a nice clear, cold stretch for a few weeks in January where the sun shines every day. It's glorious."

I saw Michael and Vivianne exchange a look. I knew they were thinking about the Kaslo land, where the sun disappeared in the winter.

"How much are you asking?" Bill said.

"Five thousand," Bob answered.

At $250 an acre, it was half the price of the South Fork land.

We followed Bob back to where we'd started. "Come in and have a coffee," he said.

"Are you sure?" I said, picturing us barging in on Pat with the two little kids.

"Sure, no trouble."

We filed into the kitchen. Bob fetched extra chairs, and we crowded around a wooden table. Nelson played with blocks on the floor, while Pat, the baby on her hip, stoked the fire in a huge black woodstove, dipped water from a plastic bucket into a coffee pot, and set the pot on the left side of the stove. It grew warm in the kitchen.

While we waited for the coffee to perc, Bob told us that he and Pat and their kids had moved to Galena Bay about a year earlier from McBride, in northeastern BC, where he'd been a high-school teacher and cattle rancher. "Then the government put in a new road," he said, "and the next thing we knew, our place was overrun with hunters and snowmobilers."

"They kept breaking fences, leaving garbage around," Pat added. "Our farm was ruined."

"Everybody was talking about big developments and big bucks," Bob said disdainfully.

"How'd you end up here?" Paul asked.

"Well, we looked all over the province for a place that was isolated enough that it couldn't happen again. Galena Bay seems like a safe bet. It's far from town, there's no electricity, no telephone or TV, and enough snow and mosquitoes to ensure that it's not going to get developed in a hurry."

That's true, I thought. This place *was* isolated. The bugs were a definite drawback. There was no cleared land on the twenty acres, so we'd have to do it ourselves. And yet something about the place appealed to me. It was gentle. It didn't have spectacular views, like the South Fork land, but it was pristine, unspoiled.

Pat poured coffee and put out containers of sugar and powdered milk. *Oh, right, no refrigeration,* I thought. She filled a plate with arrowroot cookies, then sank onto a chair, turned the baby around on her lap, and gave him a cookie, which he immediately started gumming.

"How many people live around here?" Michael asked.

Bob counted on his fingers. "Well, there's the four of us. Walter and Henry Nelson. They're brothers, born and raised here. Their sister, Margaret, works away but spends her holidays here. Then there's Henry's wife, Hilda. So that makes eight."

"Eight people from Nakusp to Trout Lake?" Vivianne said.

"Yup," Pat said. "There was a bunch of kids—well, people your age—living on the other side of the back road last summer. But they're gone now."

"What happened to them?" I asked.

"They threw up a couple slapdash cabins," Bob said. "Then the couple who started the commune split up, and it fell apart. Nobody seemed committed."

Five lines of vision intersected across the table. *Not us,* we all thought.

The next day, we drove the seventy-five miles back to Kaslo to take another look at the South Fork land. We stood beside Keen Creek and felt its spray on our cheeks.

"I've always wanted to live near a creek like this," Michael said.

"It *is* magnificent," Paul said.

We hiked up the road to the second bench and looked across the valley at glaciers that gleamed in the sun.

"Once we got the flats cleared up, we could have a productive home-stead," Michael said.

"Are you kidding?" Bill said. "It would take months, maybe even years, to clear away the slash and get usable land for a house or a garden."

"And even then, the land'll be bare and scarred," I said.

"But the view ..." Vivianne said, turning again to the mountains.

Back to Galena Bay. This time we decided to look at the land by our-selves. We drove past Bob and Pat's, turning down Hill Creek Road, then left down Ward Road before turning onto Dedosenco Road and parking at the back end of the property.

As we walked the land again, I realized that something in me had changed. Before, I had thought of wilderness as something wild and chaotic, a dark place where animals ripped out each other's guts. But now I began to see that wilderness wasn't all mystery and danger. It was *this* lichen-covered rock, *that* fallen hemlock; *this* woodpecker's tapping, *that* glacier occupying *that* position in the sky. I felt the quiet spirit that arose from the gently sloping land, the broad expanse of the lake, the silence of the forest.

And I could tell that Bill felt it, too. "I like this area," he said.

"Me, too." We smiled at each other.

"It's flat," Michael said.

"That's a good thing," Paul said. "You can use it."

"Yeah ..." Michael's voice trailed off. I knew what he was thinking. Compared to the South Fork land, this place was tame; boring, even.

For the first time, I began to think that we might not have the same vision for where and how we wanted to live.

What then?

Our choice

That night, we pitched our tents on the Galena Bay beach and made a stone ring for a campfire. As the flames began to crackle, I walked with Bill to the water's edge. To the south, the ferry crossed silently, seeming to glide on the still surface. Across the lake, three snow-capped Monashee peaks towered on the western horizon. The southernmost one was the most massive, and its top was notched, forming an M shape. Bob had told us it was called Mount Odin, after the Norse god. The peak next to it, Mount Thor, was taller, with a sharp, jagged point piercing the sky. The northernmost of the three, Mount Freya, had a gentler aspect, its flanks falling away in a series of ridges, like stairs descending.

Bill put his arm around me, and we stood there, lost in the beauty.

After we ate, Paul pulled out his guitar. Sitting on a log facing the lake, he played quietly, no particular tune, just a meandering melody. It was as if he was playing to Odin, Thor, and Freya. The rest of us sat around the campfire and listened.

As the last of the daylight faded, so did the music. Michael said, "Let's rap!" Everyone laughed. We gathered around the fire, sitting on rocks or driftwood.

At first, no one spoke. Then Michael said, "It's come down to a choice between two pieces of land. Let's talk about the pros and cons of each place and see if we can . . . if we can save this thing. I'll start with Kaslo. Number one on the pro side, the creek. You can swim in it—"

Paul hooted. "Right. For three seconds. I timed you, Scar." Everyone laughed. Each of us had lasted the amount of time it took to wade in, dip, and run out.

"Okay, it's not great for swimming," Michael conceded, "but it's a dynamite fishing spot."

"So's the lake, according to Bob," Bill said.

"But who wants to live on a dammed lake?" Vivianne said.

She had a point. The beach was in shadow, but I knew that the dark shapes that dotted it were driftwood and stumps left from when the shoreline had been logged before the dam went in. "The beach *is* a mess," I said, "but the lake is still beautiful."

"The main argument for Galena Bay is the land," Bill said. "It's accessible and it gets more sunlight. Better for growing."

"And South Fork loses sun in the winter," I said. "Can you imagine how depressing it would be not to feel the sun on your face for four months?"

"Yeah, but the place would get plenty of sunlight in the summer, when you need it for the garden," Michael pointed out.

"Besides, the spectacular views make up for the lack of sun," Vivianne said.

"And the land is partly cleared," Michael added.

Bill made a dismissive sound. "Down to clay and rock. At least here there's soil."

"But there's also swamp," Michael said. "Which is why the bugs are so awful. South Fork has no mosquitoes."

"That's because the land is so steep, no water can pool on it," Bill said.

"I don't care *why* it is, it's still a fact. Are you up for swatting mosquitoes and black flies all summer?"

He was right. The bugs *were* awful in Galena Bay.

Bill put another log on the fire, and the flames crackled.

"What about isolation?" Vivianne asked. "South Fork is only four miles from town. Galena Bay is thirty. Don't you think it'd be a bit lonely here?"

"That's the whole idea!" Bill exploded. "We're going to be our own community. The isolation will bring us together."

I remembered Paul telling me, when I first came to the Farm, that Bill had wanted the group to move to Central or South America, for the same reason.

Silence.

"Bob and Pat would be great neighbours," Paul said. "They'd help us and teach us a lot."

"That's true," Michael said.

I knew everyone was thinking of Wilf Ziegler. If there was anyone who would make a *terrible* mentor, it was him.

Paul grabbed a long stick and poked the fire. Sparks rose into the air. "There's one thing we haven't talked about. Money. Galena Bay is half the cost for the same amount of land."

"Paul's right," Bill said. "If we buy this place, we'll have lots of money left over to get things going. Buy tools. Building materials. It'd buy us time while we figure out what the hell we're doing. With Kaslo, we'd have less of a margin."

"And five thousand seems more reasonable," I said.

"Especially when you consider the condition of the land," Bill said. "If you ask me, Kaslo is a rip-off."

"It is not!" Michael said. "It's just a question of what you value."

That's it, I thought. *The core of the problem. It's what you value.* And it was looking like we valued different things.

"Maybe we should wait," Paul said. "Not buy either one. Something better is bound to come along."

"No!" Bill and Michael said at once.

"Prices are going up," Michael said. "I'm afraid that if we wait, we won't be able to afford anything."

"I'm with you there, Scar," Bill said. "We've looked at dozens of places. We know what's out there. We've got to move now."

Silence fell. I sensed that we were all reeling, trying to make sense of what was happening. How had we gone from that feeling of joyous unity in Naramata, just a month ago, to being on the verge of collapse now?

Paul snapped off a piece of stick. "We can talk about pros and cons all night, but in the end, it comes down to your gut feeling. And ever since we came to Galena Bay, this place has felt right to me."

"Ever since I saw the creek, I knew South Fork was for me," Michael said quietly.

"Me, too," Vivianne said.

I felt Bill stiffen. It was up to us. If we voted for Kaslo, Paul would come along. Not happily, maybe, but he would. My heart was so full of conflicting feelings, I felt sick. I sincerely preferred Galena Bay. But I had a selfish motive, too. I would much rather live in a commune of three than a commune of five, and if I had to live with anyone in addition to Bill, I preferred Paul. I knew that Bill was leaning toward Galena Bay, and that, if I said those words, he would join me.

And yet, it wouldn't be right for me to choose for selfish purposes. The commune was so important to Bill. It was what he had been working toward for the last two years. If I truly loved him, shouldn't I help him achieve his dream, rather than pull him away from it?

There was a long pause. Bill and I spoke almost at once. "Galena Bay," I said, as he began, "I have to pick this place. I think it's a better piece of land. I think we could make a good homestead here."

Silence. The only sounds were the crackle of twigs, the murmur of a creek emptying into the bay, the hoot of an owl in the woods behind us. Our commune had just fallen apart, and not one of us could tell why. The silence seemed to be waiting for someone to say, *Hold on, I didn't mean that, I want to change my vote.* But no one did.

"So now what?" Michael said.

"Let's sleep on it," Bill said. "Maybe we'll ... we'll check in in the morning."

Ever since the five of us had met up in Naramata, Paul had continued sleeping in Michael and Vivianne's tent. This night he moved in with Bill and me. No one commented. No one missed the symbolism.

Lying there sleepless, I examined my conscience. In my wish to have Bill to myself, was I responsible for divisive vibes? Maybe so. But I wondered if Vivianne felt the same way. Maybe she was pulling away, even unconsciously, as much as I was.

And what about Bill and Michael? Childhood buddies, teammates in sports, workmates, fellow dreamers. They had conceived this project together. Why, now, would they be willing to move apart?

A thought hit. Both men were strong leaders. Though Bill was more assertive and Michael was more laid-back, both had firm ideas about the homesteading experiment. Maybe there wasn't room for two "alpha" males in the group. Maybe, without realizing it, each was carving out his own position of authority.

None of these theories made me feel better. My whole body felt tense. By the unrelaxed sounds of Bill's and Paul's breathing, I knew that they were wrestling, too.

In the morning, we all staggered out of our tents, bleary-eyed. No one's mind had changed.

After a long silence, Michael said, "I guess this it. We split."

The words echoed. Tears stung my eyes. "I'm sorry," I said. "I'm really sorry."

"Me, too," Vivianne said, and then we were crying, all five of us, and hugging one another.

Strangely, after the tears, things felt easier. We sat down and discussed the division of assets. Allocating six thousand dollars per person, Michael and Vivianne would get $12,000, while Bill, Paul, and I would get $18,000. We would take the truck and they would take the Volkswagen.

"I'll miss the truck," Michael said, running his hand over the camper he and his father had built.

"I'll miss the Beetle," I said. That had been the car of my early teaching career, the car of Bill's and my romance as we sped back and forth between the Farm and my house in Richboro.

Within an hour, we had sorted out our possessions: clothes, sleeping bags, food, books, camping lanterns. Michael and Vivianne loaded up the Volkswagen.

My eyes filled, watching Bill and Michael clasp each other around the shoulders. "Scar." "Coach." Their voices were husky.

Michael and Vivianne climbed into the car. Leaning out the windows, they waved. "Bye! Keep in touch!"

Bill, Paul, and I linked arms. "Bye! Good luck!"

When they disappeared around a curve in the road, we turned to one another. We were a commune of three instead of five. We were inexperienced and unsure about what lay ahead. But we were in love with Galena Bay. We would make it work.

Many years later, long after Bill and I had left Galena Bay, after Paul had given up on homesteading and moved away, after Michael and Vivianne had left South Fork and divorced, after Vivianne and I had become good friends, Bill, Michael, and I talked about the split.

"Do you think we could have avoided it?" I asked.

Bill shrugged. "We were all young and stupid and not willing enough to compromise."

"We were in too much of a hurry," Michael said. "Everywhere we went, people told us that land prices were going up. We felt like we had to buy right away."

"I remember that feeling of pressure," I said.

Michael nodded. "It was ridiculous, of course. Paul was right. We should have waited a bit. We could have rented a house for the winter and then looked again in the spring."

"Do you think we would have found someplace we all liked?" I asked.

Michael shrugged. "I was pretty in love with the creek. You guys loved the gentle land. But maybe, with a little perspective, we all would have been more flexible."

"Not so stubborn," Bill said, and Michael nodded.

We sat there, each contemplating how differently the future might have unfolded if we had done that. If we had taken our time. Let go of our positions. Found a place we all could love.

I imagined the five of us walking on a different piece of land, a piece none of us had yet seen. Building a house together. Digging a garden. Building a woodshed. Taking turns cooking, doing chores, tending animals, learning crafts, playing music in the evenings, just the way we'd planned.

Sitting there, I asked myself if I regretted the way things had played out. Certainly, if the commune had stayed together, I would have felt good about fulfilling our ideals. I would have worked hard to contribute. We would have learned from one another, grown closer, achieved something remarkable.

And yet. Looking back, I have to acknowledge the private part of me, the part that shied away from being in a group. The part that craved alone time. The selfish part that wanted Bill to myself.

Yes, I regret not having given the experiment a chance. No, I do not regret the choice of Galena Bay.

Still, I can't help but wonder: What if . . . ?

4

Building

Clearing land

Late August, 1972. Bill, Paul, and I, along with Bob and Pat Harrington, sat around the massive desk in the lawyer's office in Revelstoke. The three of us were dressed for the occasion in our hippie best: I in an embroidered peasant blouse and blue bell-bottoms, Bill and Paul in clean jeans, checkered shirts, and combed hair. Bill, already balding at twenty-five, wore his straight hair shoulder-length. Paul's frizzy auburn mane encircled his head like a teased-out steel wool pad, which he attempted to tame with a floppy felt hat. Our attire contrasted with that of Bob and Pat, who were dressed in tailored slacks, shirts, and skirt, and even more starkly with that of the lawyer, in a three-piece suit, complete with a watch chain dangling from the vest.

I took the lawyer's heavy black fountain pen and signed Ellen Rosenberg on the deed in my neat schoolteacher's handwriting. Bill and Paul did the same, followed by Bob and Pat. She handed the pen back to the lawyer, an elderly British gentleman, who witnessed the proceedings in the elegant script of a bygone age.

We shook hands all around. "Congratulations," the lawyer said to Bill, Paul, and me. "You are now landowners."

We smiled, elated but also terrified. Now what? We owned twenty acres of bush. We had to clear land, build a cabin, dig a garden. Did I forget anything? Oh yeah, put in an outhouse. Lay a water line. Where do we begin?

How about buying tools? The three of us made our way from the lawyer's office to the Co-op Store. I unfolded the shopping list we'd compiled the night before with Bob and Pat's help. Or, rather, at Bob and Pat's dictation. "Swede saw? Could you spell that?" (What's a Swede saw? Too embarrassed to ask.) The list took up two pages.

"Excuse me," I said to a sales clerk in a red jacket, "could you ... uh ... where do we find a plumb line?"

He took one look at the list, fetched a shopping cart, and began to walk up and down the aisles, the three of us following like ducklings. Plumb line, hammers, screwdrivers, axes, hatchets, shovels, stepladder, nails, Swede saws in three different sizes (not to be confused with a handsaw or a rip saw or a crosscut saw), levels, chisels, planes. Plus a big speckled-black canning kettle (just like Pat's), Mason jars for canning, orange rawhide work gloves with bands of blue and green canvas on the back, and heavy, high-lacing work boots for each of us.

The cashier's eyebrows lifted as the laden cart approached the checkout—$175 later, we loaded our purchases into the truck and stood at the tailgate, admiring the gleaming blades and grainy wood handles. We didn't know how to use half of the tools, but already new vocabulary was tumbling out of our mouths: double-bitted axe ... balance level ...

Returning to Galena Bay, we drove around to the back end of the property. Although the front end bordered on the highway, and was where Bob and Pat had situated their house, we'd already decided to build back here. This wasn't a convenient choice. It meant we'd have to drive extra distances to the mailbox and the ferry. Hill Creek Road was plowed in the winter, but Ward and Dedosenco Roads weren't, so we'd have to park our truck on Hill Creek Road and snowshoe or ski a mile and a quarter in and out. Carrying groceries. And supplies. And laundry. But it would be worth it, we felt, to avoid the noise and dust of the unpaved highway and to have more privacy.

Bill, Paul, and I sat for a few minutes in the cab, smoking a joint, then got out and followed an old skid trail, mostly overgrown with bracken, thimbleberries, and hemlock seedlings, uphill for about fifty yards. We wandered about in the bush, seeking a likely spot to locate the cabin. On one side of the skid trail I noticed a clump of birch trees whose trunks all converged at the base, as if a single seed had yielded five stalks. *Those would be nice to look at from the cabin,* I thought. Standing on the trail, I looked around. There were lots of trees that would have to be cleared to make room for a cabin, but no huge ones. The land sloped uphill to the east, downhill to the west, from where sunlight was now filtering through the forest. From where I was standing, I could just make out the back road.

"Hey, you guys, come here," I called. When Bill and Paul emerged from the woods, I flung out my hand. "How about right here?"

"Pretty spot," Bill said.

"Do we want to be so close to the back road?" Paul asked.

"It's not like there's much traffic on it," Bill said.

This was an understatement, since Dedosenco Road turned into a dead end a short distance past our property and faded into a woodland trail.

"The farther away from the road we build, the longer the driveway we need," I said. "And if we build right on the skid trail, we won't have to cut so many trees."

They looked at me admiringly. "This girl's got it all figured out," Bill said, poking me with his elbow.

Not exactly true. I was stoned. The spot looked pretty. It gave off good vibes. I'd said the first thing that had come into my head. Still, I didn't mind taking the credit. I grinned. "Well?"

"Sure," Bill said.

"Fine," Paul said.

And so the cabin site was chosen.

Pleased with ourselves, we drove back to our temporary home, a 1950s-vintage cabin on 160 acres of land ("a quarter section," I liked to say, showing off) a few miles away, on Hill Creek Road. The farm, originally settled by the long-gone Dedosenco family, was now owned by a wealthy couple from Minneapolis called the Ebins, who had no plans to move there and agreed to let us stay rent-free in exchange for keeping bears out of the gnarled apple trees.

Ebin's cabin was a white-painted, wood-frame building. It was divided into two rooms, a bedroom in the back and an open living room and kitchen in front. It came equipped with a woodstove for cooking, a tin wood heater for heat, propane lights, and running cold water. No toilet, but there was an outhouse, as well as a large woodshed. The cabin stood on top of a hill that sloped down to the west, where Hill Creek ran through a culvert beneath the road. A large, cleared area, formerly farmland, now covered with weeds, stretched to the east beside the cabin.

Bill and I claimed the bedroom, flopping our newly purchased double mattress on the floor. A wooden crate turned on its side served as a night table. Paul was stuck sleeping in the living room, propping up his twin mattress against the wall during the day and lowering it at night. I was delighted that the bedroom had a door. This afforded more privacy than Bill and I had had at the Farm, where our sleeping quarters were separated from the rest of the living room by a curtain.

Our first job was to clear land. At the time, a temporary three-man sawmill was located about half a mile down the road from Ebin's cabin. Typically, once the tract was logged over at these smaller mills, the mill and crew packed up and moved on.

In this case, the owner's name was Floyd Fitzgerald, a logger and saw-miller from Revelstoke. Floyd had classic Irish good looks: medium build, a shock of thick white hair, and the most gorgeous cornflower-blue eyes I had ever seen. He smoked a pipe, and the fragrant tobacco smoke curled up around his head. Although Floyd was probably pushing fifty, I had a secret crush on him.

Walter Nelson, one of the long-time residents of Galena Bay, had told us that Floyd did good work, so we hired him to clear about a quarter-acre of land: some on the north side of the skid trail, for a garden; some on the south side of the skid trail, for a woodshed; and some right in the middle, for the cabin. Floyd showed up with an enormous chainsaw. He pulled a cord, the chainsaw snarled, and the noise blocked out every-thing: birdsong, words, even thoughts. He moved from tree to tree. With one or two swipes the tree was down, falling gracefully like a fainting maiden or, in some cases, knocking down a neighbouring tree with it. Bill, Paul, and I followed, hacking off branches with axes and hatchets, gathering armfuls of boughs, and carrying them to the edge of what was becoming an open space.

The land-clearing took several days. For the first half hour each morn-ing, my arms felt light and loose. Little by little, the axe grew heavier. My arms began to ache. My shoulders. My back. My neck. Whenever I thought that I'd surely limbed the last tree of the day, the chainsaw buzzed and another tree fell, another stump oozed piney resin. Sweat rolled down my back and itched. Mosquitoes buzzed and bit. My arms screamed as I lifted the axe for another swipe, and another.

I can't do this, I thought. *I've made a terrible mistake. I didn't know it would be this hard. I deserve to quit. I'm a girl. I don't have the same muscles the guys have.* (Ashamed to think it, ashamed to abandon my feminist prin-ciples, but desperate enough to use it as an excuse.) *Is it time for a coffee break? Should I get the thermos? I just peed five minutes ago; I can't do that again.*

Paul, too, looked exhausted, pausing frequently to blow his nose or roll his shoulders or adjust his hat. I could tell that, like me, he felt defeated by the gruelling work and yearned to quit. Only Bill worked incessantly, chop-ping and lifting and carrying and coming back for more. His arm muscles bulged when he lifted a load. I admired his strength. To be honest, it turned me on. But at the same time, I was peeved. *Can't he show a little goddamn mortal weakness?* I thought.

Back to the tree. The next. It was only the fear of letting down my side that kept me going.

I can't do this . . .

Days later, when there was nothing left but stumps in that quarter-acre, I stood in the clearing, stretched out my arms, and felt sunlight directly on my skin. The land was changed. The chainsaw had transformed a tiny part of the wilderness into a homestead—or the beginnings of one.

Once we had carried all the logs out of the way, stacking the thick, straight ones to be used for building and the others to be cut into firewood, Floyd came back to pull up the stumps. The distant drone of a skidder announced his arrival long before the machine came into view, lumbering up the driveway like a yellow dinosaur. Floyd perched in the cab, pipe clenched in his teeth. He looked like a sea captain, not a man of the woods.

Bill, Paul, and I set a choker chain—a heavy chain of cast-iron links with a hook at one end—around a stump, Floyd pushed a button, and with an electric whirr the cable tugged and strained, the stump moved, and roots emerged from the earth like great snakes rising from the mud. We unhooked the chain and wrapped it around another stump. Floyd pulled that one out and dragged it over to the first. When he had a pile of four or five stumps, he raised a huge curved blade and pushed the stumps to the edge of the woods, their roots sticking out at crazy angles as they toppled in slow-motion somersaults. Then back for another stump, one screech for forward, another for reverse. Back and forth all day in a haze of noise, smoke, and dust. In the late afternoon, Floyd waved his pipe at us, leaned his head out of the cab, and called above the roar of the engine, "Catch you later." He swivelled the skidder around and rumbled down the driveway and onto the back road, the drone growing fainter.

I turned and looked and the clearing. Grey-brown earth, gouged with wide, criss-crossing tread marks. No more stumps, no more boughs, no more topsoil. I couldn't decide whether the clearing was a raw gash or an open door.

Self-made architect

In October, Bill started designing our cabin. The fact that he had no experience in architecture or carpentry didn't deter him. None of us knew how to do any of this stuff, and wasn't that part of the adventure?

He stood in the spot where the cabin was going to be and imagined the dwelling that might stand there. He paced around Ebin's place, snapping a tape measure and scribbling dimensions on the backs of envelopes. He consulted with Bob Harrington about different building styles and materials. He made drawings, sketched doors and windows, and erased sinks and moved them from one wall to another.

Bill showed his drawings to Paul and me. "What do you think? Put the front door here," he thrust another paper forward, "or here?"

I had no idea. What did I know of building design? Would it be better to have the front door facing the driveway or facing the woods? I shrugged. Paul shrugged. Bill erased and made more lines and came back and showed them to us again. Little by little, as if I were learning to read music, I began to see actual shapes in those lines, to see a house in those pencilled walls. "Yeah, the door'll work great over there. But I want a window over the sink. Now, where's the chimney going to be?"

What emerged was a plan for a sixteen-foot by sixteen-foot wood-frame cabin, with a loft upstairs under a steeply pitched roof, the better to shed snow; 256 square feet. I had no idea how much room 256 square feet was, but it sounded like a lot. It sounded like just the right amount.

After receiving detailed instructions from Walter, we dug eight holes around the perimeter of a sixteen-foot by sixteen-foot square, plus one in the centre. We built wooden forms, stirred the gritty, gloppy cement mixture in our new wheelbarrow, and poured it into the square holes. As we filled the ninth hole, the form broke apart and we frantically propped rocks against the sides as cement oozed out at the corners. After a few days, we removed the forms, and nine more or less square pillars poked up out of the ground like widely spaced grey teeth.

Now for the framing. Again, we had no idea how to do this. And then help arrived. Our friend Kevin Murphy, from Bucks County, had driven out to British Columbia to visit Bill, Paul, and me, to visit Michael and Vivianne, to check out land to buy. Kevin had grown up in Levittown, along with Bill and Michael. Tall, slim, and almost unbearably handsome, he had been the alluring bachelor of our close-knit group of friends back east. Gifted with a beautiful tenor voice, he, along with Aileen, had been the stars of our sing-alongs back at the Farm. (I'd had a mad crush on him before I hopped into Bill's bed and fell in love with him instead.)

Now here was Kevin, just when we needed an extra pair of hands. Even better, he had brought his friend Eddie, known as Fast Eddie because of his rat-a-tat-tat style of talking and his non-stop energy. Eddie had also grown up in Levittown but now lived in California.

The two friends were a study in contrasts. Where Kevin was tall and dark, Eddie was of medium height, stocky, and blond. Kevin, who had been raised in a Catholic family and attended Catholic school, had completely rejected religion. Eddie was a born-again Christian who started each day by reading parts of the Bible to himself. Eddie had served in Vietnam, while Kevin (like Bill and Paul) had avoided the draft by securing a bogus letter from a shrink saying he was unfit.

No matter. Eddie, who had done some house framing in the past, possessed more building experience than Bill, Paul, Kevin, and I combined. He scrambled up and down ladders and leaped from stud to post like a cat sailing from fence to garden wall. He pounded in the studs. "Praise the Lord!" He attached the sills. "Thank you, Jesus!"

No, thank *you*, Eddie. In three days, using only hand tools, since we had no electricity, the framing was done. Eddie took off, Bible in hand, bound for California or who knows where. Kevin followed, heading down to Kaslo.

By now, we were on our way. One day the cabin was a skeleton of horizontal sills and vertical studs and diagonal rafters. A few days later the spaces between those wooden outlines began to fill in. Our constant symphony was the hammer's staccato tap-tap-tap, the rasp of a saw slicing wood, and the rippling thud of sheets of plywood being slapped into place. My wrist and forearm and shoulder ached, and I watched the thumbnail on my left, nail-holding hand turn yellow and then purple and then blue-black.

Plywood sheathing, windows, insulation, plastic vapour barrier, aluminum roofing, tarpaper. In a month, the outer shell of the cabin was completed. Bill, Paul, and I stood at the bottom of the driveway and saw a child's drawing of a house: square sides, slanty roof, chimney poking up.

One day, Ray Chartrand, a friend of Bill's, showed up. Ray, who had met Bill in San Francisco and had travelled with him in Mexico, was slim and slight, with a brown goatee and green eyes that had a subversive gleam. He was a Québecker with strongly accented English. He was a vagabond, a dreamer who roamed around, whispered his ideas to his friends, and then, when they were halfway through building the yurt or the alfalfa seed sprouter or whatever thing Ray had gotten them all whipped up about, disappeared.

"Raymond, how you been, man?"

Spacey grin. "Terrific. Listen, I got this idea ..."

That was Ray, and, as luck would have it, he was a fairly decent carpenter, just when we needed one. He helped us put in the windowsills, hang the door, and panel the inside walls (we used rough, un-planed fir boards, mainly because Floyd had sold us a load of them cheaply). Ray even made us a silverware drawer, which actually slid in and out like a real drawer. The only drawer in the cabin. Luxury.

And then he took off.

Walter told us about a cabin up in Beaton, an abandoned mining town on the northeast arm of Arrow Lake about ten miles north of Galena Bay. The cabin was to be torn down and burned. Bill and Paul drove up there and came back with an enamel sink, a scrapbook whose yellowed pages held faded photographs of loggers standing three abreast in front of twelve-foot-diameter cedars, a copper ash pan with a long-handled scraper, and, the prize, a Findlay woodstove. It was the quintessential woodstove: white enamel warming box, curved steel legs, lacy filigreed edges, and a small round thermometer embedded in the oven door. (The thermometer didn't work, but that didn't matter.) It was a woodstove one could fall in love with. And I did.

By late November, the cabin was livable. But almost a foot of snow now covered the ground. Every day for the last several weeks, as Bill, Paul, and I travelled from Ebin's place to our cabin, and then back again, we'd been slogging down Ward and Dedosenco Roads in four-wheel drive. It was questionable whether we could move in before the back roads became completely impassable. Paul had already announced that he planned to go back east for the winter, to work as a substitute teacher and save money for our enterprise; he would rejoin us at the end of the school year. Bill and I decided to stay in Ebin's cabin for the winter and move into our own cabin as soon as possible in the spring.

A tidy little homestead

The winter of 1972–73 had an unusually low snowfall. (At the height of winter, there was still four feet of snow on the ground, but Bob and Walter assured us that this was far less than usual.) By late March, our truck tires made two ruts down to bare gravel on Hill Creek Road. But because Ward and Dedosenco Roads had been neither plowed nor driven on all winter, their snowpack lingered longer. Every time Bill and I drove by, we stopped and measured the snow. Two feet ... sixteen inches ... a foot ...

In April, when the snowpack was down to nine inches, Bill said, "I think we can make it in four-wheel drive." I climbed in beside him, and the truck began to churn through the grainy, slippery snow. Snow scraped along the bottom with a sound like sandpaper rubbing. The engine whined as it strained to push the vehicle forward. We skidded, lurched forward with sudden ease, then plowed through slush again.

We made it.

A few days later, we carried the last few boxes into the cabin. We had said thanks and goodbye to Ebin's cabin. How strange it was now to enter our own cabin, which had stood empty all winter. That night, for the first time, Bill and I slept in the loft. Downstairs, our first fire crackled in the woodstove. I lay awake for a long time.

The pale sun of winter became yellow again, the snow became grainier, shrank, and was swallowed by patches of dark, bare earth. New leaf buds clung to the branches of the birches, still tightly closed, waiting for warmer weather to coax them open. But the birds knew. The winter Steller's jays had moved up the mountainside, and the birds of spring—robins, thrushes, a rare mountain bluebird—were back, trilling from hidden branches.

Arms around each other, one day Bill and I counted all the jobs that needed doing. First, a tool shed that would go in the northeast corner of the clearing. An outhouse; the present hole in the ground wouldn't last much longer. A woodshed ...

Suddenly we heard the sound of singing. A moment later, Kevin Murphy, our Bucks County friend who'd helped us frame the cabin, appeared on the trail, shouldering a knapsack. Wandering Kevin, singing Kevin, back from the winter on the East Coast with a few dollars in his pocket, looking for a woman, looking for some musicians to sing with, looking for some friends who needed help building a tool shed.

Bill handed him a hammer and a carpenter's apron, and they walked over to the tool shed site, talking basketball, carpentry, tales of winter east and west. I watched them go, then returned to the cabin.

It was chilly inside. The cabin, shaded by trees to the east, was in morning shadow. I started a fire in the woodstove. Already I was learning that each woodstove had its own personality, required its own special treatment; that the combination of paper, kindling, and wood that would blaze instantly in one stove (say, the one in Ebin's cabin) would, in another (say, this one) fizzle into smoke. The Findlay was a fussy lady (with her filigree trim and dainty, curved legs, I couldn't help but think of her as female), insisting on a large appetizer of crumpled, dry newspaper followed by a helping of the slenderest sticks of kindling and thinnest morsels of fir or hemlock before she would consider digesting something as hearty as a chunk of wood. On this morning, she favoured me, and without hesitation began to crackle and snap.

I surveyed the boxes stacked against the wall, searching for the carton that contained our kitchenware. I opened boxes, rifled through their contents. No—that one held books. No—that one was full of linens. No—that was our summer clothes. Finally, I found it. I removed pots, salad bowls, casserole dishes, and lifted out the prize: a coffee pot. After months of drinking cowboy coffee (water and coffee boiled in a pot, then left to sit, to let the grounds settle), this was a luxury. I filled the pot with water, set it on the stove, and continued unpacking.

Ah, the delicious agony of deciding where everything should go. Not that there was much space in my kitchen; it was only a corner of the one-room cabin. Woodstove, white enamel sink with a drain bucket beneath, bucket of water on the plywood counter, rough fir shelves. But it was mine, every splintery inch of it. Should the plates go here or here? This looks like a good shelf for the cups. But should the granola go on this shelf or that one? And look—here's a perfect spot for this little vase.

The coffee started to perc, and the aroma reminded me of my childhood when the smell of my parents' coffee symbolized something mysteriously grown up. When it was ready, I poured myself a cup and sat down at the table that we'd built from a telephone cable spool with a square of plywood nailed to the top; the chairs were cedar stumps with vertical planks for backrests. The sun had crested the treetops, and light streamed in the back window, warming my face and striking the chrome of the woodstove. From outside, the sounds of Bill's and Kevin's voices, their hammer blows, and an occasional peal of laughter carried across the clearing. The coffee tasted rich and strong. I sat there, warmed by the sun and the fire, filled with contentment. Sunshine, the cabin, the land, my man, a funky table at which to sit and drink a cup of coffee ... I needed nothing more.

There was a knock at the door. For a moment, I thought Bill and Kevin were fooling around. Cup in hand, I opened the door. A Royal Canadian Mounted Police officer stood there.

Oh, no, the dope, I thought frantically, trying to remember where we'd stashed our small bag of marijuana. *It's probably in one of these boxes, and the cop is going to march in and spot it right away and haul us off to jail—*

"Mrs. Schwartz?" he said pleasantly.

"Mmm-hmm." I snuck a look in Bill and Kevin's direction. They were hammering away, oblivious to the presence of our visitor. I hadn't heard a car. He must have parked some distance down the back road.

The officer pulled a sheet of paper from his pocket. "My information says that you are a landed immigrant. Is that correct?"

Maybe this isn't a bust after all—or is he just setting me up for deportation? By this time, we had applied and been granted landed immigrant status.

"Yes, it is," I said. "My paper's in here somewhere." With a sweep of my arm, I indicated the array of boxes. "I might be able to find it, but ..."

That's it: he's going to trick me into opening boxes and then pounce on the stash.

"No, that's all right. We're trying to track down illegal immigrants. I understand there was a group of 'em around here. Are they still here?"

I let out a breath. He was referring to Lee Harding and his pals, a group of Americans who'd bought a plot of land across the back road from us the year before. They'd built a ramshackle cabin and a treehouse, squabbled, and taken off, back to California—all before we arrived.

"No, they're gone," I said. "The place is empty. Has been ever since we got here."

I didn't add that even if they were still in BC, I wouldn't rat them out. Bill and I were legal now, but we'd lived here illegally ourselves for several months before immigrating. Solidarity still counted for something.

The officer put the paper back in his pocket. "That's what I thought." He looked over my shoulder and smiled. "Just moving in, eh?"

I grinned. "Yeah. It's a little disorganized at the moment." I remembered my manners. "Would you like a cup of coffee?"

"Smells good, but no thanks. Got to catch the ferry. Good luck with your place, eh?"

He left. I watched him until his blue uniform blended with the dark green of the forest and disappeared. I was still looking out the window when Bill came in. His cheeks were rosy, and bits of sawdust clung to his sweatshirt. "Who was that?"

"A cop."

"A cop?" His voice immediately became mistrustful. "What'd he want?"

"He was looking for illegal immigrants."

"Lee and that gang?"

"Yeah. Bill, you know something? He was really nice."

I leaned my head against the door frame. The idea of a nice cop contradicted my conception of police officers. Cops arresting freedom fighters in the South. Cops busting friends for an ounce of grass. Cops bashing protesters in Chicago. A cop as nice guy? That was a new one.

"And you know what he said? 'Good luck with your place.'"

Bill grinned. "Really?"

"Really."

"Maybe cops here are different," Bill said, turning toward the door.

"Maybe," I said. "By the way, Bill, where's the dope?"

He pointed over my shoulder. "Right there."

I turned. All by itself on a bookcase was a Players tobacco tin. A bit of plastic stuck out beneath the lid, and a package of matches sat on top. I looked at Bill, feeling my face turn hot.

Bill smiled. "Didn't you know that?"

I shook my head and poured myself another cup of coffee.

Bill and Kevin finished the tool shed. It was twelve by sixteen feet. They built shelves and hammered in nails to hang tools. Soon each shovel and hoe and axe and saw had its place on the wall. We bought half a dozen galvanized-aluminum, mouse-proof garbage cans and stored foodstuffs in them: sacks of oats, rice, soybeans, lentils, powdered milk.

Bill and I stood in the middle of the tool shed and gazed around. It was tidy and well equipped. We felt rich. We felt like experts in country living—even if we had yet to use many of the implements for the first time and weren't quite sure how.

The job finished, Kevin took off once again. Paul returned from the East Coast with a stash of money for our joint bank account and his familiar floppy felt hat. The cabin quickly became even more cramped. As in Ebin's cabin, Paul had to sleep on the floor, propping his mattress against the wall during the day.

I was glad to have him back with his excruciating puns and his splendid guitar-playing. But I was not happy about the loss of privacy. At least at Ebin's, Bill and I were able to close our bedroom door. In the cabin, to reach the loft, you climbed a ladder, and there was no door at the top of the landing. Bill's and my sleeping spot was directly over where Paul lay downstairs. If he'd looked up, he could have seen the bottom of our mattress through cracks between the floorboards. I tried to make Bill wait to make love until I could no longer hear Paul stirring, but the creak of the floorboards and the rustle of the mattress must have been obvious. Paul tactfully said nothing.

Now that the cabin and the tool shed were built, the next job was to put in a water line. A large creek, MacKenzie Creek, flowed past the eastern end of our land, on the other side of the main road. Our cabin was located at the western end, half a mile away. Bob already had an intake in a spring that emerged from the ground near his driveway and flowed back into MacKenzie Creek a short distance farther south. He said we could put our intake in the spring—a generous offer, since it would cut fifteen-hundred feet off the total length of our line and save us the trouble of having to lay the pipe through the culvert under the road.

We went to town and came back with huge coils of one-inch and three-quarter-inch black pipe and a box of brass fittings, T-connectors, elbows, reducers, clamps, and valves. The next day we made the connection into Bob's system and laid the pipe on top of the ground, fifteen-hundred feet of it, joining section to section, all the way down to the cabin. We connected it to the intake pipe on the sink—and oh, the luxury of running water. It felt almost decadent to saunter over to the sink and turn on the tap. No more pail and dipper on the counter. Fresh, ice-cold water that, mere minutes ago, was gurgling in the creek, instead of room-temperature water with a slightly stale plastic taste. The first day, just for the thrill of it, we drank cup after cup. That night we filled our chamber pots.

Now, of course, we had to bury the water line. Bob and Walter advised digging at least a foot deep, though eighteen inches would be better. Bill, the organizer, decreed that we would dig fifty feet a day, and it was a good thing he did, because the job was such drudgery, the trail so infested with roots and rocks, the air so thick with mosquitoes, that without a daily quota the task never would have been completed.

"Fifty feet a day" was branded onto our foreheads. It echoed in our footsteps as we marched up the trail, spades over our shoulders, pickaxes dangling from gloved hands. "Take this hammer, carry it to the captain ..." Yeah, it felt like being on a chain gang, but the captain was Bill, and he was working harder than anyone else, doing more than his share, so how could you bitch about your load when the captain was sweating and grunting and not saying a word?

Well, actually, you could bitch—silently. Paul and I were getting incrementally stronger, but we still tired more quickly than Bill did. Sometimes, when Paul paused to catch his breath, I thought I saw unhappiness in his eyes. I couldn't tell if it was because of the miserable work, or because Bill was bossy, or because Bill and I had each other and Paul was lonely, or because Paul didn't like being here. I didn't ask, and he didn't say.

For my part, I tried to keep going, but sometimes, exhausted, frustrated by a thick tree root that would not yield to the pickaxe, I felt that if I had to swing that thing one more time I was going to fling it into the woods. Fed up, I'd yell, "Break!"

Paul would shoot me a grateful look, and Bill would look surprised. "Really? Already?"

"Already! We've been going for an hour!"

"We have? Oh, okay." He'd flop down beside me with a grin.

I couldn't be mad at Bill. Intent on completing the job, and powered by his incredible strength and fitness, he really hadn't noticed that Paul and I were wilting.

"Fifty feet a day." The trench snaked down the trail, finally reached the back of the cabin, detoured around the side, and ended below the intake. Where an elbow made a right turn upward and through the floor, we wrapped the pipe in fibreglass insulation to keep it from freezing. (This would turn out to be inadequate and, in some winters, our water line would freeze right at that spot—but for now we thought it was ingenious engineering.)

We hiked back up to the intake with hoes and spades. All fifteen-hundred feet down, we nudged the pipe into the ditch and covered it up with dirt. And drank a glass of water to celebrate.

Next on the list: a woodshed. This went in on the south side of the driveway, about fifty feet from the house. It was a three-walled structure, open on the fourth side, basically just a wooden shell with a slightly sloping roof. Since this was our third construction project, we were getting handy with tools, and the woodshed went up quickly. We filled it with the wood Bill and I had bucked during the winter from the trees that Floyd had cut down. Three rows of firewood, each about four-feet wide and six-feet high. Thin rounds of pale hemlock; split pieces of fir, orangey-red and oozing resin; lighter-coloured cedar, good for starting fires; and, most valuable, thick chunks of birch, our longest-burning wood, for nighttime fires. Riches, indeed.

Finally, the outhouse. We located this about a hundred feet from the cabin, facing away from it, of course. We dug a three-foot-deep hole. We decided to make the outhouse a two-seater, complete with a white plastic toilet seat on one side. The other side was for squatters. The side-by-side design never caught on, though. We hadn't considered that most people preferred to do their business with a magazine, not with a companion.

When Bill and I got married, one of our wedding gifts was a mobile of translucent fish swimming lazily through the air. I hung it from a tree facing the outhouse. On sunny days, when splotches of light illuminated the fish, a trip to the outhouse became an aesthetic experience.

By the summer of 1973, we had a tidy little homestead: a small clearing, a cabin, a tool shed, a woodshed, and an outhouse. As with most of our other endeavours in Galena Bay, we embarked on these projects without having the faintest idea how to pull them off. Thanks to helpful books, advice from our neighbours, and the timely arrival of friends with more advanced skills, or at least willing hands, we figured it out. We made mistakes. Not every building ran true. Over the years, the outhouse listed to the side, pushed by the heavy snowpack, and we had to brace it from the opposite side it so it wouldn't topple over.

It never occurred to us that we couldn't build these structures. "We'll figure it out," we said optimistically, and plunged in. This attitude—"I don't know how but I can learn"—became our motto, not just in building but in everything else we undertook. It is perhaps the most important lesson we learned in Galena Bay.

And the cabin, I'm proud to say, was so soundly constructed that we never had a single mouse. Fifty years later, it's still standing.

Love, Marriage, and Immigration

Immigration

I considered myself a liberated woman. Marriage, in my view, was a bourgeois institution for people who needed the security of a legal commitment. Not I.

But Bill and I *did* need to immigrate to Canada. When we first entered the country, in June 1972, crossing from New York State into Québec, we lied at the border, saying that we were just visiting. Now it was September. Our visitor's visas were running out. We needed to acquire legal status to remain in Canada.

At the time, you could apply to immigrate at the border. Canada's immigration system was based on points. So many points for speaking French and English, the two official languages; so many points for your level of education; so many points for your occupation and the level of demand for it; so many points for the assets you were bringing into the country.

Bill and I reviewed our qualifications and decided that I was the better bet. We both had bachelor's degrees, we both spoke English (I had high-school and college French, but couldn't claim to be fluent), and we had assets in common of about $10,000. Bill had a degree in business administration with a major in marketing. He had mostly worked as a youth development counsellor in a reform school in Philadelphia before we moved, a worthy occupation but not one that he was officially qualified for. I was a special education teacher with a year's experience. Special education teachers were always in demand.

So we made a plan. I would cross back into the US, approach the Canadian border as if I were entering the country for the first time, and apply to immigrate. Once I received landed immigrant status—surely I was a shoe-in—we would get married, and Bill would immigrate as my husband.

I wasn't sure I wanted to get married under these circumstances. Not that I didn't want to commit to Bill—I loved him deeply and couldn't imagine life without him—but it wasn't the most romantic reason for getting hitched. Plus, bourgeois, etc. But no other likely option for immigrating presented itself.

I duly crossed and drove to the Canadian border. I filled out forms, produced my documents (birth certificate, US passport, teaching certificates from Wisconsin and Pennsylvania, and teaching reports) and was interviewed by a friendly, young, clean-shaven official with military-short hair.

After the interview, while the official added up my points, I leaned back in my chair, certain that his next words would be, "Congratulations, and welcome to Canada!"

Instead, he frowned. "I'm very sorry, Miss Rosenberg, but I'm afraid you don't qualify."

"W-what?"

"You didn't score enough points."

"But—but I have a college degree. And I'm a special ed teacher. And I have teaching certificates from two different states."

He turned the forms around so I could read them. "True. But you didn't receive any points for your occupation because you don't have a British Columbia teaching certificate. Your US certificates don't count. And without those points, your total isn't high enough."

My heart was pounding. "Now what?"

He gave me a smile. "I suggest you go home and apply for a BC teaching certificate. Once you get it, you can reapply. And you should be successful next time."

Go home?

Of course, I didn't tell him that I was already living illegally in BC.

I sat in the truck, shaking, then did the only thing I could think of: drove to another border crossing and entered, again saying I was just a visitor.

"Have a pleasant stay," said the border guard, waving me north.

I returned to Galena Bay and told Bill what had happened. He was surprised, and a little shaken. If *I* hadn't qualified, how would he? It was unlikely that any immigration officials would find us in Galena Bay, so we weren't in immediate danger of deportation. But our prospects for acquiring landed immigrant status looked dim.

At the time, Floyd Fitzgerald, who had cleared our land for us, was operating his three-man sawmill about half a mile down the road from Ebin's cabin, where Bill and I were staying. Floyd employed two fellows: Gordy, a tall, lanky man of about forty with shaggy light-brown hair, who looked like he had seen the inside of many sawmills and even more pubs; and Andras, a short, stocky Hungarian who spoke fractured English with a strong accent.

A few nights a week, Floyd took the ferry and drove up to Revelstoke to be with his wife, returning on the first ferry the following morning to begin operations. Gordy and Andras bunked in a small cabin at the mill.

In October, after Paul had left for the East Coast, to substitute-teach over the winter, our friend Kevin Murphy showed up. Kevin was always happy to plunge into whatever tasks Bill and I were working on—at that time, cleaning up the log slash from the trees that Floyd had cut for us earlier in the fall.

One evening, while I made cookies, Bill was playing the guitar and Kevin was singing Buffalo Springfield's "For What It's Worth." He had, ironically, just gotten to the line "Stop! Hey, what's that sound?" when we heard a vehicle coming up the driveway at great speed. We looked at one another in surprise: Who could possibly be visiting us?

A beat-up Chevy screeched to a halt in front of the cabin, and Andras jumped out, a panic-stricken look on his face. Waving his arms, he yelled, "Come, come! Help, help!" He shouted some words in Hungarian. Then again, "Come! Help!" His breath smelled strongly of booze.

We calmed him down long enough to get the gist of the story. He and Gordy had had a few beers—probably more than a few—and Gordy had come up with the bright idea of starting up the sawmill and processing a load of logs. While operating the skidder (a machine that moves logs from one part of the mill to another), he had tried to make too tight a turn and had toppled the skidder over on himself. Now he was trapped beneath it. This was one of the nights when Floyd was in Revelstoke, so Andras had come to us, the nearest neighbours.

Bill and Kevin hopped in our truck and followed Andras back to the sawmill. Fortunately, Bill, who had worked in factories in the past, knew how to operate a forklift. He used the forks to lift the skidder just high enough so that Kevin and Andras could slide Gordy out from under it.

While Gordy alternately sobbed and moaned in pain, Bill and Kevin loaded him into the truck. They drove the three miles to the home of Walter Nelson, who had a radio telephone for emergencies. Walter called the ferry, which had closed down for the night and was docked on the other side of the lake, at Shelter Bay. The ferry crew fired up the vessel, made the twenty-minute trip across to Galena Bay, and carried Bill, Kevin, and Gordy back to Shelter Bay. Bill then drove to the hospital in Revelstoke, a forty-five-minute ride, Gordy swearing at every bump.

Gordy had a broken leg and several cracked ribs. He slept off the rest of his drunk in the hospital.

The next day, Floyd came over to Ebin's cabin. "Thank you so much," he said, shaking Bill's and Kevin's hands. "I'm sorry you had to go to all that trouble. You probably saved Gordy's life, the idiot."

"That's all right. Glad to help," Bill said.

Floyd gave a sly smile, and his blue eyes crinkled. "So now I'm short a worker." He looked at Bill. "How'd you like a job, at least until Gordy gets back on his feet? And you, too?" he added, nodding at Kevin.

Bill pulled me into the bedroom for a whispered conference. "I'm not anxious to work in a sawmill."

"I know," I said. Even from Ebin's cabin, we could hear the whine of the saw and the roar of the equipment. And then there was all the smoke and sawdust, plus the sad sight of all those trees being reduced to boards. "But . . ." I said as an idea struck, "you might be able to immigrate."

Bill's eyes lit up. "True." He elbowed me. "Guess I'll have to, since you weren't good enough to get into Canada."

So it was that Bill and Kevin went to work at Floyd's sawmill, Kevin on the "green chain," unloading sawn lumber from the conveyor belt, Bill as a log bucker and forklift operator.

Floyd wrote Bill a letter formally offering him the job, which Bill took to the border. There he met with an immigration official named Felicity Appleby. He told me he remembered her name because she was one of the most adorable women he had ever seen: "If I hadn't been madly in love with you, I would have run off with Felicity," he teased. He filled out the paperwork; with the job offer, he had plenty of points.

Bill returned to Galena Bay a landed immigrant. He gave me a mischievous look. "Since I was going to marry you to immigrate, I guess I'll have to return the favour."

I smacked him.

The wedding

A few months later, in January 1973, Bill and I went back east to get married in my parents' living room in Linden. Bill had wanted to go to a justice of the peace in Revelstoke, just the two of us, but I had insisted that we give our families the joy of seeing us get married.

I flew in about a week before the wedding. One day I went out for lunch with my mother, my sister Audrey, and my Aunt Ruth. As we walked into the restaurant, twenty or so women yelled "Surprise!" A wedding shower! My first reaction was to be embarrassed. How conventional. How materialistic. Then I was amused. How could I not have guessed? And then I got into it, and I had a ball. My best friend from the University of Chicago, Kate, who now lived in Seattle, was there, and so were friends from Linden, and my mother's friends, well-to-do Jewish women in their jewels and fancy suits. I may have rolled my eyes at their values, but they had known me all my life, and I felt their love surround me.

Later, Bill told me that, a month earlier, my mother had written to him in a panic, because all her friends were calling her in a panic, because what do you give a girl who's living in a cabin in the woods without electricity? "Really, Ruth, it rather limits the scope of possible gifts," they said. So Bill had compiled a list (I remember his asking me, casually, "Say, what kinds of kitchen stuff could you use?"—and I still didn't clue in) and snuck it off to my mother. The women were extremely relieved to find out that there were regular items to choose from, like pots and pans and salad bowls, and they didn't have to search for something weird like a battery-powered chafing dish.

All brides, I suppose, have nerves, but I felt like the most unattractive bride in the world. A year earlier, I had quit smoking, a pack a day habit. It hadn't been my first attempt, but this time I wanted to do it for Bill, who (surprisingly, considering his other smoking habits) had never smoked cigarettes and had stoically put up with my stale-tobacco taste and smell for a year and a half. At the Farm, on New Year's Eve 1971, I took my last precious, delicious, delicious drag.

It had been difficult. I'd craved cigarettes for months, especially that first one in the morning ... and the one with morning coffee ... and the mid-afternoon one ... and that last one before bed. To my own amazement, I'd stuck with it, and never took another puff from that night on. But, as with most people, something had to replace the cravings. And, as with most people, that something was food. Over the course of the next year, I gained nearly thirty pounds. I felt fat and ugly.

That wasn't the worst thing. Before coming east, I had gotten a spectacularly bad, short, shaggy haircut. But there was still something worse than that —my dress.

Of course, there was no way I was going to do something as conventional as go to a bridal salon, so I had had a wedding dress made by a new friend in Revelstoke, Nancy—Nancy, whose diet consisted of marijuana brownies and carrots, and whose vocabulary ran to "Far out" and "Yeah, like, later," and who had assured me that she was an expert sewer. She wasn't. The dress was made of white velvet, with a low-cut front that showed a great deal of cleavage, short puffy sleeves, and a loose, long gown. It was hideous.

On the morning of the wedding, I sat in my parents' room and bawled on my mother's shoulder. "I'm fat! I'm ugly!"

"Shush, *mommie-shainie*," she said, using the Yiddish endearment for "Mommy's pretty one." "You're not. You're beautiful."

I knew she was just saying it, but it made me feel better. I dried my eyes and marched down the three steps from the upstairs to the living room on my father's arm.

Bill didn't own a suit and had had to borrow one from his father, Eddie. Eddie was built like a basketball player, tall and lanky, and Bill had had to stuff his football-player shoulders into the jacket. Still, he looked dashing. He had lost weight from all the physical work, and was trim and handsome with his clipped brown beard, even with his thinning hair. *It's not fair that the groom looks better than the bride,* I thought bitterly.

We had a Jewish wedding with forty guests. Rabbi Feldman, who'd headed our synagogue when I was growing up, officiated. Bill and I stood under the *chuppah*, the wedding canopy, which was held up by Paul, Michael, Kevin, and my little brother, David. The first three were stoned out of their minds, with red, bleary eyes, while fourteen-year-old David, who sported wavy, shoulder-length hair and the first shadow of a moustache, was the only straight one in the wedding party.

Bill and I said the prayers, smashed the glass, and kissed. We were husband and wife.

The next day we set off for home. When we arrived in Toronto, after the first leg of our flight, we stopped at an immigration office. As Mrs. Ellen Schwartz, I applied to immigrate. In fifteen minutes, the paperwork was stamped and I was officially a landed immigrant of Canada, having ridden in on my new husband's coattails.

Years later, I regretted having changed my name. What was I thinking, a feminist like me, abandoning my birth identity for that of my husband? All I can say is that, at the time, it felt like the most romantic gesture in the world. I was in love, newly married, about to embark on a grand adventure with my man. I couldn't wait to be Ellen Schwartz. And then there was the issue of children. It would be awkward, I feared, if our children had a different last name than I did. By the time I had a change of heart, I had already published several books under my married name, and all my official papers were filed in that name, and it made no sense to change back. But if I had it to do over again, I would have stayed Ellen Rosenberg.

From Toronto, Bill and I flew to Calgary, then took the train to Revelstoke, picked up our truck, drove down to Shelter Bay, took the ferry across, and drove back to Ebin's cabin. Forget Bermuda, Niagara Falls, Honolulu. This was a True North honeymoon, a honeymoon by icy moonlight and propane light, by airtight wood heater and four feet of snow.

The honeymoon

Every day began with chores: splitting wood (thinner pieces for the wood-stove, bigger chunks for the airtight) and hauling drinking water from Hill Creek—while we were away, the water line into Ebin's cabin had frozen, so we had to fetch water. To do this, you walked down the hill to the bridge over the creek, carrying two metal buckets, each with a long rope tied to its handle. You threw the first bucket over the side of the bridge (sometimes repeating this a few times to crack the covering of ice that had formed overnight), allowed the bucket to fill, and hauled it back up, trying to spill less than half of the contents. The same with the other bucket, and then back up the hill.

That is, Bill did it. Generally, I stayed inside, made breakfast, and washed up while he split wood and hauled water. I felt uncomfortable about this. Our roles were so stereotyped: little woman stays in the kitchen while big man does the big-muscle jobs. I proposed that, once a week, we exchange chores. Bill agreed.

My first morning on outside duty, I spent half an hour splitting six arm-loads of wood and learned all about knots and the many ways in which axes glance off them. By the time I had made two trips to the creek (necessitated by my spilling most of the water on the way back up the hill the first time), I was exhausted. Of course, I wouldn't admit it. This switch had to work. The future of equal rights for women depended on it.

The next week I tried again, and my mood, upon trudging up the hill with a good portion of that day's water supply in my boots, was not improved by the sight of Bill in his long johns, feet up while he read a book, having finished the washing up twenty minutes earlier.

I persevered for a few more weeks. Finally, I admitted that some kinds of muscles were better suited to some kinds of jobs, and we resumed the old regime. Bill was decent enough not to say I told you so. I felt ashamed, as if I'd let down my sisters. But the truth was, I was glad to get back in the kitchen. I was good at cooking, I did a better job of washing up than Bill did (he always managed to miss a mug or two: "That wasn't there, I swear it!"), and I could start the day with energy to spare. The traditional division of labour may not have been the most liberated approach, but it suited us.

After chores, Bill and I strapped on snowshoes or cross-country skis, depending on the condition and amount of snow, and swooshed across Ebin's field, along an overgrown logging trail through the bush, then half a mile down the back road to our land. There, we sawed up the logs that Floyd had cut in the fall. We stood across a sawhorse holding opposite ends of a Swede saw. (I finally learned what this tool was good for. With a two-foot-long saw blade attached at either end to a curved handle, two people can pull back and forth, allowing the other person's push to become your pull, and vice versa, thus cutting through the wood more quickly.) Push-pull, rasp, rasp, sawdust spraying onto our boots, dusting the snow all around, push-pull ... We stacked the cut pieces between trees. I learned to identify the rough, deeply grooved bark of fir, the sweet smell of cedar, the pale yellow heart of hemlock.

We sawed for weeks, with sore shoulders and cold feet, but I didn't mind. This wood would warm us next winter. And Bill and I had wonderful conversations across the sawhorse: about ourselves, about whether being married was really different from living together (we thought so, but weren't sure), about Michael and Vivianne and whether they'd succeed with their land as we were sure we'd do with ours, about Paul and the survival of our commune, about our parents and friends and how many children we wanted to have (Bill: two; me: three). Mostly we talked about the land, about how we'd plant fruit trees and shrubs and flowers, and how someday we'd clear more land and have a pasture and maybe a few goats.

Bill and I would put down the saw, tramp through knee-high snow to the edge of the clearing, point, look around, imagine. Then we'd go back to work.

The evenings of our honeymoon would have appeared dull to an outsider. We hung out in matching white Stanfield thermal tops and long johns. As the winter wore on, and my feeble hand-scrubbings removed less and less of the dirt, they took on a grungy grey cast. Dinner was vegetarian fare, homemade bread, home-canned fruit for dessert or, for a special treat, cookies.

We had a battery-powered short-wave radio (which I still listen to in my kitchen today) and followed news of Nixon, Vietnam, Watergate, and some weird brand of British Columbia politics called New Democrats versus Socreds.

Then Bill played his guitar. He was already a competent player, but he wanted to improve, so he had sent away for a Mel Bay Blues Guitar instructional tape and was learning to play runs. He had also purchased a metronome and was trying to follow its rhythm as he practised the tricky fingering.

The metronome, a handsome wooden instrument with a silver time-keeping hand, went *tick-tick-tick-DING!, tick-tick-tick-DING!* For the first five minutes, this was charming. The regular rhythm was soothing, the chime a sweet punctuation. Then it began to get annoying. Rhythm was not Bill's strong suit as a musician. He came in a shade behind the metronome, so the effect was something like *tick*-note-*tick*-note-*tick*-note-*DING!*-note.

The discrepancy was just enough to divert my attention, no matter how engrossed I was in a book. After fifteen minutes, I wanted to smash the metronome with a hammer and fling its pieces into the woodstove.

At the same time, I loved the sight of Bill's big shoulders hunched over the reddish-brown Guild, plugging away, not giving up. Now and then, I said, "You're getting better."

"I am?" he said, his face awash with pleasure.

When we packed to move into our cabin in the spring, the metronome mysteriously disappeared, never to be seen again.

On bath nights, we melted extra snow, scooped out the floating twigs and bits of bark, filled a couple of pots, and set them on the airtight. Then we stripped, lathered up with Dr. Bronner's peppermint castile soap, and washed ourselves off. We stood naked in front of the wood heater and washed each other's backs. No curtains on the cabin windows—there was nobody within five miles. Besides, it was just skin, rosy, fire-warmed skin.

After the bath, Bill plugged a tape into our battery-operated cassette player. We turned off the propane lights and let the reflected brilliance of the snow illuminate our moves. We grooved to "Dancin' in the Moonlight" by King Crimson. We rocked out to BTO's "Takin' Care of Business." Finally we put on "our song"—"Crazy Love" by Van Morrison—and slow-danced in each other's arms.

Not exactly the kind of honeymoon that most couples would wish for. But for us, it was perfect. A chance to be alone together. A chance to work hard during the day and relax at night. A chance to really get to know one another.

That may sound strange. After all, Bill and I had just gotten married. We had been together for a year and a half. But this was the first time we had been alone. No Michael and Vivianne and Jon and Aileen and Paul at the Farm. No Paul in the cabin. No Kevin visiting. From the moment I had fallen in love with Bill, as much as I believed in the communal ideals, I had been craving time for just the two of us.

That honeymoon winter of '73, I got my wish.

It was wonderful.

Making a Living

At the Farm, when we planned to move to British Columbia, we estimated that we would have a "self-sufficient homestead" within five years.

No one knew exactly what "self-sufficient" meant. But we did expect to grow, raise, or fish for most of our food. We would heat our home with wood from trees we cut down. We would raise chickens for eggs and goats or cows for dairy, and feed them on forage we grew. We would weave or knit some of our own clothing. Maybe we would even put in a water wheel to generate our own electricity. To the greatest extent possible, we would drop out of the consumer society and live on whatever we could provide with our own hands.

"Of course, we don't expect to be one-hundred percent self-sufficient," we said wisely. "If we want to drink coffee and run a vehicle and wear shoes, we're going to need some money."

This was not an immediate problem. When Bill, Paul, and I had divided the commune's savings with Michael and Vivianne, the three of us ended up with about eighteen-thousand dollars. After buying the land, which cost five-thousand dollars, we had a good stash in the bank, and there was no urgency to earn more.

That first winter, Paul went back east to substitute-teach. When he returned in the spring of 1973, he added most of his earnings to our joint bank account. That gave us an additional cushion.

By that fall, though, our savings were dwindling. In addition to building the cabin, we had built an outhouse, a woodshed, and a tool shed. We had bought tools; food to take us through the winter (and then some); winter gear; and the woodstove and wood heater. We had been running the truck into town once a week or two, where we'd done laundry and bought groceries. We'd bought manure and garden seeds. And we had plans: we wanted to build a chicken coop and a sauna, clear more land, build and furnish a summer kitchen, and get chickens and honeybees.

It was time to go to work.

Back in the US, Bill had worked as a social worker, first at an orphanage and later at a reform school. Although his degree was in marketing and he had no qualifications in social work, those institutions had been so desperate for employees that they hadn't demanded a specialized degree.

In BC, the story was different. Jobs in social services came through the provincial government, and, to work for the province, you had to be a Canadian citizen. (We were landed immigrants, now called permanent residents, but not citizens.) Plus, to do social work, you needed appropriate qualifications.

That fall, Paul moved to Nelson to take a year of education courses and get his teaching certificate at Notre Dame University, a small post-secondary institution.

That left me to be the earner. I had worked for a year as a special education teacher in Pennsylvania before we moved, and, since we arrived, I had applied for and received my BC teaching certificate. So, in the summer of 1973, I put on the only skirt and blouse I owned and visited the Revelstoke school district office. On the spot, I was offered a job teaching a special education class at Mountain View Elementary School. Because of the ferry schedule, the distance to Revelstoke, and the snow load, it wasn't possible to commute daily, so I would have to live in town for the year.

That summer we were growing our first garden. We decided that, when I moved into town to start teaching in September, Bill would stay in Galena Bay. He would finish harvesting the garden and put it to bed (that is, turn over the soil and dig in the organic matter left from the summer), split enough wood to fill the woodshed, and finish work on the tool shed. When the snow fell, likely in mid-November, he would move into town and look for a job. In the spring, he would move back to Galena Bay to get the garden ready while I finished the teaching year.

I found an apartment with two other young women, both nurses, one from Britain and the other from Goa, the former Portuguese colony off the coast of India, which I had never heard of and found fascinating.

My living situation was fine. My teaching situation was not. The school district where I had taught in the US had tested children to determine what kind of special education they needed. My degree was in learning disabilities, characterized by children who, because of neurological factors, could not learn in the usual way. They might have difficulties in reading, spelling, writing, or processing numbers, but they were bright kids who usually responded to special teaching strategies.

In Pennsylvania, I had a pre-screened learning disabilities class, with ten children from ages six to eleven. The school was new, and my classroom was large and bright, with its own bathroom and its own exit to the playground. I had a full-time aide, who knew a hundred times more than I did and was a tremendous help in managing the individualized learning curriculum I devised for each child. Every few months, my principal called me into his office and said, "You're not spending enough. What learning materials would you like to order?"

In Revelstoke, I also had ten students, but there was no testing to sort out their special education needs. The class was a grab-bag of kids with learning disabilities, emotional disturbances, and cognitive deficits. Essentially, every kid who couldn't hack it in regular classrooms had been dumped into my room. And they were between ten and thirteen years old, a less tractable and more difficult age range.

My classroom, on the third floor of a 1910-era brick school, was a former nurse's office. It was so small that there was no way I could arrange the desks so that the kids couldn't reach out and touch each other. And touching each other was the least of it: they hit and punched and knocked each other's books and lunches off desks. Needless to say, I had no aide. The books were Dick and Jane readers from the 1950s.

Learning disabilities I could deal with. But I didn't know how to handle kids with emotional and psychological problems. One boy in particular, Oskar, was a torment. A beautiful blond kid of German extraction, he threw books, pencils, and rulers. He screamed. When I tried to get him to sit down, or do his work, or stop poking his neighbour, he threw himself on the floor and pounded his hands and feet.

When Oskar became completely unmanageable, I sent him to the principal's office. But that backfired, because the principal, who was a year away from retirement, disciplined Oskar by letting him sit at his desk and play with his ink stamp. Thus rewarded for his misbehaviour, Oskar came back to the classroom and did it all over again.

And it wasn't only Oskar I fretted over. David, a tall, husky thirteen-year-old, was as sweet as could be and couldn't read a word, no matter what I tried. Nick, a bright boy, tried to get out of doing his work by engaging me in conversation. "Mrs. Schwartz, did you know that bats are the only mammals that feed on blood?" "Mrs. Schwartz, how far do you think a semi-truck can go before it needs a new engine? Huh? Huh? A million miles! Isn't that amazing?"

The only bright spot of my week was when I took my class to the library. The librarian read aloud to them—and she didn't read "baby" books at their reading level, but serious literature that challenged and engaged them. My kids, who couldn't sit still for five minutes while doing arithmetic problems, sat rapt through Farley Mowat's *Owls in the Family* and Lucy Maud Montgomery's *Anne of Green Gables*. And so did I, discovering Canadian classics along with them.

I lived for the weekends. Every Friday afternoon, I hitchhiked from Revelstoke to Shelter Bay, the ferry landing on the west side of Arrow Lake, a distance of thirty-five miles. Mostly I got rides with loggers who were also heading south for the weekend.

Bill picked me up on the Galena Bay side. The first night at home, I cried on his shoulder, letting out my frustration at being such an ineffectual teacher. Bill held me and assured me that I was doing a good job. Saturday morning, things looked better. I threw myself into jobs around the homestead, digging the garden or stacking firewood or organizing the tool shed. Sunday morning was relaxed. By Sunday afternoon, however, my anxieties started to return. Late in the afternoon, Bill drove me to the ferry, where I checked out the occupants of the vehicles waiting in line before choosing a driver and asking for a ride into town.

Amazingly, in all the weeks I hitchhiked, only once did I have a scary experience. On the Galena Bay side, I asked a middle-aged man driving a brown sedan if he would give me a lift into Revelstoke. "Sure," he said. During the ferry crossing, he put his hand on my thigh. I said, "Oh! I see someone I know," even though I hadn't. I hopped out of the car, approached a vehicle full of young people, and explained the situation. "Get in," they said, and I rode with them.

As luck would have it—bad luck for me, good luck for Bill—the snow came late that year. Bill kept putting off the date when he would move into town, arguing that he might as well take advantage of the good weather to get more work done. When the snow finally fell, in mid-December, he decided to stay in Galena Bay through Christmas. I would soon be home anyway. He would move into Revelstoke with me in the new year.

Christmas vacation was a glorious respite. I put my students out of my mind and relaxed into cross-country skiing, baking, reading, and being with Bill. As vacation drew to a close, I returned to Revelstoke with a positive attitude. I was rested and refreshed, and now I would have Bill with me to buffer the daily frustrations.

Only I didn't. Bill searched for a job, trying sawmills, warehouses, and construction sites. Nothing was available. Finally, he got a job with Parks Canada in Rogers Pass. Every year, hundreds of trees were swept down mountainsides by natural avalanches, and other avalanches were preventively shot down with cannons by the Canadian Armed Forces. Bill was in charge of a crew that cut the trees into firewood for summer campsites. The problem was that Rogers Pass was ninety miles east of Revelstoke, in the heaviest snowbelt in Canada. He couldn't commute. He had to live in an Armed Forces camp at the pass. So, once again, Bill and I saw each other only on weekends, when he came into town.

I became more and more discouraged with my job. Oskar was still a handful, and other kids were acting out. Despite my twelve-hour workdays, most of them had barely improved.

I began to eat less. I had always had a medium build: about five-foot six, 125 or 130 pounds. Weight started falling off me. Staff members commented on how thin I was, asking if I were okay. Too proud to admit my failures as a teacher, I insisted I was. I went down to 110 pounds, rail-thin for my frame.

In the spring, Bill moved back to Galena Bay to plant the garden. Once more, I commuted on weekends, counting the weeks, then the days, until the school year was over.

At the end of the year, I made a decision: I was through with special ed. I loved teaching, but I just didn't have the heart to put up with another class like that one.

Bill and I now had enough money put away to last us for the next couple of years. I packed up my apartment in Revelstoke and headed back to Galena Bay. Headed home.

6

Walter and Margaret and Henry and Hilda

The Nelsons

When Bill, Paul, and I moved to Galena Bay in 1972, we became the ninth, tenth, and eleventh residents in a fifteen-square-mile expanse. The eight others were Bob and Pat Harrington, who had sold us our land, and their two young sons; three siblings, Walter, Margaret, and Henry Nelson; and Henry's wife, Hilda.

The Nelsons had grown up in Galena Bay. Their parents had emigrated from England in the early twentieth century and had homesteaded on fertile land flanking Arrow Lake. When the children were growing up, the area was even more isolated than it was when Bill and I arrived. The road to Nakusp was gravelled and rough, unplowed in winter. A steam tug plied the lake in summer. In the winter, when the lake froze over, you could drive a horse-drawn sleigh across to the western shore and then embark either north to Revelstoke or south to the small town of Arrowhead.

The winter of 1920 was unusually mild. Arrow Lake didn't freeze solid. This meant that the few families of Galena Bay were truly isolated, unable to cross to get supplies. The Nelsons' cow stopped giving milk. Perhaps there was no one to trade with, or perhaps the parents were too proud to ask. In any event, all three Nelson children—Walter, who was about six at the time, Margaret, four, and Henry, a baby—developed rickets. Walter was the most severely affected, developing weak, stiff arms, deformed legs, and a teetering limp. Margaret was moderately afflicted with bowed ankles. Henry was fed what little milk there was and escaped with a bad back and a stiff gait.

In the 1960s, the Canadian government agreed to build a series of dams on the Columbia River to prevent flooding on the American side of the border. Under the terms of the treaty, the United States pledged to compensate Canadian homeowners whose properties would be flooded by the dams.

The Nelsons were among these. Their farm, on the shores of Upper Arrow Lake, was a thriving operation with orchards, dairy cattle, and gardens. By the time the High Arrow Dam was constructed, at Castlegar, the Nelson parents had died. Walter, who subsisted on a disability pension, lived in the original farmhouse and managed the homestead with the help of hired labour.

"BC Hydro came and bought us out, my place and the other lakeside farms," he told us. "They didn't give us what the land was worth. I watched as they bulldozed my house and barn. They cut down my orchard of one-hundred apple trees and burned them. Then, as the reservoir slowly filled, water covered everything up."

As he said this, Walter gazed out the window at the lake, his face a stern mask. I could tell that it wasn't the paltry settlement he minded, but the loss of those trees, now lying under twenty feet of water.

This conversation came later, though. At first, no one in the Nelson family was talking to me.

Walter was in his early 60s and was the eldest of the Nelsons. Although he was not handsome in the movie star sense, his face had a rugged beauty to it: cool blue eyes, prominent nose, grey hair cropped short above the ears, and a blunt jawline that hinted at a man who would not easily be moved from his position. A year earlier, in 1971, he had sold sixty acres of bush across from our place, along Dedosenco Road, to Lee Harding, a young bearded fellow from California. Later the Nelsons found out that Lee was a draft dodger evading the Vietnam War. He and his then-wife, Nancy, turned the place into a hippie commune. Flower children drifted in and out, looking for a place to crash. They smoked pot, bathed nude, and shacked up in ever-changing couples. The commune lasted only a year. By the time we arrived, all that remained were a couple of slapdash cabins and a treehouse precariously perched in a cedar.

"That was no way to treat the land," Walter told us later. "I wished I hadn't sold the land to them."

So when another band of long-haired hippies—Bill, Paul, and I—came along the following year, the Nelsons instinctively mistrusted us. And then I made matters worse.

Bill, Paul, and I were camping on the beach at Galena Bay while we looked for a place to rent. Being a health-food fanatic, I was into making my own whole wheat bread, and had been doing so all the way west, mixing up batches of dough and baking the loaves in the kitchens of friendly people whom we met along the route. Now, in Galena Bay, we were out of homemade bread.

One day, the three of us went to Walter's wood-frame house on a hill with a sweeping view of Arrow Lake to ask for advice on buying tools. The conversation meandered to our camping arrangements, and Bill joked that he was sick of eating oatmeal and almost-cooked rice, just about the only meals I could manage on a campfire. That gave me an idea. I blurted out, "Hey, Walter, could I use your oven to bake bread?"

There was an awkward silence. Walter changed the subject. I sat there, embarrassed and confused. I'd committed a faux pas, that was obvious, but how? What was wrong with asking so simple a favour?

I quickly said, "That's okay, never mind." But the damage had been done. I could see it in Walter's eyes: *Another thoughtless, intrusive hippie.*

On the way back to our campsite, Bill, Paul, and I discussed what had happened. They were as baffled as I was. We stopped at Bob and Pat's and related the conversation.

"What was wrong with that?" I asked.

Pat gave the indulgent smile of a mother correcting a child. "You just don't ask."

"Why not? I'd do the same for him. I'd let him use my stove in a minute—if I had one."

"That's not how it works in the country," Bob said. "When you're the newcomer, you don't come out and ask for favours. You don't make the first move. If he offers, that's fine. If not, you leave it alone."

"But that's dumb," I argued. "People should be open with each other. If he says no, that's cool. I won't be insulted. Why should he be insulted by my asking?"

Pat shrugged. "That's just how it is."

Society's rules are so stupid, I thought. *People should be honest with each other, trust each other, love each other. How else will we change the world?*

At the same time, I was ashamed. I should have been more sensitive, more aware.

For several months, Walter's attitude toward us remained cool. When we saw him at the twice-weekly mail delivery, he nodded hello but did not offer conversation. He briefly answered our questions, then fell silent.

Later in the winter, the relationship began almost imperceptibly to thaw. At the mail, Walter exchanged a few sentences with us—more than bare civilities but less than a conversation. When the assembled residents gossiped about the ferry crew, Walter mainly directed his comments at Henry and Hilda, but he glanced in our direction as if including us in the circle. When Bill mentioned that we had seen a pileated woodpecker, Walter said, "Oh, yeah," in his laconic way and then added, "Could be it's the same one I've been seeing around home." Bill squeezed my hand. A whole sentence.

By spring, if Walter drove past while we were out walking, he pulled over and rolled down his window for a chat. He asked questions when we told him of our plans for the land. He offered advice.

I was forgiven.

That was my beginning with Walter. Things got off to an even worse start with Henry and Hilda.

Henry, the baby of the family, was a taller, slimmer version of Walter. Straight nose in a thin face, short light brown hair, straight-gazing grey eyes. Hilda, short and solid, with frizzy reddish curls, was built like a lumberjack. She looked like she could level you with a punch—and wouldn't mind trying. Henry worked on the Galena Bay–Shelter Bay ferry, and they lived in a house near the ferry landing.

Before Bill, Paul, and I started building our cabin, we heard that Henry and Hilda had a trailer for sale. That sounded like a good temporary housing option, so we went to see it.

First, we had to make obligatory small talk.

"So, where you people from?" Hilda said, hands on hips.

"Pennsylvania."

"Oh, yeah." (In that singsong Canadian way in which people digest new information without acting the least bit surprised.) "What're you doing out here?"

"We want to go back to the land."

Snort.

She unlocked the trailer and started showing us around. "I've just finished cleaning this thing from top to bottom," she remarked, leading me into the kitchen. I opened a cupboard door and reached in to feel how deep the shelves were.

"I said it's clean," she snapped.

"Yeah, I'm sure ... I just ..." I mumbled.

We left soon after, and decided not to buy the trailer when Ebin's cabin became available. But the damage had been done. At the mail, Henry and Hilda barely gave us a nod before turning away. In order to participate in the conversation, we directed our comments at Walter, who more or less included us, along with Henry and Hilda, in his responses. It was like talking through an interpreter.

This went on for three or four years. Eventually, Hilda warmed up— slightly. I don't know whether she respected us for having stuck around, unlike the other hippies, or came to appreciate all we did for Walter. Maybe, at one point, Walter said, "You know, they're not so bad," and she reluctantly agreed. At any rate, a day came when I remarked on how well the tomatoes were doing, and Hilda, without looking at me, said, "Oh, yeah, you get good sun over there." At the next mail day, Bill mentioned that he'd seen a marten hanging around the chicken coop. Hilda nodded. "Cheeky little buggers."

We never became close with Hilda, and had almost no relationship with Henry, who was taciturn and usually absent, working on the ferry. But at least Bill, Paul, and I were no longer pariahs.

Along Walter's driveway stood a row of sheds, each crammed with the accumulation of sixty-odd years of country living. Pieces of harness from horse-pulled tractors. Motorboat engines, all of which needed just a little work to make them run like new. Spools of wire of every gauge manufactured. Welding equipment. Screwdriver sets whose wooden handles were burnished with skin oil. Nails, screws, bolts, washers, and nuts in Squirrel peanut butter tins and tobacco tins that were themselves antiques. The stuff filled shelves, was piled in corners, hung from the ceiling on hooks. To an outsider, these sheds looked like repositories of chaos, but Walter knew where everything was and, furthermore, could tell you precisely where to find it: "Garage shed, left-hand wall, second shelf from the top, two-thirds of the way back, in an Empress raspberry jam tin."

Walter spoke slowly, deliberately, with unhurried precision. At first, his measured way of speaking drove me crazy. I wanted to hurry him along, fill in the words, yank the sentence out of him. I mentally tapped my toes, formulating ten more questions by the time he had answered the first one. But there was no rushing him. He answered at his own pace—and his wisdom was worth waiting for. He knew how to garden and how to build, how to use and repair tools. He knew the wildlife and the trees and everyone who had ever lived in the area. Most important, he knew Galena Bay: how the seasons worked, how the land could be lived on.

Because of his disability, Walter walked slowly, hobbling from side to side on deformed ankles, and his arm movements were awkward. To compensate, he had made adjustments around his place. He couldn't do the normal digging, hoeing, and weeding that a garden required, so he had a tractor with attachments for plowing, mowing, and hauling heavy objects. He had a gasoline generator that ran electric lights—everybody else had propane lights—and an assortment of power tools. He hired someone to cut his firewood and load it into the basement near the furnace. He had a radio telephone for emergency calls.

One day in March 1973, during our first winter, Bill was splitting wood and the axe handle broke. He chipped away the fragments of splintered wood but could not remove the portion wedged in the axe head, which was held in place by an epoxy glue. We drove to Walter's and asked if he could get it out with his acetylene torch. "Ye-e-s-s," he replied, and went straight out to the shed where he kept his welding equipment. When the repair was finished, he said, "That'll be a dollar seventy-five." Bill, who had been unsure whether or not there would be a charge but, thankfully, had stuck some cash in his jeans, paid. Walter brought out a small spiral-bound notebook. "July 20. W. Schwartz. Axe head repair. $1.75," he wrote.

Soon after, the bottom of the ash pan in our wood stove rusted out, and Walter welded a new sheet of metal in its place. He charged us two dollars and recorded the transaction in the notebook.

A few months later, Walter cut a length of plywood for our kitchen counter with his table saw. Three dollars and twenty-five cents. Then he fixed a metal reinforcing plate with his drill press. Two-fifty.

I brought him a loaf of bread, baked in our newly-installed woodstove. He didn't remark on the irony. "How much?" he asked. "Nothing," I said. "It's free." He insisted. I took a dollar. "October 3. E. Schwartz. Bread. $1.00," he recorded on the deposit side of the ledger.

So it went. Every job, every payment, was entered into the notebook.

One summer day, Walter greeted us with a request. He needed to cut his hayfield. He could do it with the tractor, but he needed someone to sit on the back and guide the mowing blade to make sure it ran straight. Would Bill consider doing that?

"Sure," Bill said.

When the job was finished, Walter reached for the notebook. Bill put up a hand. "Walter, instead of paying me, why don't you just mark it down as a job done? I'm sure there's something I'll need you to do for me. It'll balance out."

Walter hesitated, looking uneasy, but he agreed. For the first time, no cash exchanged hands.

Soon after, Walter rode his tractor over to our place and we had him move some tree stumps into a pile. He marked the job in his notebook. Now there were new headings. Jobs Done by W. Nelson. Jobs Done by W. and E. Schwartz.

Walter gave us tomato seedlings. I gave him pots of oregano and savoury. He fixed an old generator for us. We loaded his firewood into the basement. Sometimes I saw him eyeing the two lists, calculating values to see if they balanced out.

In 1975, Margaret, Walter's younger sister, retired from her provincial government job in Fernie and moved back to Galena Bay. Margaret, five years younger than Walter, was soft and round where Walter was angular. She wore her brown hair curled in a 1950s-style pageboy. Her eyes, a deeper blue than Walter's, were warm and curious.

Neither Walter nor Margaret had ever married, and Margaret had stayed in touch with Galena Bay by returning every holiday.

With her permanent arrival, Walter's house changed. Piles of magazines and old receipts disappeared from the end of the kitchen table. Plants replaced bits of hardware on the windowsills. China displaced chipped mugs, tobacco tins, and wrenches. The kitchen began to smell like zucchini muffins and blackberry pie.

Now, when Bill and I stopped in to use the radio phone, the kettle was automatically filled. When Margaret dropped by to pick up the nails they'd bought for us in town, we went home with a bag of early peas as well as the nails. We played Scrabble with them on long winter nights. At "formal" visits, which were preceded by Margaret inquiring whether we were free Thursday evening, and which required clean shirts and combed hair, we knew we would be served tea in the best cups and at least three kinds of homemade cookies.

I wanted to reciprocate, but it was hard for Walter and Margaret to come to our place. Even during the summer, when you could drive in, the rough, uneven path leading from the parking spot to our cabin was difficult for them to walk on. Sometimes I brought them pots of homemade soup, and we ate meals together.

Our discussions with Walter and Margaret ranged over circumscribed terrain: the weather ("Have you ever seen a rainier May?" "Oh, you should have been here in '58—now, *that* was rain."); the gardens ("The cukes are flowering nicely, but the tomato leaves are blotchy—hope it's not blight."); the bugs ("Are this year's black flies equally, more, or less vicious than last year's?" "More."); rumours ("Is the highway crew really going to get a new grader?"); and Galena Bay gossip ("Did Bob go to town yesterday or the day before?" "I think it was yesterday. He said he had a dentist appointment." "Oh, yeah.").

But if our conversations were predictable, the feeling that underlay them was not. A surprising bond developed among us, one that spanned our generations and wildly disparate upbringings. Walter and Margaret realized that Bill and I were not like those fly-by-night hippies but were here to stay, that we loved the place like they did. The four of us shared an unspoken philosophy that had something to do with the notion that less is more, that material things and status don't matter much in the long haul, that if you stop rushing around, nature will show you how to live. In some ways, I reflected, I had more in common with these two shy, country-born elders than I did with my own parents.

Somewhere along the way, Walter abandoned the notebook. Now we did favours for one another without recording jobs done or jobs owed. Bill and I bought a flock of chickens and brought Walter and Margaret fresh brown eggs. Margaret gave us Christmas cookies. We gave them jars of fireweed honey from our hives. Walter mowed our new hayfield.

There was no need to keep track of anything. Friends don't need to tally the score.

The mail scene, circa winter 1973

Our mailing address was Galena Bay via Revelstoke, BC. (This was in the days before postal codes.) Galena Bay was too small to have its own mail delivery depot, so all mail went to Revelstoke. It was delivered to Galena Bay on Wednesdays and Saturdays. Everyone gathered at 12:30 at a green group mailbox that stood at the intersection of the road to the ferry and the main road.

Bill and I arrive at 12:25. Walter is already there, sitting in his pale green Scout, a Jeep-like vehicle, wearing his khaki cap and yellow and brown checked woollen jacket. Seldon Daney, the mail carrier, is also there. He's got his red Ford pickup parked beside and facing Walter's Scout so they can roll down their windows and talk without having to get out.

Seldon, who is in his sixties, is the quintessential country codger. Born and raised in Trout Lake, he has practised every occupation that can be done in the bush: logger, miner, mule skinner, farmer, tourist guide. Seldon chews tobacco and spits tobacco juice, and he curses freely. He limps as a result of a horse-logging accident in the 1950s.

He frowns when Bill and I get out of our truck. *Those long-haired hippies,* I can tell he's thinking. But at least there's just the two of us now. Things looked goddamned unnatural when that frizzy-haired fella—what was his name? Oh yeah, Paul—was hanging around. (Paul at this point is back east, working for the winter.)

Bill and I walk over to the two parked vehicles. Seldon nods and spits. Walter returns our hello. (Things have just recently thawed between us.) We stand there, kicking the snow.

"Snowed two inches last night up at Ebin's," I venture, referring to the cabin we are living in this winter.

Walter nods. "Oh, yeah. One and three-quarters inch at home. Dedosenco's place always gets a little more." He never refers to the property as Ebin's, preferring to call it by the name of the original owner.

"Shit, that all?" Seldon says, amused. "We had four inches if we had an inch, and that's the goddamn truth."

Everyone nods wisely. No one dares to contradict him. Trout Lake always gets more snow than Galena Bay.

A blue pickup pulls up. Henry and Hilda do not get out. Seldon exits his truck and limps over to trade friendly insults with Hilda. Brothers Henry and Walter exchange monosyllables. Bill and I offer quiet hellos. Henry acknowledges us with a curt movement of the head. Hilda ignores us.

"Two inches up at Dedosenco's," Walter informs Henry.

Henry nods. "Two and a half up our way."

"Not like last winter, eh?" Walter says.

Henry chuckles, shaking his head. "I'll say."

Last winter set records for snowfall. So far this winter the snow is below average. Bill and I are frequently reminded, "This is nothin' compared to . . ."

A tan pickup pulls up and parks on the other side of Henry and Hilda's truck. Bob, in the obligatory checkered woollen jacket, gets out and joins Bill and me. Gypsy, his German shepherd, runs around in the bed of the truck, barking shrilly. Bob's alone with the dog. His wife, Pat, had left in the fall of 1972 with their two young boys.

Everyone is now here. The six of us constitute the population of Galena Bay.

"Mild, eh?" Bob offers.

Walter and Henry nod. "Warmest night last night for that date since '56," Walter says.

"Wow," I say. I'm impressed not by the record-setting temperature but by the fact that Walter has retrieved that statistic as easily as his birthday.

"Say, Walter," Bob says. "What do you know about Pippin apples? Think they'd do well in this country?"

A smile softens Walter's square jaw. "Dad had a few Pippin trees on the old farm. Juicy and sweet, eh, Henry?"

Henry nods. "Good apple."

"I'm thinking about putting in a few along my driveway, where they'll get morning sun," Bob says.

Walter nods. It's not just a small nod, which would merely acknowledge the idea. It's a big nod, conferring approval.

"Think we get enough sun for apple trees?" I ask him.

He ponders, then shakes his head. "Better wait till you've cleared more land."

"Bears'll break down young fruit trees," Bob says. "I figure Gypsy'll keep them off mine. You might have to put wire fences around them. Eh, Walter?"

"Not much stops a bear," Walter replies.

He looks at his watch. "Ferry traffic should be coming soon." A moment later, the first car appears, then veers to the right, toward Nakusp. It is followed by a stream of vehicles, pickups mostly, with the odd logging truck whining up the hill and spouting blue-grey smoke like a coal-fired locomotive. Finally, a blue van appears. It pulls over to where we are waiting. The driver hands Seldon three large canvas bags, then drives away.

Seldon tosses the bags marked Beaton and Trout Lake into the back of his pickup, opens the one tagged Galena Bay, reaches shoulder-deep into it, and pulls out a handful of letters.

"Nelson," he calls. Walter and Henry both put out their hands. "Hold on, hold on," Seldon grumbles. "Gotta see which one." He peers at the envelope. "Mr. and Mrs. H."

"Ha!" Hilda says, smirking. "Got one on ya, Walt."

"Swartz," Seldon calls, pronouncing it Schwartz incorrectly. He jerks his hand in our direction and Bill takes the letter.

"Harrington . . . W. Nelson. There you go, Walter, that'll shut Hilda up . . . . Swartz . . . H. Nelson . . . Harrington . . . Galewitz—who the hell's that?"

"We'll take it," Bill says, shooting me a look. Seldon's been delivering mail to us for six months and still doesn't know—or want to know—Paul's last name.

Seldon looks at Bill suspiciously, as if wondering whether he ought to entrust this bearded hippie with someone else's mail. Finally, with a shrug, he hands Bill the letter.

Seldon shakes out the bag to make sure he hasn't missed any, tosses it, empty, into the back of his truck, and with a spit that turns the snow brown and a warning to the assembled company not to get into too much trouble till next time or he'll tan our hides, leaves.

The rest of us linger for a few minutes, chatting and surreptitiously checking the return addresses on our envelopes. No one opens a letter at the Mail Scene. It would be rude.

One by one, people get into their vehicles and drive away. Bill and I riffle through the letters. A fat envelope from my father—his weekly letter, no doubt complete with the usual cut-out cartoons and an article warning of the perils of a vegetarian diet. An array of magazines: *Audubon, Organic Gardening, Country Living.* A couple of letters from friends back east. A seed catalogue. A letter for Paul, which we will forward to him. An air mail envelope from a friend doing aid work in Guatemala.

As soon as we get home, I will make coffee for me and hot chocolate for Bill, and we will sit down and read our mail.

Making a Living

In our second year in the Kootenays, Paul was still in Nelson studying for his teaching certificate at Notre Dame University. For the next few years, he taught in Revelstoke, coming back to Galena Bay on weekends and in the summers.

Even though Paul wasn't living in Galena Bay, the three of us kept up a communal financial arrangement. After taking out what he needed for living expenses, Paul deposited the rest of his salary in our joint back account. "I'm happy to contribute this way," he said, letting Bill and me decide what projects to pursue and what expenditures to make. This support gave Bill and me a cushion and enabled us to put off worrying about money.

But not forever. Over the years, we wracked our brains trying to figure out a way to make a living in Galena Bay.

"We could have a mail-order business," I suggested.

"Good idea," Bill said. "What would we sell?"

We sat there in silence. Neither of us could think of anything.

Another time, I said, "How about crafts?"

"We're not exactly crafty," Bill said. "We don't sew or knit or do ceramics or woodwork."

"What about hammocks?" I asked. Bill had learned to weave hammocks while living in Mexico. We had a beautiful pink, blue, green, and yellow one in a box upstairs, waiting for warmer weather.

Bill perked up. "That might work." He scribbled on an envelope. "Materials ... shipping ... labour ..." He put down the pencil. "I figure I could produce six hammocks a year. At 250 apiece, that would bring in fifteen-hundred dollars. Less after expenses."

I groaned. "Not exactly a living."

"Nope."

One year, our small herb garden was doing well, so I decided to try to grow extra herbs, dry them, and sell them to the health-food store in Nakusp. I carefully tended thyme, oregano, and savoury plants, harvested them, hung them in bunches upside-down to dry, and stripped off the leaves. The plants yielded three small bags of dried herbs. After selling them, I calculated that, for my time, I had earned eighty-nine cents an hour. That was the end of that experiment.

With our neighbour Bob Harrington, Bill and I brainstormed ideas for how to bring paying customers to Galena Bay.

"How about an ecological summer camp for teens?" Bob said one day as we sat around his kitchen table, the ever-present cups of bitter coffee at hand. "We could take them for hikes, teach them trees and birds, show them how nature works. Lord knows city kids need that type of education. They'd love getting out into the wilderness for a while."

"That's a great idea," I said. "They could pick wild huckleberries and we could make jam, or dry them, like Native people did."

"And teach them about the other plants that Native people subsisted on, like Oregon grape," Bob added.

"Make nettle tea."

"Take them up above Beaton to see old-growth trees."

"Learn about succession species in the forest."

"Where would they stay?" Bill, ever the pragmatist, asked.

"We could build cabins," I said. "Or one big bunkhouse."

"And put it where?" Bill said.

No answer.

"And how would we feed them?" Bill went on. "Teenagers need a lot of food. We don't have the cooking facilities, or the refrigeration."

"But ..."

"And can you see a dozen teenagers lining up to use an outhouse?"

Bob and I deflated. Bill was right. And when we calculated the costs of setting up such a venture versus the potential revenue, it looked even less promising.

The idea fizzled, and Bill and I faced the reality that, at some point, we would have to leave again to work.

Food and Gardens

<u>Food</u>

I come from a long line of great cooks on my mother's side. My maternal grandmother, Gussie, a tiny, barrel-shaped woman with dyed auburn hair and a strong nose, was a natural in the kitchen. The only cookbook I ever saw her use was *The Settlement House Cookbook*, published around the turn of the twentieth century by an immigrant settlement organization whose charity her own family had received. Otherwise, she was a "little bit of this, pinch of that" cook. She made the most tender pot roast, the most flavourful chicken soup, the lightest matzo balls. Every Passover, she waited for everybody to take a bite of a matzo ball, then said, "I think they're a little heavy this year," waiting for all of us to protest, "No, Grandma, they're delicious. Better than ever."

My parents and I, and later my sister Audrey, lived with my grandparents during the years when my father was establishing his medical practice. From my time in "the old house," I have a memory of my grandfather being sent outside to grind his own horseradish, to go with my grandmother's homemade *gefilte* fish. I couldn't stand the taste of the horseradish but loved the sharp, acrid fumes.

My mother, Ruth, though college-educated, was a classic stay-at-home mom of the 1950s. She was completely responsible for the kitchen: she did all the grocery shopping, prepared all the meals and school lunches, did all the washing up—at least until we kids became old enough to be assigned that chore. My father never tackled any culinary task more challenging than pouring himself a glass of iced coffee—coffee that my mother had brewed.

In my teens, I questioned this division of labour

"It's not fair that you have to do everything in the house. Dad doesn't even get his own breakfast."

My mother smiled. "It's my pleasure to fix meals for him."

I gritted my teeth and vowed that I would never fall into such a stereo-typed role.

We ate a typical middle-class diet for the time: pot roast and roast chicken, sloppy joes and kosher hotdogs, sirloin and, my favourite, tuna casserole topped with crushed potato chips. The only exotic dish in my mother's repertoire was sukiyaki. In the early 1950s, during the Korean War, my parents and I had lived for a year in Japan, where my father was serving as a doctor in an American field hospital. There, our housekeeper, Yoko, taught my mom a few Japanese dishes. My mother's sukiyaki was highly Americanized: slices of strip steak sautéed with peas, carrots, and green beans, served over white rice, with crunchy chow mein noodles on top.

Every Sunday morning, my grandfather rose early and visited a local Jewish deli to pick up the fixings for brunch: fresh hard rolls, bagels, lox, tomatoes, and onions. When he climbed our back steps and knocked on the kitchen door, all three of us kids and my mother ran to answer it. We adored him, especially my mother, and he doted on her, his only daughter. He'd step into the kitchen, handing my mother the bags. "So, what'd you and Bernie do last night?" he'd ask, eager to know what fine restaurant his daughter and successful son-in-law had dined in the night before. They'd speak for a few minutes; then, with a kiss and a wave, he'd disappear down the back steps to make his delivery at my aunt and uncle's house, a few blocks away.

We rarely ate salad; when we did, it was iceberg lettuce with sliced cucumbers and tomatoes. Most other vegetables—green beans, peas, corn—were frozen (except in the summer, when we got delicious Jersey corn from nearby farm stands). We had apples, pears, bananas, and oranges in the house, but dessert was typically canned fruit, instant pudding, or Jell-O.

A special treat was Swanson's TV dinners, which we kids ate when my parents went out. I loved the slim aluminum trays and the way each food—the turkey, the mashed potatoes, the cranberry sauce, the little mound of peas and carrots, the tiny slice of cake—had its own well to sit in, so that it didn't contaminate the others. Audrey, David, and I sat in a row on the couch, our TV dinners propped on tray tables, spooning processed food into our mouths while we watched *I Love Lucy*, *The Dick Van Dyke Show*, or *Gunsmoke*.

By 1967, when I graduated from high school, I was a healthy, well-fed girl with no sense of where her food came from or how it was produced. A typical breakfast, which I threw together before dashing out the door to school, was a slice of toasted Wonder Bread, topped with Skippy peanut butter and dusted with Nestlé Quik powder.

In college, all that changed. One of the first influences was the book *Silent Spring* by Rachel Carson, which was making the rounds among my friends. I picked it up and began to understand the environmental consequences of our society's use of pesticides. Although organic farming had of course been practised for millennia, the organic food movement was just beginning to gain traction in North America. I started patronizing natural food stores, buying organic, steel-cut rolled oats and friendly-bacteria-laden yogurt. I wasn't sure if these foods tasted better, or if I felt healthier, but I certainly felt righteous.

White rice out. Brown rice in. Fast food bad. Homemade food good. Sugar: white death. Honey: nature's bounty. By my junior year of college, when I was living in Madison with my boyfriend Ned, I was baking my own bread (read: bricks), cooking thick, sludgy pots of lentil soup, and making my own granola.

The biggest change, however, came when I read *Diet for a Small Planet* by Frances Moore Lappé. The author described not only how to eat a healthy vegetarian diet but also the environmental depredations and cruelty of the North American meat industry. I was horrified—and inspired. Next time I went home for vacation, I declared, "I'm a vegetarian."

My parents, especially my father, were alarmed. "But what will you eat instead of meat?"

"Rice. Vegetables. Lentils."

"That's not enough to stay healthy," he argued. "You need animal protein."

"No, I don't, Dad. That's just propaganda put out by the meat industry. You can get complete protein by combining stuff like beans and rice." I showed him some of the recipes in the book. "See, if you combine soybeans with whole wheat flour, the amino acids balance out."

"Inferior protein."

I brushed that argument aside. "Did you know that meat production uses more energy per pound and produces more waste than any other type of farming?"

"No, I didn't. But meat is a highly concentrated protein, so a small amount is enough to meet your nutritional needs."

"Dad! It's a matter of justice. Why should a tiny percentage of the world's population, like us, be able to eat meat while everyone else starves or is malnourished? If the millions of acres now devoted to meat production were converted to grains and legumes, everyone on the planet would have enough to eat."

"So everyone should suffer with a plant-based diet?"

"Suffer! You want to talk about suffering? How about the animals?" I recited the appalling facts about animal slaughter. That chickens were kept in cages so small that they couldn't turn around—before being gassed to death. That cattle and pigs stampeded in terror, sometimes crushing one another, as they were led down the ever-narrowing chute to the abattoir. That, even after their throats were cut, they sometimes survived, screaming in pain and writhing in one another's blood, until they were given a mortal blow to the head.

"How can you eat meat knowing that?"

"Those conditions are terrible," my mother acknowledged. "That's why I buy kosher meat. The animals are killed under humane conditions."

"There's nothing humane about murder!"

After I returned to school, and for years afterward, my father sent me a steady stream of articles from medical journals with such titles as "Malnutrition in Infants Fed Vegetable-only Diets" and "Macrobiotics: A Generation Faces Nutritional Peril." But, since these were from the medical "establishment," which in my mind was in the same dubious camp as polluting industries and our war-mongering government, I brushed them off and continued to eat a vegetarian diet.

Until 1978, that is, when I became pregnant with our first child. Now, all of a sudden, I craved animal protein. And, I admitted to myself, those articles from my father sprang back into my mind and frightened me.

One day early in the pregnancy, when Bill and I were in town grocery shopping, I put a package of chicken breasts into the cart.

He frowned. "What's this?"

"I need the protein," I said.

"We always said we could get enough protein from vegetables," he argued.

"My body is telling me to get animal protein."

"But the environment ... slaughter ..."

"I want meat."

Who's going to win an argument with a pregnant woman?

So chicken and fish crept back into our diet. Bill ate them sparingly, unenthusiastically—but since I was cooking he didn't have much choice. To this day, we don't eat beef, pork, or lamb—not so much for environmental or ethical reasons, but because we don't like them. And although we continue to rely on legumes, dairy, and eggs for most of our protein, we still eat moderate portions of poultry and fish.

After Bill and I arrived in Galena Bay, we heard, through the hippie grapevine, about a health-food guru named Arnold Ehret. One of his books, *The Mucusless Diet Healing System*, advocated a diet based on fruits, starchless vegetables, and leafy greens. While *Diet for a Small Planet* advised on what foods to combine, Ehret counselled on what foods *not* to eat together: for example, no citrus with nuts, because that combination produced "mucus," a slodgy, unhealthy substance in your blood that caused lethargy and disease.

Certainly, I didn't want mucus in my body. But Ehret's food-combination recommendations and prohibitions were complicated. I sat there, with *Diet for a Small Planet* and *The Mucusless Diet Healing System* open in front of me, trying to come up with menus that would follow both prescriptions. No nuts with spinach—but Lappé's rice casserole called for those two ingredients. And how could we get protein without mixing beans and cheese, a no-no in Ehret's eyes? Finally, I put *The Mucusless Diet* away. If Bill and I had to have mucus, so be it.

Another of Ehret's books made a deeper impression. In *Rational Fasting*, he argued that the digestive system needed a rest to recuperate and recharge, and suggested a weekly fast.

Bill was in favour of this. I was less sure. "What if we get hungry?" I asked.

"We'll drink lots of water."

"How are we going to work without eating?"

"We have plenty of reserves."

Reluctantly, I agreed to give it a try, and we instituted a weekly fast. After eating dinner on Wednesday night, we did not eat all day Thursday, though we drank plenty of water and herbal tea, and broke our fast on Friday morning with Ehret's recommended meal of grated carrots and cabbage.

"Don't you feel terrific?" Bill would ask as we sat down to our cleansing salad.

"Yeah," I admitted. I felt light and clean after a day without food, and cabbage never tasted so delicious.

But I hated fasting. Hated the denial. Had coffee withdrawal. Secretly, I used to sneak into the cabin and lick a spoonful of honey. Sometimes I even snuck a handful of granola.

After about a year of weekly fasts, I told Bill I was quitting. I could tell he was disappointed, but he didn't criticize me. He carried on for another few months, during which I felt even guiltier eating while he was going without—though not guilty enough to resume fasting. Then he quietly let it go.

When Bill and I moved to Galena Bay in the summer of 1972, we knew that our back road would not be plowed in the winter and so we would not be able to get into town often to buy groceries. That meant we had to stock up on staples to see us through the snowy months. But how much would we need? I had no idea. *Better too much than not enough*, I thought, and on a trip to Vancouver that fall, I purchased fifty-pound bags of oats, rice, lentils, powdered milk, and soybeans. We loaded the huge bags into mouse-proof galvanized-aluminum garbage cans in the tool shed. As we fastened the lids, I felt secure. *It could snow all winter and we'd still have enough food*, I thought.

I had never eaten soybeans before, except as a fried, salted snack food, but was excited to incorporate them into our diet, since *Diet for a Small Planet* said that they contained more protein than any other legume. One day I cooked a batch of the pale yellow beans. It took three hours of boiling to get them to an edible stage. They were bland and unpleasant in texture, even when drowned in tomato sauce (and, as we soon found out, were highly gaseous). I tried soybeans in a couple more recipes, but each time Bill and I found ourselves picking them out of the dish and leaving them on our plates.

Guiltily, I left the barely used bag in the tool shed. Eventually I dumped forty-eight pounds of them on the compost pile. Over time, moths flourished in the oats, and the brown rice went rancid. They joined the soybeans. Most of that initial purchase went to waste.

No young woman, especially a rebellious one, wants to admit that she is just like her mother. But in one significant way I was: I did all the cooking.

Secretly, I was happy. I loved cooking, loved trying new recipes and ingredients, loved putting healthy meals on the table. So I brushed off the embarrassment of falling into a stereotypical role and threw myself into my next challenge: learning how to cook on a woodstove.

Our first woodstove, a Findlay, which we salvaged from a tumble-down cabin in Beaton, was a relic of old-time craftsmanship, with scrolled iron filigree around the edges, and white enamel doors on the oven and on the warming oven above the stove's surface, which was perfect for proofing bread. It was also extremely inefficient. Even after I got the hang of starting the fire in the woodbox—crumple newspaper, criss-cross thin sticks of kindling over that, lay on a slim piece of fast-burning cedar, *remember to open the flue*, and light the fire—either the woodbox smoked or the fire burned out too quickly or the pieces of hemlock I placed on top of the cedar didn't catch. The fire was always too cool or too hot, resulting in food that was either undercooked or burned. When the fire was too hot and the pancakes I was cooking turned black underneath, Bill christened them "carbon cakes." Even I had to laugh, because that's exactly what they were.

Then there was baking. A woodstove's oven receives heat from the firebox, which is typically located on the left side of the stove. This means that the oven is hottest on the left. And that means that you have to turn your baked goods around a few times to make sure they cook evenly.

It took me a while to learn this. For the first several months, my cakes tended to rise quickly on the left, forming a small mountain that burned on its left flank, while the right-hand side fell into a doughy, uncooked valley. I can't count the number of times I went, "Oh, shit!" and dashed to open the forgotten oven door, only to discover a half-burned, half-raw mess of a cake or bread, which went straight into the compost.

A year or so later, we bought a brand-new Enterprise Woodsman woodstove. This was a large, square, black, unlovely beast. It had no filigree, no curves, no enamel, but it was well designed and very efficient. A water reservoir hooked onto the left side of the firebox, so I could get warm water for washing up by dipping into that instead of having to heat pots of water on the stove.

By now, I was much more competent. I had learned the properties of different species of wood and knew how to use them to get the result I wanted: cedar to get the fire going, hemlock for a low, steady fire, slightly hotter fir for stovetop cooking, and beautiful birch, our longest-burning wood, for steady baking heat. I had also learned where to place things—for example, to put a pot of water directly over the firebox to bring it to a boil, then move it about a foot to the right to keep it simmering for soup or stew. And I mostly remembered to turn my baked goods. I felt like an accomplished pioneer woman, wise in woodland lore.

I still produced carbon cakes—just not as often.

Through one of my cookbooks, I learned that commercially ground flour lost nutrients when the germ—the oily, healthful part of the grain—became exposed to air over long periods. This wouldn't do. I decided that we should grind our own flour so as to get it at optimum freshness. At a farm supply store, we purchased a hand-operated wheat grinder and a fifty-pound bag of hard spring wheat, the best kind for baking.

The wheat grinder was a small, cast-aluminum device, similar to a meat grinder. You clamped its base to a countertop, poured wheat kernels into the hopper, and turned the handle. Easier said than done. The resistance was strong, and it was hard to grind wheat with any degree of fineness. I could manage maybe thirty turns of the handle before I had to rest my arms and catch my breath. I enlisted Bill and Paul. They were stronger than I was, and could do more grinding before getting tired, but it was still an onerous chore. Soon we hit on an ingenious idea. Whenever friends came to visit, we showed off the wheat grinder and invited them to take a turn. "If you want pancakes for breakfast ..." Bill would begin, leaving the rest unsaid. Our visitors complied, providing us with a short-term supply of flour.

Actually, "flour" is too generous a term. The grinder couldn't produce anything as finely ground as commercial whole wheat flour. Instead, it yielded a coarse meal dotted with bits of cracked wheat. My bread, muffins, pancakes, cookies, and pies came out heavy, dense, and crunchy. No, let me be honest: they were leaden.

But healthy!

One summer, during the reign of the wheat grinder, Bill went backpacking with our friend Kevin for a few days, leaving Paul and me in the cabin. Paul was a big fan of pasta, and he also loved peanut butter, so I decided to make him a treat for dinner: homemade whole wheat noodles with peanut sauce.

Having never made pasta before, I followed the directions, mixing flour, eggs, and water. Then I started rolling out the dough. Because the flour was coarse, I couldn't roll the dough out very thin; in fact, the thinnest I could get it was about a quarter-inch. When I had a fairly flat sheet of this, I sliced the dough into ribbons and dropped them into a pot of boiling water. Meanwhile, the peanut sauce—a mild version of *gado-gado*, since I didn't have any of the Indonesian spices called for—simmered on the stove.

"Surprise!" I said as Paul sat down, setting a steaming plate of noodles topped with sauce in front of him.

"My two favourites," he said. "Thanks!"

I sat across from Paul with my own plate. We both took a bite. We chewed. And chewed. And chewed. The noodles were dense and gloppy. The sauce was lumpy.

Paul finally swallowed. He kept his eyes averted.

We took another bite. Chewed. Swallowed.

We looked at one another across the table and burst out laughing.

"It's awful," I said.

"Horrible."

"Disgusting."

"Inedible."

We scraped the remains of our dinner into the compost pail and ate peanut butter and honey sandwiches for dinner.

After that, I quietly retired the wheat grinder to the back of a shelf, and we went back to buying commercially ground flour.

I think my grandmother made pickles when I was a child—I have a vague memory of a ceramic crock with a weighted lid in a corner of her kitchen— but my mother didn't do any preserving. With all the frozen, canned, and pre-packaged foods available, she had no need to.

But I did. Without electricity, we couldn't freeze food, and we couldn't plan on going into town to stock up on groceries more than once a week during the summer and once every couple of weeks in the winter. I had to preserve fresh fruits and vegetables for the winter. But how? "Can them," Pat Harrington told me. I envisioned aluminum cans of food. How could I possibly produce those? No, she corrected me, canning meant preserving food in glass Mason jars.

Under Pat's tutelage, I bought the necessary equipment: a 21-quart enamel canning pot with a wire rack, large enough to hold 8 one-quart jars at a time; several dozen boxes of Mason quart and pint jars; canning lids, and screw tops. I took a trip to the Okanagan Valley—BC's premier fruit-growing region—and filled the truck bed with boxes of produce: cherries, peaches, and apricots; peas, green beans, and corn. Then I went up to Bob and Pat's with a flat of apricots for a lesson.

Patiently, Pat walked me through the steps. Wash, pit, and cut the fruit in half. Fill the jars nearly to the top with apricot halves. Pour over them a boiling sugar-water mixture. (I balked at using "white death," but Pat said it was necessary in order to preserve the fruit.) Wipe the jar rims. Place on canning lids and screw on the tops. Put eight jars in the canner. Pour over enough hot water to submerge the jars. Bring to a boil. Keep at a rolling boil for twenty-five minutes. Remove the jars. Listen for the delightful *ping* that indicates that the seal is complete. Repeat with the next batch.

The process was the same for vegetables, I learned, except that you used a mixture of water and salt rather than sugar. And vegetables required longer processing times because of the lack of natural preserving sugars and the presence of harmful bacteria that had to be killed through prolonged exposure to heat.

Thanking Pat, I returned to the cabin to tackle the rest of the produce on my own. And that was when, gazing at the dozens of boxes of produce I had brought back from the Okanagan, I said to myself, "What was I thinking?"

For the next week, I washed, cut, peeled, pitted, shelled, snapped, sterilized, cleaned, poured, lifted, sweated. We had purchased a two-burner propane stove, so I had sugar water boiling on the woodstove while the canner bubbled on the propane stove. As fast as I emptied cardboard boxes of clean, new Mason jars, I refilled them with processed jars of food. Some nights I didn't finish the last batch of canning until one or two o'clock in the morning. Bill and Paul nicknamed me "the Energy Queen."

The grand total that first summer: three hundred jars of fruits and vegetables.

We stacked the boxes in the "the little room," a corner of the cabin that we had walled off to create an alcove where we stored firewood, gumboots, and hand tools. The stacks reached the ceiling.

Oh, those jars of food! Opening a quart of peaches on a snowy winter day brought the taste and aroma of summertime into the cabin. Spooning home-canned corn and peas into a pot of soup made me feel thrifty, satisfied that food preparation had come full circle, from my summer labour to our winter meal.

But it didn't take long to realize that I had canned way too much. Bill and I ate maybe two dozen quarts of fruit and a dozen quarts of vegetables over the course of the winter. The rest of the jars sat. And sat. Some of them got so old that, although the seals were still intact, I figured that the food must have lost all flavour and nutritional value, and dumped them onto the compost pile (joining the still-undecomposed soybeans). The trick of figuring out how much food we would need in a season was proving more difficult than I had imagined.

Still, I had learned a valuable food preserving technique. A few years later, I bought a cast-aluminum pressure canner, which processes food in much less time. And, five decades on, I still preserve summer's goodness every year, filling my shelves with ruby cherries, golden peaches, spicy applesauce, and the scarlet hues of my homemade tomato sauce.

Gardens

One of our first priorities, after building the cabin, was to put in a garden. Bill, Paul, and I knew almost nothing about gardening, so we chose a pretty, sun-dappled, relatively flat spot about a hundred yards down the slope from the cabin. We hired Floyd Fitzgerald, owner of the sawmill that had employed Bill (and thus enabled us to immigrate), to clear about a quarter-acre.

"Dig about a foot and a half deep," Pat Harrington advised us. "Get rid of any rocks bigger than an egg. Anything smaller you can leave."

No problem, I thought. The garden space was only about twenty feet by thirty feet. *It shouldn't take more than a few days to dig it up. And how many rocks bigger than an egg can there be?*

Bill, Paul, and I marched out to the plot with spades and stuck them in the ground.

Clink.

We each hit a rock. I dug mine up. It was the size of a medium potato. Paul's was the size of an orange. Bill's was the size of a grapefruit. We tossed them to the side of the demarcated area. *Thump, thump, thump.*

Spade in again.

Clink. Scrape. Screech.

The tip of my spade lost purchase under the rock. I moved it slightly to the side and dug again. This time I manoeuvered it underneath. I pulled back on the handle. It didn't budge. I tackled it from the other side. First I had to remove a bunch of smaller stones before I could get the blade under the other end. *Creak.* I finally pried up a rock the size of a spaghetti squash. I needed two hands to lift it and toss it aside.

We lay down our spades and used pickaxes and grub hoes. When we whacked them into the ground, the bones in our arms shuddered. I wondered if all forest soil was like this, or if there was something aberrant about this patch. Muscles in my arms that I had never used began to ache. Paul stopped frequently to blow his nose, making it a longer and more drawn-out procedure each time. Sweat glistened on Bill's bald spot.

After a couple of hours, I was on the verge of tears. Bill caught my eye. "Hey, it's a rock festival."

I just groaned.

Paul leaned on his spade. "Yeah, I'm pretty stoned."

"Rock out," Bill said.

A giggle escaped me. I gave in. "Everybody must get stoned."

Paul: "Rock around the clock."

Bill: "They'll stone you when you're trying to be so good."

Me: "Rockin' robin, tweet, tweet, tweet." I held the handle of my spade like a dancing partner and jitterbugged.

By now we were all laughing hysterically. This couldn't be happening. It was. What else could we do but laugh—or cry?

Later, we went up to Bob and Pat's. Pat took one look at us and invited us in for lemonade. We sat at the table, trying not to scratch our mosquito bites, and told them about the rocks. They exchanged a look. Bob said, "Sounds like you hit an old creek bed."

"You mean, a creek used to run through there?" I asked.

Pat nodded. "And deposited rocks along its bed."

Bill's voice was tight as he asked, "Would it have covered the whole lower part of the property?"

"No way of knowing," Bob answered. "You could dig a hundred feet away and find good, rich soil."

There was a pause. We sipped lemonade. Pat said gently, "Didn't you dig up some soil samples before you decided where to put the garden?"

Bill, Paul, and I looked at one another. "No," Paul said in a small voice. "We didn't think of it."

"We thought it was a pretty spot for a garden ..." My voice trailed off.

Back at the garden patch, we hefted our pickaxes and stood there, gazing at the cleared area. We didn't speak but I know we were all thinking, *How stupid could we have been?*

Pretty damn stupid. But there was nothing we could do about it now. This was the area we had asked Floyd to clear. This was the area we had to work with.

Day after day. *Clink. Scrape. Screech.* Reddish, iron-flecked rocks. Yellow stones. Grey, brown, black. Stones with rings, stones with flat sides, stones piled on top of one another, one, two spades deep in the earth. Some of them were so large that it took half a day of digging just to clear enough space to get under them. We couldn't lift them out—we had to wrap them in ropes and use a come-along hooked up to the truck to winch them out and pull them aside.

When rocks came up easily, I was grateful to them, mentally thanking them for their cooperation. Those that were difficult I remembered long after I'd dug them up. "That's the one that took me fifteen minutes," I'd tell Bill. "That's the one I cut my thumb on." "That's the one with the funny little notch."

Week after week.

That was the first—and practically the only—time I felt like giving up on the whole back-to-the-land project. Hitting yet another rock, and another, I thought, *I don't know if I can do this.* Then, *I can't do this. I don't want to do this. I want to—*

I didn't know what I wanted to do. *Go home* crossed my mind. But what did *home* mean now? Not the United States. Certainly not Linden. Home was where Bill was.

But this—this endless digging, these fucking stones—isn't what I signed up for.

It wasn't so much the physical work that was gruelling; it was the sheer drudgery of finding another, and another, and yet another stone. It was not knowing if it would ever end. It was feeling that I was not capable of doing this task, and being afraid to fail.

I didn't quit. Quitting, not doing my share, being inadequate to a task—all of these are some of my deepest fears. So I forced myself out there, day after day, and after three brutal weeks, we finished. We had taken out so many rocks that the level of the soil in the dug-over part was lower than that of the surrounding earth, and what remained was clayey and grey, or rusty-red from iron. It didn't look like it would support any kind of growth.

And it didn't. That first year we planted broccoli and peas, carrots and beans, cabbages and zucchini, corn and potatoes. The shoots came up—and then dwindled to spindly, anemic-looking stalks.

When we consulted Walter to find out what the problem was, he said that forest soil was low in nutrients in the first place and that ours had become even more depleted when the top layer had been scraped off by Floyd's skidder. "Build up the soil with compost, manure, and mulch," he advised. But we didn't have any compost. We had started a pile beside the garden, but its contents (including the forty-eight pounds of soybeans) had yet to decompose. It was too late in the season to apply manure; if we dug it in now, it would burn the plants. We didn't have any mulch, either. Desperate, I went into the woods and picked armfuls of bracken ferns and layered them between the rows of plants. Unwittingly, I made the soil even more acidic than it already was.

We even collected hair clippings from barber shops in Revelstoke— natural! organic!—and dug them into the garden, hoping that their protein would enrich the garden. Hair, however, doesn't decompose very quickly, and when, months later, we found creepy clumps of blond, black, and brown hair lingering underground, we abandoned the practice.

That summer we harvested a few spindly carrots and a handful of beans. Slugs got the cabbages, and the corn didn't even tassel, let alone produce ears. Walter gave us excess produce from his garden. "I can't use it all," he said, though I suspected he was just being kind.

In the fall of 1973, we set out to build up the garden in a serious way. By then we had a small but rich pile of compost. We bought three truckloads of horse manure, along with several bales of hay, and dug all of it into the garden. By the following spring, when we turned the garden over, the dirt was actually beginning to look like soil. We even spotted an earthworm or two.

The next summer's garden was better. We harvested modest crops of peas and beans, carrots and cabbages. We started a small herb garden, with garlic, thyme, oregano, savoury, and basil, which, amazingly, thrived. By then we had our first flock of chickens, and we dug the manure-rich straw into the garden at the end of the season.

We became manure experts. Chicken shit was the richest and most concentrated. You had to use it sparingly—but that was okay, because we accumulated it sparingly, dropped here and there in the chicken coop, mixed in with straw on the ground.

Horse manure was a good balanced manure, nicely mixed with straw. When it was aged, it crumbled beautifully and had—I really mean this—an almost aromatic smell, of barns and earth.

Cow manure was stinky and rich. It too was also mixed with straw, but also contained grass and undigested seeds that cropped up later as weeds in the garden. Cow shit was a good, all-purpose fertilizer.

Probably the best manure was pig shit, because pigs ate a varied diet of grains, vegetables, kitchen scraps, hay, you name it. Their manure was concentrated and smelly, and performed wonders in the garden.

Each year our garden became lusher and more abundant. By 1975 or '76, the soil was loose and dark, full of earthworms. We dug baskets full of thick, long carrots and beautiful round potatoes. We experimented with pole beans and bush beans; learned to put out containers of salt to trap the slugs and harvested large, heavy green cabbages; grew globular beets and turnips; sowed a succession of greens: lettuce, spinach, chard, lambs' quarters, mustard greens, and New Zealand spinach; and even managed to grow a row or two of corn, despite the fact that the garden, bordering the forest to the west, didn't get much late afternoon sun.

We made one major mistake: we planted zucchini seeds directly in the compost pile. The zucchinis exploded. They grew inches every day. We couldn't give them away fast enough. We couldn't even feed them to the chickens fast enough. They kept growing, to the size of baseball bats, cudgels. I made stuffed zucchini, zucchini pickles, zucchini bread, zucchini cake. One night, after I had served the third zucchini dish in a week, Bill said, "You know what? I really hate zucchini."

I nearly clobbered him with a club-sized zucchini.

After Bill and I had been living in Galena Bay for a couple of years, we wanted to clear more land. We wanted goats for milk, and that would require room for a barn, forage, and hay for winter feed. We wanted to put in a fishpond and to grow nectar-producing plants for our honeybees. We wanted to build a house—a real log house with *rooms* and an indoor bathroom and a view of the Monashee Mountains to the west. And, in this new clearing, we wanted to grow a larger garden that would enjoy greater exposure to sunshine than the original one, which backed onto the forest.

One afternoon in the fall of 1974, Bill and I walked through the bush to the east of the original clearing and paced out an area roughly 150 feet on the east–west axis and 220 feet on the north–south axis. We dug up a spadeful of dirt in the middle of the rectangle. It yielded clay-like soil—*with no rocks*. Bill and I grinned at each other.

"Yes!" I said.

We spent that winter cutting trees in a one-and-a-half-acre area, then hired a friendly earth-mover-operator from Nakusp, Charlie Howe, to pull the stumps. By late spring, we had a rough clearing.

The first thing we did was to plant a cover crop of buckwheat, which not only is a terrific source of nectar for bees, producing delicious, dark, smoky honey, but also concentrates nitrogen in its roots, nourishing the soil.

The second thing we did was to dig a new, larger garden, which we called the "upper garden," approximately thirty feet by forty feet. We placed it on a flat stretch at the base of a small incline, at the top of which would go our future log house. The spade slipped into the ground like velvet.

And now we had a new manure supplier: Minnie Marlowe.

Minnie was a single woman about forty years old who lived on a small farm outside the village of Trout Lake, about twenty miles northeast of Galena Bay. She had immigrated from England with her two brothers, Alan and Bill, when they were in their twenties. Minnie's brothers logged, mined, and generally hustled. Walter never said so explicitly, but I got the impression that he thought they were ne'er-do-wells, the type who would—and probably did—cut down ancient, old-growth cedars to make a quick buck. They were slim, shifty-looking fellows who radiated disdain for tree-hugging hippies. Minnie stayed home, fed and cleaned up after her brothers, and raised a few dairy cows.

Minnie was what the locals called "bushed"—so accustomed to living in the bush that she couldn't function in society. According to Walter, she had never travelled farther than Nakusp in twenty years. She dressed like a hillbilly, in a checkered flannel shirt with overalls several sizes too big, gumboots on her feet, and a floppy hat on her head, beneath which brown hair frizzed out. Minnie had protruding, crooked teeth that pointed in different directions.

Minnie was so shy, especially of men, that she refused to talk to them. If a truck drove by when she was leading her cows from the barn to the pasture and back, she dived into the bush and hid until it was gone. Rednecks from Trout Lake used to drive back and forth, just for the cruel sport of making Minnie duck for cover.

But Minnie had cows, three or four animals, which she loved; she stroked their noses and crooned endearments to them. And her farm was the closest source of manure to our homestead. So one day, Bill and I headed up to Trout Lake to see if she would sell us some.

As we pulled into the driveway, we saw her dash into the barn. Bill and I slowly approached, stopping several feet from the doorway.

"Hello, Minnie?" Bill called. "It's Bill and Ellen Schwartz, from Galena Bay."

"Go away," a raspy voice shouted.

"We only want to buy some manure," Bill said.

"I'm not talkin' to ya."

Bill and I exchanged a look. *Let me*, I mouthed. I motioned him to return to the truck.

"Minnie? It's me, Ellen."

Silence.

"I sent Bill away. He's in the truck."

"Hmph."

Encouraged, I went on, "Would you sell us a truckload of manure?"

"Well, Lord knows I got plenty ..."

"We'd really appreciate it."

Another silence. "Well ... okay."

"Terrific. Can we back the truck up to the barn?"

She peeked out. Giving me a crooked grin, she said, "Can't load it up if you don't, eh?"

I smiled back. "Uh, Minnie, is it okay if Bill helps me shovel it? I don't think I can do it all myself."

She frowned. I waited.

Finally, "Okay. But not till I scram."

Minnie showed me where in the barn to take the manure from, then scampered back to the weathered wood-frame house she shared with her brothers.

Bill was incredulous when I told him she'd agreed. We quickly unloaded our wheelbarrow from the bed of the truck and propped a wide, sturdy plank against the open tailgate as a ramp.

The cows, in their byres, lowed comfortingly as we entered the barn. The manure was liberally mixed with straw and gave off a pleasant, earthy smell. We filled the wheelbarrow and then Bill pushed it up the ramp into the bed of the truck and upended it.

The work was exhausting. Soon my arms and shoulders ached. I kept going by thinking of all the lovely vegetables that would grow from this manure. Once or twice I saw Minnie peeking out from the doorway of her house, but she didn't come over, and I knew better than to spook her by saying anything to her.

When the load reached the top of the truck bed, we spread a tarp over it and placed the wheelbarrow and the shovels on top. Our gumboots were caked with cow shit, and our work gloves were soaked and stinky. And we still had to unload it when we got home.

I went over to the house. Minnie scurried into the shadows.

"Thanks so much, Minnie. How much do we owe you?"

"Ten bucks."

"That's all? Are you sure?"

"Yup."

I reached my arm into the shadows. A hand snatched the bill.

A few days later, I came back—by myself—and dropped off a couple of loaves of homemade bread.

Several years later, in 1979, after nearly a year of living and working away, Bill and I came back to Galena Bay with our infant daughter, Merri. Both gardens needed rebuilding, so we made another trip to Trout Lake.

Minnie dived into her house, as usual. But when I got out of the truck with Merri in my arms, Minnie came out and tentatively approached us. To my amazement, she didn't shy away from Bill. Instead, her attention was wholly focused on Merri, who was about five months old.

"And who's this?" Minnie said, grinning at the baby, her teeth sticking out crookedly.

Merri gave one of her adorable baby smiles, while I told Minnie the story of her premature birth.

"Well, she sure looks healthy now, don't she?" Minnie said, running a dirt-encrusted finger down Merri's leg.

Bill elbowed me. Minnie had never been this friendly. It was disconcerting.

"So, Minnie, we were wondering if we could buy a truckload of manure," I said.

"Sure."

"Great. I'll just put the baby in her car seat—"

"Oh no, you don't," Minnie said. "You're a new mama. You shouldn't be shovelling manure. You just hold on to that sweet little one."

"But Bill can't do it all—"

"I'll help," Minnie said firmly. And she did. Despite my protests, she shovelled shit with Bill while I stood there holding Merri. Mind you, she didn't *look* at him, or *talk* to him, but she worked beside him until the truck was full.

This time she charged us fifteen dollars. And she waved goodbye.

With liberal lashings of Minnie's manure, plus our own compost, the upper garden was soon thriving. Because that plot received considerably more sunshine than the lower garden, we learned to plant suitable crops in the two locations: early, shade-tolerant plants like lettuce, spinach, peas, broccoli, cauliflower, onions, and cabbages in the lower garden; sun-loving, heavy-feeding vegetables in the upper garden like corn, squashes, potatoes, carrots, peppers, tomatoes. We happily gave our excess produce to Walter and Margaret and Bob, repaying them for the generosity they'd shown us when our garden was a pitiful, barren patch. We built drying racks out of screening stapled to wood frames, and dried peas and beans in the new sauna, heated by a low fire. (When we later took a sauna, a pleasant soupy smell wafted from the cedar walls.) I canned dozens of jars of corn, beans, and tomato sauce, pleased that I could now preserve my own produce. We stored potatoes, carrots, beets, cabbages, and squashes in the root cellar, and enjoyed them all winter.

Our next gardening adventure was the new trend of planting by the phases of the moon, which we had heard about in a back-to-the-land newsletter that made the rounds of the West Kootenays. My first reaction was, "Ridiculous! Whoever heard of such a crazy thing?" But as I read the article, it began to make sense. The moon controls the tides, and even has influence on ground water. And whether the ground water is rising to the surface or retreating to the depths can affect your crops.

I learned that moisture levels are highest during the new and full moons; at those times, seeds will absorb more water and thus germinate more reliably. The article laid out specific instructions for planting certain crops during the four phases of the moon. For example, during the new moon, plant above-ground crops that produce their seeds outside the fruit, like lettuce, broccoli. and cabbage. After the full moon, while moonlight is decreasing, plant root crops such as beets, carrots, and onions.

Planting by the phases of the moon became all the rage among the hippie community. When I met up with acquaintances at the food co-op we had joined, someone would invariably say, "I planted peas in the second quarter and they did great, but when I tried planting another row of peas in the third quarter, they didn't come up at all!"

"Far out," someone else would say, and everyone else would nod knowingly and contribute their tales of moon-influenced boom or bust.

I became a believer. Bill was more skeptical. "What difference can it make when you plant what?" he said. "We just need to get the damn seeds in the ground."

"But it makes sense," I argued. "Different plants do better when the water level is rising or falling. Besides, it can't hurt to try, can it?"

Reluctantly, Bill agreed. But working out a schedule was harder than it sounded. The weather in April and May could be cool and rainy, or it could be sunny and warm. We had to grab planting days where we could find them.

Then there was the complication of planting complementary, or companion, crops. This was the idea that certain plants did well when planted next to one another, while other combinations repelled and weakened one another. For example, tomatoes did well when planted near carrots, but not next to corn. Peas and beans made good neighbours, but peas and onions were bad bedfellows.

Organic Gardening magazine said that companion planting was important. But how to reconcile all these requirements? We should plant carrots next to tomatoes, but tomatoes should be planted during the new moon and carrots two weeks later, after the full moon. I grappled with the lunar calendar, trying to slot different vegetables into different weeks, while accommodating the complementary plants that would work well with them. Finally, I came up with a workable, if complicated, schedule.

We diligently planted according to the phases of the moon, and the garden did well.

"See?" I said to Bill. "It works."

But the truth was that I didn't know whether the garden's success was attributable to the moon's phases or to the companion plantings or to both or to neither. When weather interfered and we couldn't follow the schedule, the garden did well anyway. As much as I wanted to believe, I had too much scientific skepticism in me to accept the results unquestioningly.

We planted by the phases of the moon for a year or two. Then, without discussing it, we let the method slip away and went back to planting what we could when we could.

The garden bloomed anyway.

Gardening with a child was a new experience. Bill and I had been living, working, and gardening in Galena Bay for the better part of seven years by the time Merri was born. We were used to following our own rhythms, working long hours if the job demanded it, getting our chores done on our own schedule. Now we had to figure out how to do everything with a kid in tow.

Merri was born in February, so that first spring she was a baby. We didn't have a stroller or a playpen, so when we needed to work in the garden we opened up a suitcase on the ground and laid her in it. (I knew that if my mother had seen this, she would have killed me.) We covered Merri with a piece of netting to keep off the mosquitoes. She slept peacefully in the suitcase until it was time to nurse again.

The following season, however, she was just over a year old. How were we going to get any gardening done with a toddler?

At first, we tried putting her down on the ground with a pile of toys while we tried to hoe or plant. This amused her for about ten minutes, and then she wandered after us, walking over the seeds we had just planted or trampling the tender shoots that had just come up. One time, I was planting potatoes. I dug a trench, then went down the row placing the seed potatoes a foot apart down its length. When I turned around, I saw that Merri had crawled after me and removed every potato from the row.

Merri loved berries, and the woods in Galena Bay were full of wild huckleberry bushes. We could get some relief by plunking her down in front of a bush within eyesight. She'd happily pick huckleberries one by one, ripe and unripe, until she had stripped the bush. Then she'd squawk, and we'd move her to the next bush.

Merri also loved fresh peas and beans, and I was glad to let her eat them raw from the garden. The trouble was that she didn't know how to pick them carefully, and in pulling a pea or bean from the vine she'd pull up or tear down the entire plant.

"At this rate," I said to Bill, "the garden's going to be wrecked."

We puzzled over what to do. Finally, we hit on the idea of building a sandbox. We placed it next to the upper garden, where Merri could see us and we could keep an eye on her. The sandbox did the trick. She'd dig and play with her toys for twenty minutes at a time. When she got unhappy, we'd give her a pile of pea pods (which she'd carefully open, popping the peas one by one into her mouth) or a raw ear of corn (which she'd munch until she dropped it, at which point she'd get a mouthful of sand and wail).

Something from those early days took root in Merri. She developed a keen interest in food; now she grows a garden of her own.

When I arrived at the Farm in 1971 and started helping Jon tend the fields, I knew nothing about gardening. I had never planted a seed, never handled a gardening tool, never harvested a morsel of food.

At Galena Bay, I became a student of horticulture, nutrition, and food preservation. Every year I learned more, tried new plant varieties, experimented with different planting configurations.

I discovered that I loved gardening, especially planting. I loved setting the seeds in the dug-over trenches, carefully sprinkling dirt over them, and waiting for the first shoots to poke up. I loved weeding and thinning, laying down mulch, and, of course, harvesting.

I was amazed. Here I was, the daughter and granddaughter of people who had turned away from the soil, people who preferred to hire landscapers and to buy their produce in the grocery store—and I loved digging in the dirt.

I still do.

Birds, Bees, and Bears

Birds

On a spring afternoon in 1974, Bill and I met the Greyhound bus in Revelstoke. The driver opened the baggage compartment and started taking out parcels. He pulled out a carton with holes punched on all sides. "Schwartz?"

Bill stepped forward. "That's us."

The man handed him the box. The contents shifted to one side with the sound of claws scratching on cardboard. Bill tilted the box, and the scratching noise moved back the other way. We placed the box on the truck seat between us and set out for the ferry. There was a faint odour of manure. From the holes came warbling. I had expected them to cheep, but instead they made a soft, musical, throaty sound.

We were about to become chicken farmers. Chickens were a logical type of livestock to start out with. They didn't take up much space. They didn't require pasture. They ate kitchen and garden scraps, though we'd need to supplement those with commercial feed. They produced manure—and *Organic Gardening*, our bible for all things rural, said that chicken manure was the richest, most concentrated manure there was. And Lord knew that our pathetic garden, planted in the thin soil that was left after we'd dug up a stone wall's worth of rocks, needed something rich and concentrated to happen to it.

I wondered how the chicks would like their new home. Bill and I had built a chicken coop based on a plan in *Raising Poultry for Fun and Profit*, and it was, without a doubt, the grandest building we'd yet constructed. We'd situated it right behind the garden, reasoning that we could conveniently chuck greens from the garden straight into the coop, and shovel manure from the opposite direction.

The main part of the coop was twelve feet square with a moderately sloping aluminum roof. We'd insulated the walls with fibreglass batts and the ceiling with sawdust, put in a small south-facing window, and hung a sturdy door, the better to keep out varmints such as skunks and martens. We painted the exterior a pale minty green. Inside, we built platforms for roosting (chickens like to sleep in high places, harking back to when they were wild and lived in trees) and a triple-compartment laying box, which was curtained (laying hens like their privacy) with sections of Bill's worn-out tartan-plaid boxer shorts.

We built an ingenious feed tray, constructed so that, as the chickens removed food from the tray, more pellets automatically moved down a chute and filled the tray. We bought a red and white plastic water dispenser, much like the filtered water dispensers found in offices today. You filled a container with water and turned it upside-down over a tray. As the chickens drank, more water dripped into the tray, balancing the pressure differential.

Appended to the coop was a run where the chickens could scratch for feed, dig up bugs, move around, be exposed to sunshine, and generally hang out. The run was open on three sides, with only a chicken-wire enclosure around it and a roof overhead. Sawdust covered the ground.

We hung on the wall a large glossy photograph of an immaculately white, plump Leghorn hen—"to serve as inspiration," I said. When we were finished, we stood back and admired our handsome new structure. "It's the Chicken Hilton," Bill said, and that's what we called it.

We'd debated what kind of chickens to get. Leghorns were the classic variety, white, with a pleasant pear-shaped body; they laid pure white eggs. Bantams were popular among many homesteaders we knew. They were small, with plumage ranging from white through brown, grey, and black, and they laid tiny, highly nutritious, brightly coloured eggs. But because of their small size and low body weight, Bantams, or Bantys, as they were called, could still fly. They were known to escape their coops and lay their eggs in secret hiding places, forcing their owners to conduct daily scavenger hunts.

Finally, after talking to Walter, we chose Harco Sex-Links. They were a hybrid of Rhode Island Reds and Barred Rocks, both known to be hardy birds and excellent layers. They were medium-size chickens, slightly larger than Leghorns, with brown feathers speckled with black, and they had bright red combs and feet. We ordered chicks from a supplier in the Okanagan. That was what was in the box: 25 one-week-old chicks.

We gingerly carried the box into the coop. When we lifted the lid, the chicks spilled out in a heap. They looked like small balls of fluff with beaks. Rather than the buttercup-yellow of chicks in storybooks, they were pale yellow, a dull shade that made them look as if they'd been out in a dingy rain. They huddled together, pushing and warbling and sometimes climbing over or under each other. A few brave individuals ventured out to peck at the wooden support of the laying box, then scurried back to the flock.

Bill pushed them over to the feed tray brimming with chick starter pellets, while I scooped one terrified chick into my hand and showed it the water tray. The gang discovered the food and began to gobble up the pellets. One chick, smaller than the rest, kept getting pushed aside. I picked it up and made room for it at the tray, where it joined the others in frenzied eating, only to lose its place after a moment to a larger, more aggressive chick.

"Aren't they cute?" I said. Bill gave me an oh-don't-be-a-sentimental-fool look, but I could tell that he was thinking the same thing, and would have said so if I hadn't beaten him to it.

Although some people claim to be able to determine whether an egg will yield a male or a female bird, most poultry specialists admit that it's impossible. It's only when the chicks are about a month old that the plumage differentiates sufficiently to make a positive identification. You can buy unsexed newborn chicks, figuring you'll end up with half and half, or you can wait and buy older birds whose sex is known. We'd opted for the unsexed chicks, partly for the thrill of the gamble, partly because they were cheaper.

This, of course, raised the unspoken issue overlaying the entire enterprise. Walter had said it plainly. "If you don't want the roosters for meat, you'll have to butcher them before they get too big, because they'll cheat the hens of food and take up space that you can't afford."

We'd nodded uncomfortably. We didn't want the roosters for meat—or the hens, for that matter. We were vegetarians. We wanted chickens only for eggs. But raising poultry necessarily meant that we would have to deal with the roosters, and with the hens when they reached the end of their laying days.

"'Deal with' is too mild a word," Bill said to me when we discussed this, before ordering the chicks. "We're going to have to kill them. Slaughter them."

"I know," I said. "But, after all, butchering is part of homesteading. We'll just have to do it."

"Can you see yourself chopping off a chicken's head?"

I squirmed. "No, but I can see you doing it."

"Hey!"

We laughed. "Let's not worry about that now," I said. "We'll deal with it when we have to."

Not the most responsible position, but an expedient one.

We watched the chicks grow into chickens, watched their necks elongate and their bodies take on a full-bellied contour, and hoped for more hens than roosters. In time, the hens became shorter and squatter and turned a rich orangey-brown shade, while the roosters became taller and heavier, grew larger, jigglier combs and wattles, and developed black and white speckled plumage.

There were eleven hens and fourteen roosters.

I had never had a pet as a child. Bill had grown up with dogs. Neither of us had any experience with farmyard creatures. I don't know what Bill imagined, but my vision of chickens was of plump, pretty birds that would follow me around, eagerly pecking up the corn that I scattered in graceful arcs, cackle in soft tones, lay warm brown eggs, and generally lend a pastoral atmosphere to the homestead.

Wrong.

Two things quickly became clear. One was that the expression "bird brain" was accurate. The chickens were startlingly stupid. Every time we entered the coop, they squawked and clucked in alarm, as if they had never seen us, or any human being, before. They defecated in random locations, then stepped in their still-moist manure. They spilled great quantities of food out of the feeder and scratched sawdust into their water. One hen would start running in a certain direction, for no apparent reason, and the others would follow, squawking. Then another one would veer off in a new direction and they would bump into one another, scrambling to follow the new leader.

The other revelation was that the chickens were cruel. No cute, sweet little chickies here. The phrase "the pecking order," which I had thought a mere figure of speech, turned out to be based in reality. The chickens pecked at one another constantly, usually on the back of the neck. The bigger ones chased the smaller ones away from the food, away from the water, just *away*. The powerful ones squawked, flapped their feathers, and snapped their beaks at those that were weaker, and so it was repeated down the line, an ever-diminishing echo of power and aggression, from the largest to the smallest.

This unfortunate bird turned out to be the runty chick that I had tried to help that first day. She was a petite, delicate hen, only half the size of her sisters. We nicknamed her the Little Hen, and she became the target of the other hens' cruelty. They chased her away from the food and water. She took to darting in when no one was looking, grabbing a quick mouthful, then scurrying away and hiding in the corner. The other chickens pecked at her mercilessly, pulling out the feathers on the back of her neck and eventually piercing the skin. The Little Hen cowered, clucking in fear, vainly trying to escape. At times, her skin was so mutilated that we had to place her in a separate enclosure while she recovered.

Meanwhile, the roosters ate, the roosters grew, the roosters, as Walter had predicted, began to take up more space than we could afford. Bill and I tried to ignore this. We studiously avoided saying the word "slaughter" or "butcher" or "kill." But finally, we couldn't pretend any longer. In May, two months after we'd brought the chicks home, the coop had grown too crowded and the feed bills had become too high. We looked each other in the eye and said, "It's time." *Later* had come.

But how do you kill chickens? Chop their heads off? Break their necks?

That year, I was teaching in Revelstoke and coming home on weekends. One day when I was in the staff room, I mentioned that Bill, Paul, and I were planning to butcher our roosters the following weekend. "Good luck," one of my colleagues said, while another grimaced and said, "Better you than me."

John Campbell, the vice-principal, happened to be in the staff room. A tall, wiry guy with curly black hair, John was about ten years older than I was, and he had taken an interest in the hippie lifestyle Bill and I were leading in Galena Bay.

John and his wife lived on a small rural property on the outskirts of Revelstoke. They kept a couple of horses and a flock of chickens. When he heard me, he said, "Oh, that's a coincidence. We're going to be butchering some of our chickens, too."

"How do you do it?" I asked.

"I pith them. It's easy, it's bloodless, and it's instantaneous, so the chickens don't suffer. Come out to my place and I'll show you how."

The next day after school, I went home with John. The sun was shining, the lilacs were blooming, and it was a lovely day for walking, canoeing, marking papers—anything but killing chickens. John, carrying an ordinary steak knife, not an axe, I noticed, offered me some advice as we walked out to the barn. "Don't think of them as chickens, or even as birds. Just think of them as things. As a job that has to be done."

He walked calmly into the midst of the milling flock, grabbed one of the roosters, and carried it over to a stump set up in the middle of the yard. He lay the bird's head on the stump, using the palm of his hand to hold the head down while forcing the beak open with the thumb and forefinger of the same hand.

"In the roof of a chicken's mouth, there's a soft spot," John said. "The brain is right above that. All you have to do is thrust the knife upward through that spot and give it a twist. That instantly severs the spinal cord and destroys the brain—and the chicken is dead."

He inserted the knife. He twisted. The bird jerked once or twice, then lay still. John tossed it into a plastic bucket. He turned to me. "Quick and easy, eh?"

"I didn't know it was going to—" I motioned with my hand. "You know."

"Twitch, you mean? Oh, sorry, I forgot to warn you about that. It's a reflexive movement. The bird is already dead and can't feel a thing, but it takes a second for the message to get from its brain to its muscles."

This scientific explanation did not comfort me. I followed John back into the coop, where he caught another rooster. The whole procedure, from the time he grabbed the bird to the time he threw it into the bucket, took about a minute.

"Now it's your turn," John said, handing me the knife.

My stomach fluttered.

"What if I miss?"

"You try again."

"What if the bird gets away?"

"You catch it and hold on tighter."

"What if—"

John gave me a look. I followed him into the coop. Kindly, he caught a rooster and handed it to me. I tucked it under my arm. It thrashed, nearly breaking free.

"Hold it tight," he said.

I pressed my elbow against the bird's body, and it subsided. I carried it to the stump and lay the neck down. The rooster jerked and nearly got away, but I caught it and pressed the neck down against the stump. I pried the beak open and inserted the knife. On my first stab I missed the hole and pierced through the cartilage on the roof of its mouth. A strangled cry came from the rooster's open beak. Frantically I felt around with the tip of the knife. After two eternally long seconds, I found the hole, thrust upward, and twisted the knife. The bird gave one mighty twitch, then lay still. My hands shook as I tossed the carcass onto the pile.

"Don't worry," John said, "you'll get better."

Amazingly, I did. After a few more attempts, each slightly less botched than the last, I began to get a feel for it. How to hold the bird's beak open with two fingers while I pressed down on the neck with the heel of my hand. Where to thrust and how deeply. I learned that the quicker my movements, the more merciful the butchering. I became an efficient killer. I realized that I had adopted John's advice: the chickens weren't birds, they were things. Things to be dispatched.

I felt awful. I was taking lives. Innocent lives. What had these roosters ever done to me? One minute they were pecking in the yard, and the next they were lifeless carcasses. And there was something so sad about their limp, dead bodies, thrown callously into the bucket.

At the same time, I felt proud. I was good at this. Soon I could put away a bird almost as quickly as John.

I thanked John and left. On the way home, I realized that I had just made a terrible mistake. I was now the only one of our threesome who knew how to butcher chickens.

A few days before our butchering, Bill and I discussed whether to kill all the roosters or to leave one of them alive. Hens do not need to be fertilized in order to lay eggs, but if you want fertilized eggs, or if you want to raise your own chicks, then, of course, you need a rooster.

"What's a farmyard without a rooster?" I said. "It wouldn't feel complete."

Bill nodded. "And it might be fun to raise our own chicks someday. Then they can grow up and lay eggs and hatch more chicks, and on and on."

Also, there was the issue of fertilized versus unfertilized eggs. On that subject, opinion was divided. As far as science was concerned, fertilized eggs held no nutritional or health advantage over unfertilized eggs. All they were good for was producing chicks. But the new-age community was convinced that fertilized eggs were superior. The differences might not be detectable using traditional measurements, said articles in *The Smallholder* and *The Mother Earth News*, but on some subtle, perhaps even spiritual, level they were there.

I vacillated. My father, a doctor and an eminently rational man, had a scientist's mind. His constant question was, "Where's the proof?" and that mindset was more ingrained in me than I cared to admit. Still, my heart pulled me to believe in the unprovable advantages of fertilized eggs, and I was enough of a mystic to be persuaded.

So it was decided. We would keep one rooster. There wasn't much debate about which one it would be. One fellow was bigger and plumper than the others, his voice louder, his comb redder, his eyes brighter. Paul named the rooster Abdul, conjuring up the image of a sultan surrounded by his adoring harem. Abdul would be spared.

Saturday morning dawned dull and cloudy. Bill, Paul, and I arose early. All of us, perhaps sensing that it would not stay down, skipped breakfast. I fortified myself with two cups of strong coffee. I started a fire in the Findlay and placed on it two large pots of water. We set up a butchering stump, sharpened several knives and the axe, cleaned a few twenty-five-gallon plastic buckets, and tied a rope between two trees from which to hang the carcasses while they were being bled and plucked. Now all that remained was to do it.

Paul, who was a more devout vegetarian than Bill and I, declined to have anything to do with the actual killing. His job would be to scald and pluck the birds. I, the experienced one, would be the butcher. Bill would catch the roosters and help hold them down.

The water boiled. It was time to begin. Bill, donning gloves, went into the chicken coop. A loud, panic-stricken squawking ensued. I remained at the stump, gripping the knife and repeating John's words to myself: "Stay calm. Be quick. Think of them as things."

In a moment, Bill came out with a black and white rooster under his arm. He took the bird by the feet, swung it over his head like a lasso (we had read that this made the birds dizzy, which would buy me an extra second in which to find my mark), and placed its head on the block. The dazed rooster lay still for a moment, then began to squirm. I forced its beak open, thrust in the knife, and twisted. Although I shuddered when the rooster twitched after death, I knew I had done my job well. Bill chopped off its head with the axe, then carried it to the tree, where Paul waited to start plucking.

"One down, twelve to go," I said to myself as Bill walked to the coop for the next bird.

Rooster after rooster, killing after killing, press, pry, thrust, twist. Bill and I made a good team. He quickly learned how many spins it took to get a rooster dizzy (three), how to hold its body still for me, how hard he needed to chop with the axe to cut off the dead bird's head with one blow. I learned how hard to press on the neck, to lighten my grip on the knife, to work more quickly and (I hoped) humanely. The assembly line of death ground on.

Paul dipped the hens into buckets of hot water to soften the feather connections before hanging the birds by the feet from the clothesline. It was laborious work. The large feathers came out easily enough, but the smaller pin feathers were a pain to get out. And the smell! I'll never forget the disgusting stink of those wet feathers.

Once the birds were naked, we chopped off their feet, slit them open, and scooped out the entrails: the heart and lungs and liver, the gizzards, the intestines with their gross contents, shit spilling out onto the ground—and our hands—as we inadvertently squeezed. We dug a hole on the other side of the clearing, far from the cabin, and buried the feathers and innards. We hosed down the butchering area, but it still stank for days, and so did our hands, despite repeated washing.

When it was over, we had three buckets full of bumpy-fleshed, headless, footless carcasses. It amazed me how small the roosters' bodies were when stripped of feathers, beaks, and claws. I cut the meat into pieces, wincing at the crack of the bones, stuffed them into quart Mason jars, covered the pieces with boiling water, salt, and herbs, and canned them for three hours.

Those sealed jars sat on a shelf for several months. I couldn't bring myself to use the meat. Finally, I opened a jar and made chicken soup. The flavour was delicious. The chicken was like rubber. Bill and I chewed and chewed the same bite and then forced it down with a gulp.

A few weeks later, I used a second jar of chicken, this time in a stew. Across the table, Bill and I exchanged a look. Without a word, we opened the remaining jars and dumped the meat in the woods. The ravens and coyotes and skunks had a feast.

The hens started laying at about six months of age. A hen would flutter up to one of the boxes and dart inside, disappearing behind the boxer-shorts curtain like an actress exiting into the wings of a theatre. We'd hear musical clucks, then a rustling sound as the hen wiggled in the confined space, straining to expel the egg. Finally there would be an extended clu-u-u-u-c-c-k-k!, and voilà—a warm brown egg.

We had to remove the eggs promptly so the hens wouldn't go broody. A hen's natural instinct, when she lays an egg, is to sit on it and hatch out a chick. But we didn't want our hens to hatch broods right now, because during the nesting time they stop laying, having fulfilled their reproductive purpose. So every morning, we went into the coop, slid our hands into the laying boxes, and removed the eggs. Sometimes we disturbed a sitting hen, who squawked in protest and gave us a baleful look.

At first, while the hens were still immature, the eggs were small, the size of commercial-grade small eggs. After a few months, they got larger until, by the following spring, they were so big we couldn't close extra-large cartons for fear of crushing them.

Oh, those eggs! Never before had I realized that home-raised eggs could be so different from the white, thin-shelled, pale-yolked eggs I had grown up with. The shells, a rich caramel-brown colour, were so thick that you had to give them a good whack with a knife to crack them. The yolks were pumpkin-orange, and when you slid an egg into a frying pan, the white didn't run toward the edges of the pan like a store-bought egg would, but shimmered firmly around the yolk like gelatin. I had never known that eggs actually had a taste. Not only did scrambled eggs and omelettes taste delicious, so did pancakes and muffins and cookies. They tasted rich. Natural. Nutritious.

Soon our flock of eleven hens was producing ten, twelve, sixteen eggs a day, so many that I couldn't use them fast enough. We sold the odd dozen and gave the rest away—to Walter, Bob, Hilda, anyone who would take them.

The idea that roosters crow only in the morning is a myth; Abdul strutted around the run, crowing at all hours of the day. He knew his duty. He'd jump on the back of one of the hens and push his sperm glob onto her vent. The hen would give a startled, indignant cry and twist to try to shake him off, but he'd dig his claws into her body and bite her neck with his beak, hanging on until he was finished, a matter of seconds. He'd jump off with a loud crow. The hen would shake out her feathers and go back to pecking in the straw as if nothing had happened.

One day, as Bill and I watched Abdul do his thing, Bill turned to me and said, "Let's try it like that." He puffed up his chest and jerked his head. "Get over here, baby."

I smacked him in a tender spot.

If we had hoped that removing the roosters from the coop would lessen the amount of pecking, we were disappointed. In fact, it got worse. We consulted our manual. It assured us: "If hens have enough space, good food, and plenty of fresh water, pecking should not be a problem." But our hens had all three, and pecking was still a problem. A few of the hens had bare spots on their necks, and the Little Hen, the scrawniest of the flock, had a large, red gap in her feathers.

One day, when we described to Walter in gory detail our hens' cannibalistic tendencies, he mentioned a possible solution. "You can get little blinders for chickens."

"You mean like horses wear?" I laughed at the bizarre image of chickens with blinders on.

Walter wasn't laughing. "They fit through the little holes at the top of their beaks and cut off their vision to the sides. Apparently, if they can't see each other, they stop pecking."

Later, I said to Bill, as we stood by the chicken coop, "That's the silliest thing I've ever heard."

"Me, too."

The Little Hen waddled into view, looked nervously from side to side, and started pecking in the dirt. Another hen came over and jabbed her beak at the Little Hen's bare spot. With a piteous cackle, she scurried away.

Bill turned to me. "We've got to do something."

On our next trip to town, feeling foolish, I called the hatchery where we had bought the chicks. "Sure, we have blinders," the man on the other end said. "How many sets do you want?"

"Eleven," I said. "Uh ... how do you put them in?"

"Don't worry, we'll enclose instructions. That'll be seven dollars and twenty-eight cents including tax."

Each blinder consisted of two squares of red plastic connected by a thin clasp. When we opened the clasp, we saw that on one of the free ends was a plastic arrow, the kind that can be inserted into a hole but not pulled out. In the box was a slip of paper. "Separate halves. Push arrow through both holes in beak. Rejoin halves." A diagram pointed to the two nostrils at the top of a chicken's beak, one on each side.

Bill and I marched out to the chicken coop and commenced Operation Blinder Insertion. It did not go smoothly. The chickens did not appreciate having a plastic arrow inserted into their nostrils. Perhaps things would have gone better had the arrow tips not been so much bigger than the holes, and had the holes not been filled with a tough, cartilaginous fibre. It took us an hour to put blinders on eleven hens, and when we were done, we were scratched, pecked, and covered with dust.

The chickens were confused. They twisted their heads from side to side, trying to shake off these strange new appendages. When that didn't work, they cocked their heads and tried to see over the plastic squares, like aristocratic old ladies peering over their spectacles.

For a while the blinders actually worked. Pecking decreased, and the Little Hen's back began to heal. But after a couple of weeks, the chickens figured out how to see around them, and resumed pecking with equal, if not greater, ferocity.

One day the Little Hen had an open, bleeding gash on her back. "We can't let her go on like this," I said to Bill. He nodded, picked her up, and carried her to the stump.

The Little Hen did not struggle. I think she knew she was going to her death and sensed that it would be better than the misery she had endured for so long. She died quietly, without a squawk. We could not eat her. We put her body deep in the woods and let the ravens pick her bones clean.

In the fall, the hens moulted, and egg production fell. By winter they had feathered out and were laying again, this time producing fewer but larger eggs, many with two yolks.

Chickens can survive cold temperatures: in the winter their shared body heat keeps them warm. But in January 1975, a cold spell hit. The temperature went down to six degrees Fahrenheit at night. In the morning, when we went into the coop, the water in the tray was frozen. Worried that the chickens' feet might freeze, we bought a small kerosene heater and placed it under the roost.

That winter the water line into our cabin froze, too, so Bill and I had been hauling buckets of water from a nearby spring.

One night, as Bill and I were getting ready for bed, we heard loud squawks coming from the chicken coop. That was odd: normally the hens were quiet at night.

"A predator must have gotten in," I said. We'd already lost the odd chicken to a skunk or a marten. We went outside to investigate.

The chicken coop was on fire.

We ran into the coop. The kerosene heater was tipped over on its side, and flames were flickering up one plywood wall toward the sawdust-insulated ceiling. The sawdust floor smouldered with the putrid smell of burning manure. While Bill righted the heater and turned it off, I hurried back to the cabin and returned with the two buckets of water we had filled that afternoon. We doused the flames on the wall and poured water on the sawdust. When the water was gone, we threw handfuls of snow onto the now-smouldering insulation.

The chicken coop filled with smoke and steam. The hens skittered around in a frenzy, clucking and squawking, getting in our way. One lone hen sat in a box, calmly laying an egg in the midst of the commotion.

We managed to put out the fire. In the morning, we surveyed the damage. The insulation had burned up and would have to be replaced, and one wall, on both the outside and the inside, was scorched. But the building was intact and not dangerously weakened. And, amazingly, we hadn't lost a single chicken, although a few had had their feathers singed.

Bill put his hands on his hips. "It's not the Chicken Hilton anymore. It's the Charcoal Hilton."

When the first flock of hens passed their egg-laying prime, in the spring of 1976, we gave them, alive, to John Campbell and bought a flock of Bantams. They were smaller than conventional hens, and we could make up about half of their diet with kitchen and garden scraps, saving money on feed. They laid beautiful, golf-ball-size eggs: some were robin's-egg-blue, some were speckled blue and grey, some were indigo.

But that was if you could find them. What our friends had told us turned out to be true: Bantams were semi-wild, and they didn't like to be confined. They found ingenious ways of getting out of the coop, flattening themselves to squeeze under the wall, or finding a hole in the chicken-wire fence. Every day Bill and I searched the adjacent woods for eggs, occasionally spotting one, more often returning empty-handed. One by one, the birds escaped, never to reappear.

After that, we decided to go back to more conventional birds, and purchased a dozen white Leghorn pullets, hens just beginning to lay. They were flightier and, if possible, stupider than the Harco Sex-Links, and their white eggs didn't say "country" the way the brown ones did. But they were extremely productive, and the flock prospered.

When the Leghorns finally stopped laying, we debated what to do.

"I just can't face pithing them," I told Bill. "Once was enough."

"Okay. I'll chop their heads off."

This time I caught the hens, swung them around to make them dizzy, and handed them to Bill, who wielded the axe. The decapitated bodies twitched and sprayed blood. It was gross and disgusting and sad.

We gave the meat away. I didn't have the stomach to can it.

Altogether Bill and I kept chickens for three years. In the end we calculated that, with all the free eggs, our chicken operation had just about broken even.

Bees

"Bees are the easiest, most docile, and least demanding creatures to raise," our neighbour Bob Harrington told Bill and me. "All you have to do is put the hives together, put the bees into the hives, feed them a little sugar water until the local plants start producing nectar, and then sit back until it's time to harvest the honey."

Bill and I nodded our heads at this—he vigorously, I less so. It wasn't only the prospect of getting stung that scared me, although that was a real fear. It was the consequence of failing. If we grew a new variety of cucumber and the plants withered and died, it would be disappointing but not devastating. If we got bees and botched it, we'd be responsible for the demise of an entire colony of lives.

Yet beekeeping sounded so easy; the thought of producing our own honey so alluring; and the opportunity to study the social system of honeybees so intriguing, that, with a little coaxing from Bill, I agreed. Besides, honey was the only sweetener I would use. It made sense to produce our own.

Bill went to Vernon and took a three-day course with a venerable apiarist named Leo Fuhr. Leo, Bill told me, *lived* honeybees. He kept over fifty hives spread throughout the Okanagan, taught courses, sold equipment and bees, and loved everything about the fascinating insects. "He was so comfortable," Bill said, "that he worked among his hives without any protection. No gloves, no mask, not even long sleeves. Bees crawled on him and buzzed around him, and he just carried on as if they weren't there. It was like he had a silent communication with them."

Bill learned about the life cycle of honeybees, how to introduce a colony into a new hive, common honeybee diseases and how to prevent them, and how to extract honey. He came home with an apiarist certificate, a thick book by David Cramp called *The Complete Step-by-Step Book of Beekeeping: A practical guide to beekeeping, from setting up a colony to hive management and harvesting the honey, shown in over 400 photographs*, and a great deal of enthusiasm. Also, a dozen packages of equipment (supers, sheets of foundation, entrance bars, and smokers) and protective clothing (helmets covered with a veil that fit around your shirt collar, leather and canvas gloves that came up to your elbows, and white coveralls). And a jar of apple blossom honey.

The hive components came unassembled. Bill and I opened our new "bible" and followed a series of diagrams to build the hives. The first step was to nail together three supers. These were topless and bottomless wooden boxes, each of which would house ten frames of honeycomb. Then we assembled the frames, rectangles of thin wood like oblong picture frames. To each frame we attached a sheet of foundation, a flat panel of honeycomb, so that each frame was filled with a pale yellow "picture." Later, the bees would build out the foundation with their own beeswax and fill each cell with honey. Finally, we painted all the wooden surfaces with non-toxic white paint: paint to protect the wood from moisture, white to reflect sunlight away from the hive.

We set the empty supers on wooden bottom boards, which would provide a landing spot and entrance for the foraging bees. Then we drove to Vernon to pick up a few thousand colonists.

Leo had three boxes ready for us. The boxes, each about the size of a toaster, were made of wood on the sides and bottom, and covered with wire mesh on top. Each box contained a queen bee in a smaller screen box, about 2,500 worker bees (females), and a few dozen drones (males). Bill and I placed the boxes on the truck seat between us. My left thigh tingled with their vibrations, and the cab filled with a low-pitched droning sound.

As we drove along, I visualized my prostrate body, swollen beyond recognition, pierced by hundreds of tiny stingers like acupuncture needles. I knew that such incidents rarely, if ever, occurred with North American-bred bees, which were known for their docility. But too many glances at tabloid headlines—"Girl Stung to Death By Killer Bee Swarm"; "Thousands Flee Their Homes"—had made such a spectre seem possible. Also, I knew that bees, like other animals, were able to sense fear and that it made them anxious and unpredictable. I edged as close as possible to the truck door, hoping that the bees weren't picking up on my vibes.

We left the bees on the truck seat and went into the cabin to dress. A few minutes later we emerged, clad in impossibly white coveralls, gloves, and veils, with our pant legs tucked into high-lacing boots. We moved as gracefully as knights in armour.

I was armed with a smoker, an ingenious tool consisting of a small burning chamber attached to a bellows, similar to that used by blacksmiths. Into the chamber you placed damp leaves or a piece of burlap, anything that smouldered, and lit it. Each time you squeezed the bellows, a puff of smoke came out of a hole in the chamber. Smoke pacified bees: when they smelled it, it awakened in them a primordial suspicion that the tree in which their hive was located was on fire, and, to prepare themselves for the ordeal of searching for a new home, they gorged on honey. Stuffed in this way, they were unable to contract the muscles that pumped venom into their stingers and thus were unable to sting. The only trouble with a smoker was that if you overused it, the bees realized that you were crying wolf and became annoyed. "DO NOT ABUSE THE SMOKER," the manual warned. *I won't,* I promised as I lumbered down the driveway. Still, I puffed the smoker a couple of times to make sure the burlap was burning.

Because Bill had taken the course, I "let" him install the bees (read: begged him to install the bees). After lifting the lid from the first super, he opened the small screen door on a box of bees and thumped the box sharply downward onto the wooden frames. Bees tumbled down. There was a moment of silence, as if they were shocked to feel themselves suddenly dumped into some strange box. Then the droning sound rose from the depths of the hive. Bill released the queen from her small cage and put her in the super. I quickly replaced the lid. We repeated the steps with the other two supers.

We had not needed to use the smoker. I gave it a squeeze anyway. Nothing came out. I opened the cap of the burning chamber. The fire had died.

What saved me from my fears, in the end, were the bees themselves. They ignored me. They went about their business and did what bees are supposed to do: make beeswax, lay eggs, gather pollen and nectar, fly around, and buzz. I got stung, numerous times. It hurt. The spot became swollen and pink and itchy. But I didn't die. Walter said that bee venom was good for arthritis. I couldn't attest to that, not suffering from that disease (yet), but I did find that my hay fever improved. Whether it was repeated doses of venom or pollen-laden honey that acted as a desensitizing agent, I don't know, but I'm certain that the improvement was related to keeping bees.

By the end of the first season, I had become brave enough to shed the bulky leather gloves. But I never, either that year or in subsequent years, shed my veil. Such bravado I left to the grinning show-offs in the bee book, who were pictured short-sleeved and bare-headed, their heads and arms covered with bees.

The bees' social system fascinated me. Each of the three types of bee has its own clearly defined and essential role. There is only one queen in a colony. Once the queen is mature, she flies out of the hive, followed by a dozen or so drones, the male bees, who have stubbier, more rectangular bodies. As the queen and the drones perform a dance above the hive, she mates with several drones in succession, storing up to one-hundred million sperm in her body. The queen returns to the hive. From that time on, her only job is to lay eggs.

The worker bees, the females, are about half as long as the queen, with more delicately coloured bodies. As the queen crawls across the frame, pausing to lay an egg the size of a grain of rice in each cell, "nursemaid" worker bees secrete wax to cover the cell and protect the egg until it is ready to hatch. Later, the nursemaid bees chew a hole in the wax cap to release the baby bees. Other worker bees, the "gatherers," fly out every day to collect pollen and nectar, which they bring back to the hive. They do an intricate airborne dance to tell their fellow workers where the best sources are. The workers digest the nectar and secrete it as honey, which they deposit in cells and cover with wax.

I took no small pleasure in teasing Bill. "Typical. The males lie around all day, waiting until it's time for sex, while the females do all the work."

Bill winked. "Those drones may be lazy, but they're smart. Sounds like a routine I could get into."

At the end of the summer, it was time to harvest the honey. Following plans in our bee book, we built a homemade extractor. Essentially, an extractor is a chamber in which frames of honeycomb spin around, using centrifugal force to push the honey out of the cells.

We scrounged an old metal rain barrel, cut off the top so the barrel measured about three feet in height, and hired Walter to weld four metal brackets to a circular frame that fit inside the cylinder. Each bracket was sized to hold a frame of honeycomb. We placed a vertical axis in the centre of the barrel and attached a handle to it so that, when we turned the handle, the axis and the circular frame spun around. Finally, we installed a spigot near the bottom, through which we would remove the honey.

Suited up, we removed the lid from the first hive. I gave the bees a puff of smoke. As they retreated downward, Bill removed the first frame. Rapping it sharply on the side of the super to dislodge any remaining bees, he handed it to me. So we continued until we had four frames, each bulging with rounded caps of beeswax. Bill replaced the cover on the hive and we took the frames into the cabin. (We had decided to do the extracting indoors. This was inconvenient, since the cabin was so small, but it was better than doing it in the open air, where the bees might decide to try to take back their honey.)

I heated a knife in hot water and sliced it across the surface of the frame. A bumpy sheet of beeswax peeled off like the skin of a cooked squash. Liquid honey started dripping out. Quickly I placed the frame in the first bracket and heated the knife again.

When all four frames were in place, we fastened the lid on top of the rain barrel. Bill turned the handle. The axis spun, slowly at first, then faster. Because the frame inside wasn't perfectly balanced, its spinning caused the barrel to rock back and forth, threatening to topple. Frequently we had to stop, right the barrel, reposition the handle, and start turning again.

After a few minutes, we removed the lid. Golden honey was dripping down the sides of the barrel. The cells were empty.

Success!

We replaced the four empty frames in the hive and removed the next four. And so on.

That first extractor worked, but not well. The following year, we bought a used commercial extractor. This one had a shiny barrel, brackets for eight frames, and a handle that turned with a whisper. Best of all, the circular frame spun smoothly on the axis. By then, we had five hives, so we appreciated the greater efficiency of our new extractor.

The honey! Never had I tasted anything so delicious. And it was fascinating to taste the honey produced from different plants. Clover, both white and "red" (really a pink shade), grew semi-wild where farms had once flourished in Galena Bay. Clover honey was light in colour and delicate in flavour. Fireweed honey was stronger and sweeter. A few years after Bill and I started keeping bees, we cleared more land and planted buckwheat to build up the soil. Buckwheat honey, dark and smoky in taste, was my favourite. During honey harvesting season, we ate pancakes for breakfast (and sometimes for lunch and dinner) slathered with buckwheat honey.

Bees become inactive during the winter. They huddle in a ball in their hives, sharing warmth. We left them several frames of honey to sustain them through the cold, dark months. In the spring, at our latitude, nectar did not start flowing until well into May, so we had to feed the bees a sugar-water mixture until they could forage for themselves.

It was always sad to open the hives in the early spring and see piles of dead bees at the bottom. We waited impatiently for the clover and birch buds and fruit trees to bloom. As the days warmed up, we'd see one bee here, another bee there, scouts venturing out to reconnoitre and report back to the hive. Finally, spring would arrive, and our fields once again reverberated with the hum of honeybees.

As Bob Harrington had assured us, North American-bred honeybees were docile. For the first several years, we never had any trouble with our bees. They didn't mind when we opened the hives, took out frames to inspect, or even removed frames to extract the honey. If they stung us, it was only because we inadvertently brushed against them too hard.

By the late 1970s, though, we began to hear rumours about more aggressive bees. "African killer bees," so called because they had originally been bred in Africa for their superior nectar-gathering abilities, had been introduced into North America. These bees were much more easily angered than traditional North American bees, often attacking beekeepers or even bystanders, inflicting multiple stings. Articles in our beekeeping magazine warned that these colonies were overtaking milder colonies in the southern United States, killing the resident queens and installing their own, who then went on to raise more aggressive broods. And they were moving north. "Be sure to check with your bee supplier about the origin of your bees," the article warned. "If you get an especially aggressive colony, you may have to destroy it."

The winter of 1977 had been an unusually cold one, and our bees did not survive. We had to start again with new colonies. By now, Leo Fuhr had retired and his son had taken over his business. "These bees may be on the feisty side," the junior Fuhr advised us when we picked them up.

He wasn't kidding. Even the hum of the bees in their boxes, on the trip home, was louder than usual, and when we thumped the bees down into the supers, they boiled up in a throng. We quickly smoked them down and placed the lids on top.

One thing I have to say for those bees: they were incredible gatherers. We spotted them foraging early and late, and they filled the frames more quickly than our former bees had. But whenever we opened the hives to inspect them, dozens of bees rose up, circling our heads with an angry roar and darting at our arms, looking for an open patch of skin to sting. Needless to say, we had reverted to full protection: helmets and veils, gloves, coveralls, boots. When a bee did break through and sting, it hurt and swelled more than the milder stings of the past.

Bill and I were nervous when it came time to extract the honey. "If they react like this when we just take a look, what are they going to do when we actually remove the frames?" I asked.

The operation was further complicated by the fact that our hives were now located on top of a ten-foot-high platform, which we had built because of predation by bears. So it was going to be awkward and time-consuming to get the frames down from the platform and into the cabin, giving the bees plenty of time to get pissed off.

We set up a tag-team relay. Bill climbed up onto the platform while I remained within arms' reach on the ladder. He opened the hive, smoked down the bees, pulled out a frame, and handed it to me. While I hustled down the ladder, Bill closed up the hive. Once I reached the ground, I ran to the cabin, half a dozen bees following me and buzzing angrily. I brushed off the bees clinging to the frame, darted inside, and placed the frame in the extractor. Then I ran back to the ladder to receive the next frame. Each time I repeated the trip, more bees seemed to figure out what was going on, and more of them followed me. The same thing happened to Bill each time he opened the hive. Soon there was a cloud around his head.

Finally, we managed to get all the frames out of the hives. A few bees slipped indoors and they buzzed around the cabin, bouncing off windows, swooping over the extractor, until we killed them.

The harvest of honey that year was our biggest yet. But we couldn't face another season with these aggressive bees. We didn't feed them over the winter, and they died. The following year we started again with new colonies. Thankfully by this time, breeders had managed to rid their colonies of the African strains, and we once again welcomed docile, beautiful, peaceful bees into our hives.

Bears

For me, bears occupied—and still occupy—the dark, frightening territory of mysterious predators. Wolves, cougars, coyotes, bobcats. Animals that roam stealthily, appear suddenly, attack, disappear. Unpredictable. Powerful. Wild.

Galena Bay was bear territory. With kokanee trout in the lake, abundant wild berries in the woods, small mammals everywhere, and almost no humans, the valley was a bear's paradise.

Sometimes, while working in the garden, Bill and I heard a rustle and crash in the nearby bush, and looked up to see a massive black form humping over fallen logs, nosing among thimbleberry bushes, grubbing in rotted stumps. Then the bear lumbered away into the deeper shadows. In the spring, bears emerged from the forest to nibble on our fresh clover. They climbed onto the compost pile and pawed among the carrot tops and coffee grounds, thrusting their noses into the ripe stew to claim spongy apple cores. When they stayed too long for our comfort, we rattled pots and pans and scolded, "Go on, bear! Get out of here! Go on!" The skittish ones looked up, startled, and were gone almost before our voices had carried across the field. Others, the more habituated ones, who knew the difference between a shout and the retort of a rifle, lifted their heavy heads, bent down for another bite of compost, unhurriedly lowered themselves to the ground, and padded off, their rumps swaying from side to side.

When I saw a bear, I felt a tingle that was part panic and part exhilaration. They were a contradiction of heaviness and speed, clumsiness and agility. I was glad that places like Galena Bay still existed where there was room for bears. But I still didn't want to get close to one.

Our neighbour Bob Harrington carried a rifle when he walked in the woods. This puzzled me, since he often said that bears, like most wild animals, were more wary of people than people were of them.

When I asked him why, he said, "Because they're unpredictable. Almost always they'll run, but sometimes they'll charge. And if you get between a sow and her cub, she'll go after you. You and Bill should get a gun, too."

Get a gun? This was the last thing we wanted to do. Escaping the violence in the United States was a big part of the reason we had come to Canada in the first place. Guns, shooting, killing—we wanted nothing to do with any of that.

"We don't even eat meat," I said in argument. "We don't want to be responsible for killing anything."

"And after all, the bears were here first," Bill added. "We're the intruders."

Bob shrugged. "So you'll let a bear maul you, just to remain pacifists?"

When he put it like that ...

It was the word *unpredictable* that did it. No matter how peaceful our intentions, we couldn't control the reactions of a wild animal. We had to be prepared.

We sat down with Bob and looked through a catalogue from a mail-order company in Winnipeg. Trying to figure out what kind of gun to get, we narrowed down our needs. We didn't want to hunt, we didn't want the meat, we didn't want to put the fur on the floor, we didn't want any trophies. We just wanted to be able to defend ourselves.

Bob pointed. "Then this is the one you want. A .440 Marlin. It's only accurate up to about a hundred yards—"

"A hundred yards!" I repeated. "That's awfully close."

Bob nodded. "At that distance, it'll blast a hole in a bear and kill it immediately."

Bill and I looked at each other. If that was what we needed, so be it. We sent in our order, and the gun arrived a few weeks later. It came inside a black leather case whose shape was so indistinct that it might have held a trombone, or a quiver of arrows.

"This is creepy," I said to Bill when we picked it up in Revelstoke. "You send in your money and they mail you a gun. It's like ordering a winter coat from the Eaton's catalogue."

Back home in the cabin, he unzipped the case. The rifle had a long, dull-silver barrel and a polished wooden handle—the "stock," Bill told me it was called. From end to end, it was four-and-a-half feet long, and it weighed seven pounds. The brass bullets were three inches long. Each one was heavier than a large, ripe plum.

Bill knew how to shoot. Target practice had been a teenage hobby of his. He showed me the parts of the gun, how to load it, how to set the safety catch. How to sight. How to pull the trigger.

"Okay, enough, I've got it," I said, though I hadn't absorbed a word.

We put the zipped-up case in the little room—the small storage room in a corner of the cabin, where we kept firewood and canned goods—and tried to forget about it.

Our first close encounter with a bear occurred in the fall of 1972. One morning Bill went out to the woodshed, where we had piled three rows of split wood to shoulder height. As he loaded his arms with wood, a great shaggy head poked up on the other side of a woodpile. Bill jumped. The bear jumped. The wood in Bill's arms flew in all directions. The bear scrambled away.

We laughed it off as a harmless encounter.

The following spring, my parents sent us a care package of delicacies: cheeses, crackers, nuts, dried fruit. At that time, we didn't have refrigeration, so, after we gorged ourselves on the goodies, we faced the problem of how to preserve the rest. We came up with earth storage. Near the cabin we dug a two-foot-deep hole, lowered a heavy ceramic crock into it, placed on the lid, and covered that with a board topped by a large rock. Natural refrigeration.

The next morning, we found the lid cast aside and the crock empty. A bear had eaten everything—except a plastic tube of Cheez-Whiz. Evidently our bear had discerning taste.

Again, we laughed, even if the thought of a bear being so close to us while we slept was unnerving.

Things soon turned more serious. A black bear began to harass our elderly neighbours Walter and Margaret Nelson, who had both been partially crippled by rickets in childhood. Bill and I often helped them do physically demanding jobs, like stacking firewood near their furnace, and soon we would be called upon to help them with a bear too. One midsummer night, the bear climbed up onto Walter and Margaret's porch and clawed at their front door, leaving deep gouges in the wood. This went on for several nights. The bear began to show up in the daytime as well, and Walter and Margaret's shouts and arm-waving did not drive it away.

"It's terrifying," Margaret said. "It sounds like the bear is going to break down the door."

"And it doesn't react when we yell and bang pots and pans," Walter added. "It must be diseased. A healthy wild bear would run away at the noise." He looked at Bill, hesitated, then said, "Would you shoot it for me? I'd do it myself, but ..."

Bill didn't wait for him to finish. We both knew what Walter was going to say: that his arms weren't strong enough to hold and aim a gun.

"Of course, Walter," Bill said. "How do you want to do it?"

They arranged for Bill to come over that afternoon. He would wait beside the porch for the bear to show up.

For hours, Bill told me, he sat still and silent in the shadows at the side of Walter and Margaret's porch, cradling the rifle. Then came a telltale scrambling sound, and a medium-size black bear started climbing up the wooden stairs.

"I pulled the trigger," Bill said. "There was a thunderous explosion. The bear fell. Then it got up, and I realized I had hit it in the leg. I felt awful. I didn't want the damn thing to suffer. I just wanted to kill it and be done with it."

I took Bill's hand.

"It started limping toward the woods. I followed. The bear was running in circles. Must have been confused, frantic. I finally got good aim and shot again. This time I hit it in the chest. It fell with a thud. I stood there. It smelled rank, like a filthy, wet dog. Then I went and told Walter and Margaret. They thanked me over and over."

Bill swallowed. "I felt sick. One minute that bear was huge and black and wild. The next it was nothing, a slab of meat and fur with blank eyes."

"But you helped them," I said.

"Yeah," Bill said quietly.

A few years later, Bill and I were living in Nelson, a small city about ninety miles southeast of Galena Bay. Bill was doing a year of teacher training at a local college to earn a BC teaching certificate, and I was teaching a split grade one-two class in the nearby town of Slocan. By May, Bill had finished his program and moved back to Galena Bay to plant the garden and feed the honeybees. I remained in Nelson until the school year ended in late June.

The last day of school arrived. I bade goodbye to my students, packed up our apartment, and made the three-hour drive up to Galena Bay to rejoin Bill. When I got out of the car, I was surprised to see a drawn, unhappy look on his face. Where was his sexy smile to welcome me home?

"What's the matter?" I asked.

"You'd better come in."

"Bill, you're scaring me."

He led me into the cabin. I noticed that the screen on the front window looked different. Newer.

"The floor feels sticky," I said. "What's going on?"

Bill motioned me to sit down and sat across from me.

"Yesterday I went over to Walter's to help him stake his raspberries and blackberries. it was a beautiful day, so I left the windows open."

Nothing so terrible about that. I couldn't see where this was going.

"When I drove back up the driveway, I saw a large black shape climb *out* the front window and run into the woods."

"A bear?"

Bill nodded. "The cabin was a mess. The compost bucket was knocked over and compost was slopped all over the floor. It had eaten most of a box of apples. Tore open the big bag of sugar and spilled it on the floor."

"So that's why—"

"I mopped it ten times. The stickiness just won't go away."

"The hell with the stickiness! A bear was in our cabin!"

We looked at each other, both thinking what we had heard many times: where a bear has scavenged food, especially humans' food, it will return.

"I stayed up all night last night with the rifle. It didn't come back."

"Yet," I said.

Then something hit me. In two days, Bill was leaving. He would be gone for a week. I would be staying in the cabin by myself.

About a year earlier, Bill and I had started meditating. Along with Paul, we had joined Self-Realization Fellowship (SRF), an international organization focused on *kriya* yoga, a sacred spiritual science originating millennia ago in India. SRF incorporated both daily physical exercises and meditation. I had tried it for several months, but I chafed the entire time. Finally, I quit, saying it wasn't for me.

But Bill had taken to SRF. He did the exercises with vigour, and after his daily meditations he seemed calmer, happier.

Every summer, SRF held a "class series" in Los Angeles, a week-long seminar of lectures, group meditations, and chanting sessions. Thousands of people attended. The year before, Paul had gone with our friends Pam and Sandy. This year, Bill was joining them.

"I don't have to go," Bill said, reading my thoughts.

More than anything, I wanted to say, "Yes, please stay!" But I couldn't.

"No, you go," I said. "You've been looking forward to it for months."

"I don't want to leave you alone."

"Really, Bill. You've got to go."

"I'll stay up again tonight," he said. "Maybe the bear'll come back and I'll shoot it, and that'll be the end of it."

That night Bill brought the rifle upstairs and lay it on the floor beside our mattress. He sat up, looking out the window. I snuggled up against his leg but couldn't sleep. When I finally fell into an uneasy slumber, I felt Bill twitch as he nodded off and then jerked awake.

In the morning, there were deep shadows under his eyes. He shook his head.

"Time to teach you how to shoot," he said.

After breakfast, he slung the rifle over his shoulder and handed me the box of bullets, several sheets of newspaper, earplugs, and a towel. When we reached the woods, he draped a piece of newspaper over a stump for a target. Then he knelt down, lay the rifle across his legs, and pulled down a lever. "This is how you set the safety catch," he said.

I nodded. We both knew I hadn't learned anything back when we'd first bought the gun. Now I was paying attention.

"You do it," Bill said.

I pulled. The lever didn't move.

"Harder."

I yanked. The click was loud.

Bill took a bullet from the box and gave it to me. It lay heavy in my hand. He showed me how to eject an empty cartridge, load the bullet into the chamber, release the safety catch.

"Here's how you sight," Bill said, and demonstrated how to peer down the barrel so the front and rear sights lined up.

"And then you pull the trigger," he said.

"And then I pull the trigger," I echoed.

I put in the earplugs, draped the towel over my shoulder, and raised the gun. My arm wavered. I pushed the butt into my shoulder, then rested my finger on the trigger. I squeezed. There was a split second of silence, during which the recoil pushed me violently backward. Then the noise cracked the air and pulsed away: **BOOM** - BOOM - boom - boom . . .

I stood there, listening. Only when it was quiet again did I remember to look at the target. The newspaper hung from the stump.

"Way to go," Bill said.

Despite my dismay, I smiled and thought, *Not bad*. I took out the ear-plugs and handed the gun back to Bill.

"Oh, no, you've got to practice a few more times."

Safety catch on. Eject cartridge. Load bullet. Safety catch off. Sight. Pull. Again. Again.

Many shots later, my arm aching and my ears ringing, I said I'd had enough. As we walked back to the cabin, Bill said, "You did great, Ellie Oakley."

"Thanks," I said, proud. I'd managed to hit the target most times. But I was thinking that this practice session, all unhurried and orderly, with earplugs, shoulder padding, and Bill nearby, was hardly a true test. In real life, with 350 pounds of bear lunging at me—what then?

The next morning, Bill again offered to stay. Again, I refused. As soon as he left, I closed the wooden shutters over the cabin windows and kept them drawn, even in the daytime. I preferred to skulk around in the gloom than allow the bear another chance to climb through a window.

But it was June. The garden needed tending. I couldn't hide in the cabin all day; I had work to do. I carried the rifle out to the garden and propped it against a rock, silently repeating the steps to myself—safety off, sight, brace, pull trigger—as I sprinkled seeds down the rows, glancing up every minute or so, scanning the surrounding trees for a hulking black shape. At every cracking branch, every raven's caw, I startled, my head jerking up. I carried the rifle back to the cabin at lunchtime, back out to the garden for the afternoon. To the outhouse. Outside with me the next day. And the next.

Amazingly, incredibly, the bear did not come back. Summer came quickly that year; the berries ripened early up in the mountains.

I was spared.

Keeping bees is a tricky proposition in a place like Galena Bay. Bears will inevitably find them. When we brought home our first colony of three hives, Walter suggested building a "bear box." So we did. It was a plywood structure that enclosed the hives on four sides, with a large plywood lid that we opened during the day to allow the worker bees to fly in and out, and closed at night after they had returned to the hive.

That worked for a few months. Then one night we heard smash-ing sounds. We crept outside and, by flashlight beam, watched as a bear knocked down the front wall with one swipe of its huge paw. We shouted, to no avail. The bear flipped off the lid of one of the hives, then pushed over the top super. Frames sprayed on the ground. We heard the sudden hum of confused, angry bees. The bear pawed through the fallen frames and bit off chunks of comb and honey, bees and all.

Finally, by banging pots and pans, Bill and I scared it away. In the dark, we dismantled the damaged frames, threw the torn sheets of honeycomb in the compost, and replaced the intact frames in the super. The next morning, we installed a padlock on the bear box, and locked it at night. That was a temporary solution, but clearly the bear box was not the answer.

What next? Bob Harrington suggested a platform raised off the ground. It would be inconvenient, we thought, to have to climb a ladder to tend to the hives, not to mention awkward when we had to carry frames of honey up and down. But it would be better than repeating what had just happened.

The next spring, we dug four deep holes in the ground near the woodshed, and in each hole placed a thirteen-foot cedar pole, one foot in diameter. When we backfilled the holes, the poles stretched ten feet above the ground. On top of these poles we built an eight-foot-square plywood platform. As a final precaution, we wrapped sheets of salvaged corrugated aluminum around the poles to make them unclimbable. Then, laboriously, we transferred our four colonies—two of the old ones, which had survived the winter, and two new ones—super by super up to the platform.

The bee platform worked. Occasionally a bear padded over to it, sniffed, looked upward, raised a paw to lean against one of the poles, shook its head as if deciding it wasn't worth the trouble, and shuffled away. We congratulated ourselves on our cleverness.

On a summer's night in 1975, Bill and I stepped outside to look at the stars before going to bed. There was a rustling in the brush near the bee platform, and a small black bear moved into the patch of light cast by the cabin windows. The bear looked at us for a moment and then moved away, merging with the shadows. That night Bill brought the rifle upstairs.

In the dim light just before dawn, I was jolted awake by a sudden movement. Bill was on his knees, loading the gun. I looked over his shoulder. The same bear was on its hind legs at the base of the bee platform, head raised, sniffing.

"Get out of there!" Bill shouted out the upstairs window.

The bear dropped to all fours, then raised itself again, leaning its front paws on one of the poles. Bill yelled again. The bear ignored his shout. Then, while Bill and I watched in disbelief, it sank its claws into the aluminum as if it were putty and started climbing, paw over paw. In less than ten seconds it had reached the top of the pole.

Cursing, Bill ran downstairs and out the door. The bear heaved itself onto the platform and pushed the lid off one of the hives. Bill fired a shot over its head. The bear looked up for a moment, then swung its paw and knocked the top super off the hive. As the super fell to the ground, Bill fired again. The shot hit the bear in the head. Its body jerked upward. It fell off the platform and landed with a thud next to the scattered frames of honeycomb.

I ran downstairs. Bill, breathing heavily, was pointing the rifle at the bear. But it didn't move. Slowly we walked over to it. Part of the top of its head was missing. We looked between the legs; it was a young male, two or three years old. He smelled rank. Beside him the frames lay spilled like a spray of playing cards, some intact, others mangled. Honey dripped onto the clover like glistening dewdrops.

I said, "I can't believe it. He just climbed right up. The aluminum didn't stop him at all."

We turned and looked at the pole. It was pockmarked with holes.

"That warning shot went right over his head," Bill said. "He didn't even care."

I looked at the bear again. "Poor thing."

"I didn't want to kill him."

"Bill, I know. You had to."

Bill was quiet. Then he said, "He sure did a job on the hive."

"Do you think it's a total wreck?"

"Depends on whether the queen was in that super. Probably she was on the bottom, so the hive'll be okay. But I doubt if they'll be able to build back up in time for winter."

I pointed. "What are we going to do with him?"

Bill shrugged. "I don't know. Maybe Walter or Bob would want the meat—"

"Yuck!"

"I'll go ask Walter as soon as it gets light enough," Bill said. "The gun jammed on the second shot, and he's got a tool that can fix it. I'll see if he wants the meat."

We decided to leave the frames on the ground, to allow the bees to retrieve whatever honey they could. As soon as the sun rose fully, Bill took the gun and drove away.

About half an hour after he left, I heard a rustling outside. I peeked out. Another bear, a larger, rust-coloured one, was poking around the clover beneath the bee platform. Ignoring the dead body, it padded over to the fallen frames and began to lick the spilled honey. Then it shuffled over to one of the poles and reared up, sniffing.

Oh, no, I thought, *not again.*

Grabbing a pot and a wooden spoon, I stepped onto the porch and banged the pot. "Go! Get out of here, you! Go!" The bear looked up, startled, dropped to all fours, and scampered away into the bush. I watched until it was out of sight, then went inside.

Five minutes later, the bear returned. It paused beside the dead body, sniffed once or twice, turned over a frame with its large paw, and resumed licking the honey. Again, I clanged and yelled. Again, the bear looked up. But this time it didn't run away.

Just then Bill, with Walter behind him in the tractor, pulled up the driveway. At the sound of the muffler-less truck, the bear lumbered into the forest. Bill and Walter came inside. As I poured a cup of coffee for Walter, I told them about the bear.

Bill grimaced. "I don't want to shoot another bear."

Walter shrugged, as if to say, *Can't be helped*. He rose, searching for his cane. "I'll move the carcass now," he said.

"Don't you want the meat?" I asked.

He shook his head. "Too much work for Margaret and me." He paused, then added, "Good meat, though, bear meat." He limped to the door.

"Look," I said. Bill and Walter peered out the front window. The rust-coloured bear was back. It padded over to a pole, reared up, and rested its front paws on the aluminum.

I stepped onto the porch and banged the pot and spoon. The bear didn't even turn its head.

Bill fired a shot over the bear's head. It looked his way but didn't drop down. Then it began to climb up the pole. Bill reloaded and fired. The bullet hit the bear's thigh. With a great twitch it fell off the pole and staggered through the tall grass toward the back road. Bill ran after it. The second shot finished it off.

Bill walked back to the cabin as though dazed, the gun hanging from his hand. He didn't speak for a moment. "It was a female," he said at last. "She looked at me."

I hugged him. "How could we have known that the aluminum wouldn't work?"

Bill shrugged. We couldn't have known. But still, it was our fault, not the bears'. Our ignorance was no excuse, our good intentions no justification for the two carcasses outside.

"Was it worth it for four bee hives?" I asked.

"It's worth defending your home," Walter said. "You've got to. Otherwise, you might as well pack it in and turn it all over to the animals. You've got a right to live. You've got a right to a corner of the land."

Bill sighed, then smiled wryly. "There's some irony in here—the great environmentalists, killing two bears in one morning."

"Vegetarians, even," I added, smiling in spite of myself.

We sat in silence. I drank my coffee. "Now what?"

"I've got some sheets of galvanized steel around home you can have," Walter said. "Nothing'll go through that."

"I'll come get them right away," Bill said, standing up.

"What about the ... uh ... bodies?" I asked.

"I'll drag them down the skid road and leave them in the bush," Walter said, pushing himself up from his chair. He walked to the door. "Thanks for the coffee," he said as if this were an ordinary visit.

Walter's tractor had a flat wooden platform for carrying firewood. Bill helped him load the bears onto the platform, and then we watched the tractor roll down the driveway, one black paw and one rusty ear dangling over the edge.

That afternoon Bill and I removed the aluminum and wrapped sheets of galvanized steel around the poles. No other bears ever tried to climb the bee platform.

For the next several nights we fell asleep to the howls of coyotes and the croaks of ravens. We shivered at the sound, yet felt oddly comforted by the cycle of life and death.

About a week later, Bill and I walked down the skid trail. All that was left were bones, picked clean and scattered in a wide area around the brush. A year later, they, too, were gone, gnawed or decayed, returned to the earth.

Making a Living
PART THREE: 1976

By the late fall of 1975, Paul had completed his teaching certificate and was teaching high school in Revelstoke. He heard that the teacher of a grade two-three split class was leaving at Christmas because of illness. I had vowed never to teach special ed again, but this was a regular primary class. I applied and got the job. Bill and I moved into town and shared a house with Paul.

Teaching a regular class was a revelation. You showed the students how "e" disappeared off the end of most verbs when adding the "ing" ending, or how four times three could be reconfigured as three times four, and they *learned* it. It was a challenge managing twenty-eight kids and mastering both the grade two and the grade three curricula on the fly, but the absence of temper tantrums more than made up for it.

I brought in my guitar and taught the kids folksongs. I hadn't learned any Canadian ones yet, so I taught them the ones I knew: "If I Had a Hammer," "The Erie Canal," "Oh Susannah." (Good thing the citizenship police weren't patrolling.) I read them *Mr. Popper's Penguins* chapter by chapter, and they hung on every word. I didn't even cry on the weekends.

Things weren't going as well for Bill. He found a job loading railroad ties into boxcars. Bill was a strong and muscular man, and at that time he was twenty-seven, probably at the peak of his strength. But after a month, he got fired for being too slow. Undaunted, he next got a job as an edgerman at a sawmill, operating a machine that shaved the curved edges off logs to create flat boards. He worked the graveyard shift, leaving late at night when I was asleep and falling into bed next to me when I was getting up to go to school.

Working nights was bad enough, but it wasn't the worst thing. "It's so boring and repetitious," he said one morning as I massaged his shoulders before dashing off. "I'm not using my mind at all."

Perhaps a seed was planted that very day. When the school year ended and we returned to Galena Bay with another stash of money, Bill had decided that he wouldn't do mindless manual labour jobs anymore.

LEFT Ellen and Bill at their wedding (*1973*).

BELOW Bill and Ellen at a sawhorse (*1973*).

ABOVE Bill and Ellen (*1973*).

BELOW Paul, Ellen, and Bill in front of the cabin (*1973*).

ABOVE Bill, Ellen, Paul, Walter Nelson, and Ray Chartrand (*c. 1974*).

LEFT Ellen with a monster zucchini (*1974*).

ABOVE Ellen and Bill on the bee platform (*1974*).

BELOW Bill gathering eggs (*1974*).

ABOVE Bill playing guitar (*c. 1974*).

BELOW Ellen holding a bee frame (*1974*).

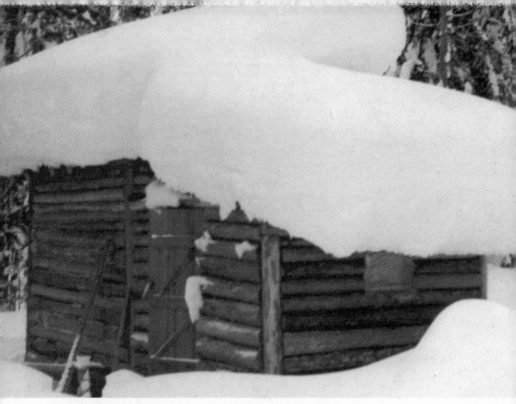

ABOVE The late, great sauna (*1975*).

LEFT Ellen gathering wood at the woodshed (*1975*).

ABOVE Abdul the rooster (*c. 1975*).

RIGHT Ellen with a
butchered chicken (*1975*).

ABOVE Walter Nelson on his tractor (*c. 1976*).

BELOW Bill with a squash harvest and cat (*c. 1977*).

ABOVE Ellen in the cabin (*1978*).

BELOW Ellen and Bill extracting honey (*1978*).

ABOVE Bill shovelling snow off the porch roof (*1978*).

BELOW Ellen and Bill with the Energy Van (*1978*).

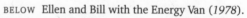

ABOVE A bear in the compost (*1979*).

BELOW Merri peeking over a hanging basket (*1979*).

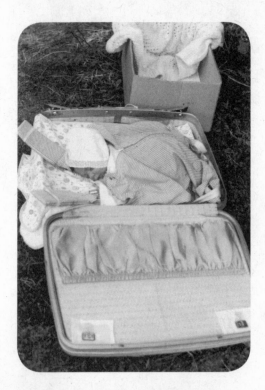

LEFT Merri sleeping in a suitcase (*1979*).

BELOW Bill building an addition to the cabin (*1979*).

ABOVE Bill and Merri (*1980*).
We call this one "Galena Gothic."

RIGHT Minnie Marlowe (*1980*).

ABOVE Bill and Amy (*1981*).

BELOW Amy and Merri in the cabin (*1982*).

9

Bob and Pat

Getting to know the Harringtons

Robert and Patricia Harrington, who sold us our land in 1972, were originally from New England: Bob from Connecticut, Pat from Maine. At the time, Bob was the same age as my parents, around fifty; Pat some ten years his junior. They had met when Bob was teaching at Bates College. I don't know the story of their romance, but I imagine that Pat, a young, impressionable student, was swept away by the knowledgeable, authoritative professor.

After leaving the US in the late 1960s, seeking a quiet life close to the land, the Harringtons moved to the McBride area of northeastern BC, in the western foothills of the Rocky Mountains. They ranched cattle, and Bob taught science in the local high school. But a few years after they arrived, the government put in a new road. Their property became overrun with hunters and snowmobilers, and the locals started talking about big logging and mining developments. In search of an even more pristine and isolated place, they found Galena Bay and bought eighty acres of mostly second-growth forest with a small clearing near the main road. They were putting the finishing touches on their large wood-frame house when we arrived.

Bill, Paul, and I hit it off with Bob and Pat immediately. Although they were closer in age to our parents' generation than to ours, they were nothing like our stodgy, middle-class parents. They were living in the woods. They had forsaken upwardly mobile aspirations for a simpler lifestyle. They were *cool*.

Bob was a tall, solidly built man with a military-style crewcut; indeed, he had served in the Marines during the Second World War. Pat was slight in build, with fair skin and short, light brown hair. At the time we met them, they had two sons: Nelson, three years old, and Christopher, a baby.

Bob and Pat occupied themselves with working on their homestead: building the house, collecting firewood, cultivating a garden patch. I don't know how they supported themselves. They didn't work away from Galena Bay, and no jobs were available right there, other than on the ferry. Pat had been a nurse, but she was staying home to raise the boys. Bob had written a couple of biology textbooks, and he contributed occasional pieces to scientific journals and radio broadcasts, but these would not have provided a living wage. Perhaps he had a pension from Bates. Perhaps there was family money. We didn't ask, and they didn't tell. It didn't matter. What mattered was that they were there to offer advice and companionship. And we needed both.

When it came to homesteading, Bill, Paul, and I were ignorant in just about every way—how to build a cabin, what species of wood to burn in the woodstove, how to grow a garden, what tools to buy, how to preserve food—and we were eager to learn. Bob and Pat were founts of information. They helped us make shopping lists, drew us diagrams, and demonstrated how to do things.

But it wasn't just the practicalities of homesteading that the three of us needed guidance in. We had grand ideas about going back to the land. By dropping out of mainstream society, we were going to make a difference in the world. But how? Our aspirations were vague, if exalted. Bob helped us see how our lifestyle fit into a larger context of environmental activism. He helped us understand not only how to live more lightly on the earth, but why it was the only defensible choice.

Bob had studied and taught biology, but his true calling was as an ecologist. That was a fairly new word at the time. In the past, science had been rigidly divided into separate fields: biology, zoology, chemistry, physics, geology, hydrology. Ecology was the discipline that pulled them all together, that showed the interrelatedness of all things. Bob was an ecologist before the term became fashionable. And for him it wasn't just an interest. It was a religion.

Bob and Pat's house was a palace compared to our cabin. It had *rooms*: two bedrooms, a study, a living room, and a large kitchen. It had propane lights. It had a full basement as well as the main floor. It had a bathroom with a flush toilet.

I didn't want a big house; I loved our cabin and didn't want to live anywhere else. Still, it would have been nice to have an indoor toilet. Whenever Bill, Paul and I visited Bob and Pat, we took advantage of theirs. Frequently.

Although Bob and Pat's living room was large and well appointed, with a wood heater, bookcases, and easy chairs, I don't remember ever sitting in there. Instead, all our visits took place in the kitchen. While the massive woodstove crackled, we squeezed around the kitchen table, drinking strong coffee from the always-perking coffee pot and eating cookies.

That is, Bill, Paul, Bob, and I sat around the table. Pat was too busy.

Here is a typical scene:

Bill, Paul, Bob, and I squeeze around the kitchen table. Bob lights a cigarette. Nelson, the three-year-old, is playing with Lincoln logs on the floor, away from the woodstove, which is burning even on this early fall day. Pat, with Christopher on her hip, pours strong coffee from a percolator into thick porcelain cups for Bob and me, then fetches sugar and powdered milk. She makes instant hot chocolate for Bill and Paul, who don't drink coffee.

ME (*seeing her shift Christopher to her other hip*): "Pat, can I help you?"

PAT (*smiling wanly*): "No, that's fine, I've got it."

PAUL: "We saw a pileated woodpecker on our way up here."

BOB: "Majestic birds. Though how much longer they'll be around, I don't know."

ME: "What do you mean?"

NELSON: "Daddy, look at the house I built!"

BOB: "With all the logging that's going on, they're losing habitat faster than it can be replanted. And those monocultures the logging companies are planting—they call it 'reforestation,' but it's no such thing—don't provide adequate habitat."

NELSON: "Daddy, look!"

BOB: "So with no dead trees for the woodpeckers to nest in—"

NELSON: "Daddy!"

PAT: "Bob."

BOB (*looking annoyed*): "Yeah?"

Pat points to Nelson.

BOB: "Very nice." (He turns back to us.) "So, with no dead trees, there are no woodpeckers, and with no woodpeckers, the insect population goes haywire, and the decomposition process is disrupted. So the humus is impoverished—"

PAT: "Bob, would you take the baby? I've got to sterilize the diapers and I don't want him near the steam."

Bob holds his arms out for Christopher without looking at Pat. She places the baby on his lap. Christopher starts pulling Bob's hair. Bob jerks his head out of the way. Pat dumps a load of cloth diapers into a large enamel pot of boiling water on the woodstove and stirs them with a long wooden spoon. Sweat forms on her forehead.

CHRISTOPHER: "Da-da! Da-da!"

BOB (*talking around Christopher*): "So the forest soil has fewer nutrients, and the new trees are less hardy."

CHRISTOPHER: "Da-da!"

Using the wooden spoon, Pat lifts the diapers one by one from the kettle and places them in the sink. Steam rises.

A clatter of wooden toys comes from the side of the room. "Look, Daddy, I crashed my house! Now I'm going to make a barn."

BOB (*glancing quickly*): "Good for you, Nelson."

Nelson smiles up at him.

BOB (*turning back to us*): "And all because it's easier and cheaper for the logging companies to clear cut whole mountainsides rather than log selectively. Never giving a thought to how their actions affect something as lowly as a bird. But that bird is connected to the whole ecosystem. As Barry Commoner says in *Science and Survival*—" (He pulls a volume from a stack of books, magazines, and seed catalogues on the windowsill. Holding the book out of Christopher's reach, he reads aloud.) "'When you pull up a dandelion, you pull the rest of the world along with it.'"

I have heard this quote before. But now its profundity hits me. The interdependence that Commoner speaks of isn't just in the abstract. It's the pileated woodpecker we saw this morning. It's the insects and the trees and the forest. It's the world.

ME (*worriedly*): "But if everything affects everything else, how can we possibly avoid contributing to the mess? I mean, we burn wood for heat, so we're emitting smoke, which goes into the air, which goes into the atmosphere, which spreads all over the Earth. We're just as guilty."

BOB: "True. Everything we do has an impact. But if you're going to live in a northern climate, you have to stay warm. Wood is a renewable resource, and it's abundant, around here, at least. So yeah, you produce smoke, but it's the least bad alternative. Better than oil. Better than coal. You just have to try not to waste wood, and to replant where you've removed trees."

ME (*thinking*): *Whew.*

PAT (*holding the percolator*): "More coffee?"

On one level, these visits made me uneasy. To see Pat working while Bob sat and pontificated was clearly unfair. Even Bill and Paul, who espoused a feminist line ("Men should do half the housework") but still managed to leave a few dishes sitting on the counter when it was their turn to wash up, and then sheepishly did them when I pointed this out, admitted as much.

I wondered why Pat put up with it. I certainly wouldn't have. But I couldn't spend time feeling guilty about her burden. I was too much under Bob's thrall.

Thrall is not too strong a word. As I sat there, feeling Bob's passion, listening to his eloquent arguments, learning new scientific ideas, watching as he moved from book to book, effortlessly finding the passage he was looking for, listening as he quoted authorities ranging from the Bible ("Esau sold his inheritance for a mess of pottage") to E.F. Schumacher ("Affluence leads to conspicuous consumption"), from memory, I was spellbound. Glancing at Pat, I wondered if this was what had made her fall in love with Professor Harrington.

Bob often quoted a friend of his, an old prospector named Paddy Carroll, who lived in northern BC: "The only honest occupation is a self-sufficient homesteader." By this, Bob and Paddy meant that you shouldn't take advantage of government services, you shouldn't work for corporations or even well-intentioned public agencies, you shouldn't rely on money as a means of exchange, but instead should forage or grow or hunt your own food, build and heat your own house, repair your own tools, make your own clothing, and do everything in your power to avoid participating in The System.

As Bob expounded this philosophy, Bill, Paul, and I nodded enthusiastically. Yes! This was what we were trying to do. This was what we would aim for. We would be pure. We would live in a way that would earn Paddy Carroll's approbation.

But at the same time, I shrank inside. What did it really mean to be self-sufficient? What about money to buy things? What about coffee, and sugar, and books, and gasoline for a car? I didn't want to do without these things. I didn't want to live on nettles and snails. I didn't want to weave my own shoes out of cedar bark.

And, of course, Bob didn't live that way either. He was full of the usual human contradictions. He slagged government interference in people's affairs but supported tough environmental regulations. He criticized corporate polluters but drove a truck. He exalted relying on the land for sustenance but drank coffee and smoked cigarettes.

Still, Bob was an inspiring and generous mentor. Every time we visited, he sent us home with books. *A Sand County Almanac* by Aldo Leopold, an eloquent treatise on conservation and the need for a "land ethic"—a human conscience toward the use of land. *The Naked Ape* by Desmond Morris, which reinforced humans' position in the family of primates and underscored the way in which we were embedded in nature, not superior to it.

One time, he held up a book (I can't remember the title) and said, "Talk about paradise lost. This is an account of the primeval state of North America before European contact. Manhattan was a pristine island covered with wild grapevines, forests full of deer, and streams teeming with fish."

"No way!' I said, visualizing how I used to walk up 8th Avenue from the Port Authority bus terminal at 42nd Street to my dance teacher's studio at 56th Street, leaping over drunks lying on the sidewalk.

Bob turned the page. "Listen to this. 'What is now the northeastern United States was so dense that a squirrel could travel from New York to Ohio by jumping from tree to tree, without ever having to touch the ground.'"

"My God!" Paul exclaimed.

"It sure ain't like that anymore," Bill said.

Bob grunted. "No place is." He grinned. "Except maybe this little corner of the world."

As Bill, Paul, and I walked back down the trail to our cabin that day, I said, "We've got to do everything we can to keep Galena Bay from getting ruined."

"Don't you think we are?" Bill said. "We're off the grid."

"Not on purpose," Paul joked, and we all laughed.

"We're doing our part," Bill went on. "We only cut trees when we need to. We hardly use our truck. We compost our kitchen scraps and put them back on the land."

"And even our shit is going directly back into the earth," Paul pointed out.

"But we should still try to waste less," I said. "Like, when I was in Europe a few years ago, I saw people going to the market with cloth bags. We don't do that in North America. Why not? Why can't we get cloth bags and reuse them every time we go shopping?"

"We can," Paul said. (And we did.)

"And we can buy our clothes second-hand," I added. "That way we're not using up resources and energy to make new clothes."

(And we did. Or, at least, I did. At the Salvation Army thrift shop in Revelstoke, I bought a camel-coloured woollen coat with a zipper and a hood. It had patches on the elbows, and the front pocket was frayed, so I replaced it with a third patch. The next time Bill and I went back east, my mother-in-law took one look at the coat and took me shopping. But I insisted on keeping the shabby coat, and used it for chores around the homestead. I saved the new coat, a thick, warm garment in plum-coloured wool, for "nice.")

Not all of our time with Bob was spent sitting and talking. He took us outside and showed us the principles of ecology in action.

One late-summer day, as we walked along the gravel road that led from the highway to our back road, he pointed to a waist-high plant with a spike of purple-pink flowers at its crown. "See that plant? It's called fireweed. Botanists call it a pioneer plant because it's one of the first plants that colonizes burned-over plots of land."

"Was there a fire here?" I asked.

Bob shook his head. "Fireweed also comes in after land has been logged, like here, to build the road. It grows fast and loves the sun. After a few years, small trees like alder and willow spring up, and the fireweed dies out because it doesn't like shade. Birds and small animals start living in this early forest. Then bigger deciduous trees come in and crowd out the alders, and finally coniferous trees, hemlocks and cedars and firs in this neck of the woods, get established and dominate the mature forest. This can take a hundred years. And it all starts with this little unassuming plant, which most people consider a weed."

We stood there and admired the fireweed, and I felt a deep sense of satisfaction to know that the forest would regenerate itself in such an orderly fashion, even if I wouldn't be around to appreciate it. (And a couple of years later, when we got our first honeybee hives, I felt as if my education had come full circle when I presented Bob with a jar of our fireweed honey.)

On other forays, Bob taught us to identify the rough, resinous bark of fir trees and the long, smooth strands of cedar bark; the short, flat green and silver hemlock needles and the varying clusters of pine needles: two needles per bundle for lodgepole pine, four for ponderosa pine, five for western white pine. He showed us how fungi and mosses grew on the north sides of trees; how new growth sprouted from rotting logs; how lichens slowly drilled down into rocks, opening them up to erosion and freeing their trapped minerals. He taught us to recognize the shrill cries of ospreys, soaring over the lake in ever-widening circles, and to listen for the liquid notes pouring from the throats of invisible Swainson's thrushes at dusk.

Pat, meanwhile, was a different sort of mentor to me. She showed me how to work a woodstove; what kind of wood to use to get the fire going; what kind to use for intense heat or for slow, even cooking. She advised me on what canning equipment to buy and helped me can my first batch of Okanagan apricots, patiently walking me through the steps. She even showed me the best kind of snow boots to purchase for the coming winter. She used a double layer: on the inside, lace-up shoes made of felted wool with a woollen sole and a rubber heel; on the outside, thin rubber galoshes that fit snugly over the shoes. This combination provided protection from the snow, yet when you removed the outer boots, your feet stayed warm and dry in the woollen shoes. Pat helped me order my own pair from the Eaton's catalogue.

It was Pat who advised me, when I had my period, to burn my bloody tampons in the woodstove rather than dropping them in the outhouse. Bears, she explained, were attracted to the smell of blood. I did what Pat suggested. The burning tampons gave off an acrid smell, and I could hear the hiss as the moisture sizzled.

After Pat

One day in early 1973, after Bill and I returned to Galena Bay from New Jersey, where we had gotten married, we went up to Bob and Pat's for our customary visit. The house seemed strangely quiet, and there were unwashed dishes in the sink. Strange.

Bob met us with a sheepish look. "Pat's left," he said.

"Left?" I said. "You mean, gone to town?"

"No, *left*. Taken the kids and gone." Looking lost and humiliated, he held a note written in Pat's small, neat handwriting.

Stunned, I plopped onto a chair. Here I was, newly married, in love, at the beginning of a lifelong adventure with Bill—and here was their marriage, broken to pieces. "Did she say why?"

He waved the note. "She wasn't happy." Then, in a low voice, "With me." He raised confused eyes. "I don't know what I ever did to her."

Of course you don't, I found myself thinking, and realized that, although Pat's sudden departure was a shock, I wasn't really surprised. Although she had never confided in me, I'd sensed that she wasn't happy. Bob paid her scant attention, treating her more like a domestic servant than a partner.

And it wasn't just that Pat did so much of the work, I thought. Bob was considerably older than she was, and of the Father Knows Best generation. He wasn't abusive, but he *was* paternalistic. Once I heard him say, when Pat ventured a comment about some environmental topic we were discussing, "You really haven't read enough to have an informed opinion about that, Pat." I saw her stiffen, and I felt embarrassed for her. Bill never would have said something like that to me, nor I to him, and I felt somehow that I should defend my fellow female. But I didn't, unsure how to respond and unwilling to intrude.

Now, as the reality sank in, I felt bereft. Pat and I hadn't been close, but she had been the only other woman I could talk to in Galena Bay. Margaret, Walter's sister, hadn't moved back yet, and Hilda wasn't speaking to me. Even though Pat was fifteen years my senior, we'd been glad for each other's company. I'd assumed that we'd grow closer as time went on. Now I was on my own.

"Where did she go?" Bill asked.

"Kamloops. She'll get a nursing job, I suppose."

"Will you get to see the boys?" I asked.

He nodded. "She says we'll work it out. She wants them to know their dad." His voice broke a little on those last words. Then he shook his head and forced a smile. "Guess I'm batching it for a while."

Bob opened the issue of *Audubon* magazine that lay on the table. "There's an article in here you've got to read, about the desertification of the high plains. You take out all the native grasses, plants that have flourished there for thousands of years, and put in a monoculture of wheat, and the soil becomes impoverished. No wonder nothing'll grow after a few generations."

We never spoke of Pat again.

Now that Bob had no wife and children to care for, his mentorship of Bill and me grew more intense. We visited him twice a week, on mail days. We'd go with him to the group mailbox, then return to his place. While he and Bill sat at the kitchen table discussing the latest book we'd read or the dire state of the world in general, I made lunch. That was the year I was experimenting with recipes from *Diet for a Small Planet*, and I made some truly ghastly soybean stews and lentil casseroles. They were stodgy and heavy, not to mention gaseous. Bob didn't mind. He wasn't one for cooking. His idea of dinner was to fry some ground beef and throw it on a plate with boiled "spuds."

After a late lunch, I joined Bob and Bill at the table for a cup of bitter coffee and more conversation. If it was a fine day, we went for a walk along the road, marching alongside ever-higher mounds of snow pushed aside by the plows.

One day in February, the sky had cleared after a foot-high snowstorm the night before. Mounds of snow sat on cedar fronds and the tops of hemlock trees, then fell to the ground with a *whump*. Sunlight sparkled on the white expanse, and streaks of blue appeared over the Selkirk peaks to the east.

As the three of us walked along the highway, talking softly, Bob suddenly held up his hand. A small black and white shape flew into the woods and disappeared in the boughs of a tree. We fell silent. The chickadee called, clear and sweet, *cheeeee-chee-chee*. Bob answered, echoing the song note for note. There was a pause. Then the chickadee replied. *Cheeeee-chee-chee*. Bob answered. The two creatures, large man and tiny bird, called back and forth for several minutes, their voices singing across the expanse of snowy forest.

Little by little, though, Bill and I began to distance ourselves from Bob. We had grown weary of his endless environmental harangues. We had heard the messages so many times—and, for goodness' sake, we agreed! We were doing what we could to live an environmentally positive lifestyle. We grew organic food. We used hand tools where possible. We planted bee-friendly forage. We rarely drove our truck. ("Less than you drive yours!" I wanted to say to Bob.) We didn't need to be lectured anymore. We were finding our own way to homestead, our own way to live on the land.

We began to cut back on our visits. I stopped cooking lunch for Bob. He, Bill, and I still chatted at the mailbox, and we still discussed books and shared news about our homesteads. But Bill and I no longer sat enthralled as Bob railed about environmental degradation and pontificated about the environmentally proper way to live. If Bob noticed that we were pulling away, he didn't comment. Neither did we. We just let the separation occur as a natural maturation of our relationship.

Decades later, I am truly grateful for all that Bob and Pat gave us. At a time when our parents thought we were crazy for moving to the middle of nowhere, the Harringtons took us seriously. They opened up our minds to big ideas about conservation, the environment, ecology, and nature. They helped us figure out how to live in the woods. I will always cherish the education we received at their kitchen table.

10

The Late, Great Sauna

The dream of steam

When we first put in the water line to the cabin, it was a luxury to have cold running water. No more hauling water from a nearby spring. No more bucket and dipper on the counter. Now we could just turn on the tap, and voilà! Icy-cold, delicious, pure water came streaming out.

But that icy-cold, delicious, pure water wasn't ideal for getting clean in. Even in hot weather, it was too cold. In the summer, we bathed under a garden hose warmed by the sun. Usually, the warm water lasted for one-and-a-half showers: by the middle of the second person's shower, the water was icy-cold again. In the winter, we heated pots of water on the wood-stove and sponge-bathed with washcloths. Baths decreased to every other day. Then every third day. We smelled funky.

In the winter of 1975, Bill and I started to clear more land. Every day, with our newly purchased Stihl chainsaw, we went out to a section of forest to the north of the cabin and cut down trees. Day by day, tree by tree, the clearing grew. Every afternoon, as the winter sky darkened, we stood at the back end of the clearing and looked at our expanding view westward, toward the lake.

By April, when the snow had retreated to slushy piles in the shade, we had a one-and-a-half-acre clearing dotted with hundreds of stumps. Cedar, fir, hemlock, and birch logs were piled around the clearing, ready to be turned into firewood, fence posts—and our future log home.

One evening in the early spring, after a day of limbing trees and carrying logs, I rinsed out the pot I had just sponge-bathed in. I sat down with *The Mother Earth News,* one of the many back-to-the-land periodicals Bill and I subscribed to, along with *Harrowsmith, Organic Gardening,* and *Country Living.* "Go Scandinavian with a sauna!" read the lead article. As I read, an idea took hold.

"Hey, Bill," I said.

Bill looked up. "Yeah?"

"We should build a sauna. It says here they're really healthy. You sweat like crazy and it cleans out your pores."

Bill looked interested.

"And you don't need electricity. It can be wood-fired. In fact, the best ones are wood-fired."

"How do you wash off all that sweat?"

I consulted the article. "Most people build a shower next to the sauna. But we could have buckets of water."

"I thought our water was too cold for you."

"I think I could stand it if I was steaming hot. And I'm sick of sponge baths."

"Me, too. And Lord knows we have enough logs to build with." He grinned. "Let's do it!"

The article in *The Mother Earth News* included a plan for a simple sauna. Theirs was wood-frame, but we adapted it for logs. We decided to build the sauna at the top of the new clearing, about a three-minute walk from the cabin, at the edge of the woods.

"It'll be a little inconvenient for now," Bill said, "but once we have our log house, it'll be right nearby."

The sauna was about ten by twelve feet, divided into a larger room for the heated chamber and a smaller outer room for changing clothes. For the walls we used hemlock logs, chinked with moss. Inside, we built cedar-plank benches at various levels for sitting and lying on. The roof was made of well-seasoned cedar shakes that we had salvaged from an abandoned cabin. We had recently bought a beautiful new cast-iron wood heater for the cabin, so we moved the old tin wood heater, slightly rusted, into the sauna. We were in business.

It takes a lot of work to get a wood-fired sauna ready to use. You have to start the fire two to three hours in advance to give the room time to heat up. Because of the location of our sauna, that meant trudging up the slope every half hour or so to feed the fire. And because our water line didn't extend up there, it meant schlepping up buckets of water to rinse off with. Guiltily (but not too guiltily), I let Bill do most of this preparation.

But once the sauna was ready, it was a delight. We stripped off our coats, boots, and clothes in the little outer room where we stashed our towels and Dr. Bronner's peppermint castile soap, and scurried into the hot chamber. Bill, who always tolerated heat better than I did (he could dip right into a hot bath, while I had to lower myself inch by inch; on the other hand, I was better in cold water, plunging into a lake while he stood thigh-deep at the shore), went straight for one of the upper benches, where the air was hotter, while I started on a lower bench and worked my way up. We stretched out and let the heat soak into our pores, into our bones, easing the aches from the day's work. Sweat dripped off our bodies onto the benches. Once in a while, Bill poured a dipper full of cold water onto the stove, creating a cloud of steam, making us sweat even more.

When we had had enough, we exited the sauna and, after a moment of fearful anticipation, jumped into the snow. We rolled around in it and rubbed it on our sweaty bodies, hooting with the shock of cold. Then we washed and rinsed off with the precious water in the buckets. Languid and squeaky clean, our hair smelling of peppermint, we wrapped ourselves in towels, stuck our bare feet into our boots, and walked down to the cabin. Often, we went straight to bed.

The sauna wasn't perfect. We found that we had made it too big, and the moss chinking shrank in the dry air, so the sauna was drafty and it cooled down more quickly than we would have liked. But it was still a treat, not only for us but for our friends who visited. We all stripped together (the hippie ethos dictated that one was not ashamed of one's nakedness), sweated together, and shrieked in the snow together. Soon having a sauna became a weekly or even semi-weekly habit for Bill and me. We had never been so clean.

By late April of 1975, the snow was entirely gone from the clearing, and it was time to have the stumps pulled so we could plant a ground cover and turn the bare patch of land into a pasture. Floyd Fitzgerald, who had done that job for us with his skidder on our first clearing, had moved away, and this task was beyond the capability of Walter's tractor.

Bob Harrington recommended a fellow named Charlie Howe, who worked for the highway crew. During the week, Charlie stayed at their camp in Trout Lake, about twenty miles northeast of Galena Bay. "He owns his own Cat," Bob said, "and he probably wouldn't mind picking up a little extra dough in his spare time. He's a hard worker, and careful. He knows how to use the machine to do the least damage to the land."

We contacted Charlie, and he said he'd be glad to do the work for us in the evenings after work. In early May, he began to pull the stumps out of the field.

Charlie was a short, husky man of about forty-five with thinning dark hair covered by a yellow Caterpillar cap. One of his legs was an inch shorter than the other as a result of a logging accident several years earlier. A cigarette butt, usually unlit, dangled from his lip. He was the quintessential Canadian: had named one of his sons Gordie, after the hockey player; said "aboot" and "hoose," and appended "eh" to nearly every sentence he uttered. Charlie had grown up in the Columbia Valley. Until the High Arrow Dam had flooded them out, he and his wife had farmed along the Columbia River. Now his family lived in Nakusp.

Like Walter Nelson and Floyd Fitzgerald, Charlie was a rural man, an environmentalist before the word came to be associated with left-wing political causes. He would not even have been comfortable with the word "conservationist." For him, conserving the environment was a matter of practicality, not grand principles. "Natural resources are there to be used," he said one time, balancing a coffee cup on his knee, the ever-present cigarette tucked behind his ear. "But you gotta be smart about it. Otherwise, Mother Nature'll shut the whole thing down." For Charlie, that wasn't a credo, it was simple common sense.

Charlie came to our place a few nights a week. He'd drive up the driveway in his red Chevy pickup, wave hello as he limped past the cabin to his Cat, which was parked at the lower end of the clearing, and start her up. (He called the machine 'er: "Start 'er up. She's runnin' good tonight," in that strange way men have of referring to their machines as females.) The roar of the engine was Bill's signal to put on his work gloves and go outside to set the choker chain around the logs and stumps.

They usually worked for an hour or two, until the evening light faded and their own hands became shadows, then came inside for coffee and cookies. Charlie lingered, soaking up the conversation. Camp life, even with diesel-generated television, was lonely, and he was in no hurry to get back.

One time, he took the cigarette butt out of his mouth and said, "Y'know, if I was twenty years younger, I'd pack 'er up and move my family out to the bush and do what you folks are doin'."

An uncomfortable thought pricked me: if I had first seen Charlie on the street, I'd immediately have taken him for a redneck. I'd have been wrong.

One afternoon in May, Bill came back to the cabin after stuffing a load of wood into the sauna's wood heater. It would be ready in about forty-five minutes. There was no longer enough snow to jump into, so we were going to have to lug extra buckets of water up there. We didn't mind. It was a cool, cloudy day. This would likely be the last sauna of the season. We wanted it to be a good one.

Half an hour later, Charlie showed up. Bill and I exchanged a look. *Bad timing.* We didn't want to mention the sauna because Charlie would feel that he was interrupting, and he'd want to leave. Yet he'd come all this way on his free time. It wasn't right to brush him off.

Bill put on his gloves and went out with Charlie. They worked for an hour or so. I quietly made trips up the hill, keeping the sauna going.

Afterwards, Charlie came in, and I offered him coffee and oatmeal-raisin cookies. He started telling a meandering story about a couple in Nakusp who had hired him to dig a foundation for a house—only the building site was on a steep hillside, and once he got started, half the hillside slid away.

"More coffee, Charlie?" I said, lifting the pot.

"Don't mind if I do." He held out his mug with a grin. "Good mud, eh?"

He rolled another cigarette, and another, for some reason in a more talkative mood than usual. I wished that we had mentioned the sauna at the beginning. Now it would be too awkward. Surreptitiously, I glanced at our little wind-up clock. We'd been sitting for almost an hour.

Shadows began to lengthen outside. I made more coffee. If Charlie stayed much longer, I thought, I was going to have to invite him for dinner. I didn't mind—I'd be glad to feed him—but what about the sauna? Would he want to take one with us? That meant Bill and I would have to dig up our bathing suits. I didn't think Charlie would want to join us *au naturel*.

Finally, I figured the sauna was a lost cause. "Hey, Charlie, would you like to stay for dinner?" I asked.

"Oh, no, thanks. I'd better get going. Thanks for the coffee, eh?"

Charlie stood up and stiffly stretched. He left. I heard his truck back down the driveway. Hurriedly I grabbed two towels while Bill filled a bucket at the sink.

A moment later, we heard the sound of a truck pulling up the driveway. *Now who's here?* I thought irritably.

A truck door slammed. Charlie poked his head in. "Do you know your sauna's on fire?"

"What!"

Bill and I ran outside. Sparks were shooting up into the black sky, and orange flames were visible through the trees. We ran up the clearing. The fire was in the roof. Every now and then a shake crackled and sent up a shower of sparks. We could feel the heat on our faces.

"Oh, my God, Bill! Can we save it?" I asked.

Bill shook his head. "Looks like it's a goner."

Another shake crackled, and a burst of flame shot up, blazing dangerously close to a nearby hemlock.

"Holy shit!" Bill said, jumping backward.

"We've got to keep it from spreading," I said.

"I know," Bill said, "but the hose won't reach this far. Come on, let's get buckets of water and dampen the ground."

As we ran back down to the cabin, Charlie was lumbering up the path in the Cat. "I'll push 'er down so the fire doesn't spread," he yelled.

Bill and I stretched the hose as far as it would go, filled buckets, lugged them up the clearing, and dumped water on the brush all around the burning building. Meanwhile, Charlie, cigarette dangling, positioned the bulldozer's blade against one wall of the sauna. He pushed. With loud creaks and groans, the wall fell into the middle of the sauna. Burning shakes tumbled in after the logs, showering sparks. Bill and I slapped them with wet cedar fronds, stamped them out where they fell on the ground, and threw buckets of snow, gathered from shady places in the woods, onto the smouldering logs.

Charlie, his face alternately illuminated by fire and darkened by shadow, maneouvred around to the next wall. The Cat engine whined and rumbled. *Crash!* That wall fell in.

Our clothes soaking and streaked with dirt, our eyes tearing from the smoke, our shoulders aching, Bill and I continued to carry buckets of water up the path. Finally, when we had saturated the ground all around the sauna, we slumped to the ground and watched Charlie finish the job. The two remaining walls toppled. Flames blazed up, but not as dramatically as before. The fire, nearly smothered by the logs that were its own fuel, was losing its vitality.

With the flat blade on the front of the Cat, Charlie scraped up the top layer of soil—dirt, brush, moss, stones, flowers—and dumped it on top of the heap of rubble that had been the sauna. The fire choked, sputtered, died. In the Cat's headlights, we saw a blackened mound of earth from which curled a few wisps of smoke. Amazingly, the forest hadn't caught fire.

Exhausted, shaking, stinking of smoke, we trooped back down to the cabin. Bill and I thanked Charlie over and over. "Please, Charlie, can I give you dinner? Coffee? Cookies? Anything?"

He shook his head. "No, thanks, it's fine. Good job I was here, eh?" With a last goodbye, he drove off into the night.

In the cold light of morning, Bill and I went up to examine the wreck. It looked worse than it had the night before. Jagged edges of broken logs jutted through the dirt. Mud-caked shakes were piled in messy heaps, surrounded by soggy ashes. The whole thing smelled like scorched, dirty timber.

"Those damn shakes," Bill said. "How stupid of us."

It was true. We'd known better. Walter had once told us, "Never put shakes on a building that will have a fire." But we'd salvaged all those beautifully weathered shakes, and we hadn't wanted to shell out for a new aluminum roof.

After the ugly, stinking pile of wreckage sat there for a long time, we finally retrieved a few dozen scorched but intact logs, carting the too-damaged ones and the shakes into the woods to decompose.

In with the new

We built a root cellar on the site of the sauna. We dug down a few feet, lined the hole with the scorched logs, and continued raising the walls several more rounds, above ground level, until it was possible to stand upright in the space. We put in shelves, and there we kept our jars of canned fruits and vegetables, as well as bins of carrots, potatoes, onions, and beets from the garden, nestled in layers of straw. The scorching of the logs acted as a natural preservative, and they never showed the slightest sign of rot or decay.

A few years later, we built a second sauna, this one much closer to the cabin, to increase the ease of hauling water and tending the fire. We constructed the walls of planed cedar, installed insulation, and put in a proper cast-iron wood heater rather than a tin model. The new sauna was smaller than the old one, allowing the room to heat up and retain heat more efficiently. Most important, we put aluminum on the roof.

The new sauna worked beautifully. It took only an hour or two to heat up, and the cedar walls and benches gave off a fragrant smell as they warmed. We even put up hooks and benches in the outer room—very spa-like, I thought.

The original sauna was like many of the projects Bill and I undertook in Galena Bay. We launched into it with great enthusiasm and not much knowledge. We made it too big. We didn't insulate it properly. We used an unsafe heater. Most foolishly, we put flammable material on the roof.

Yet we loved that first sauna. We had conceived an idea and had gone and built it. It was the product of our hands. We were proud of it, despite its many flaws.

The new sauna was superior in location, architectural design, and materials. But even as I appreciated its efficiency—and its safety—I missed the old one. Drafty, inconvenient, inefficient it may have been, but it was the first. The original. The late great.

Making a Living

In the fall of 1976, true to his vow not to work mindless manual jobs anymore, Bill went back to school to get his teaching certificate. Because he already had his bachelor's degree, he could do this in one academic year, called a professional year. He enrolled at Notre Dame University (NDU) in Nelson, the same institution Paul had attended a couple of years earlier, and we moved into student housing on the NDU campus on the hill overlooking town.

I got a job teaching a grade one-two split class in Slocan, about forty miles northwest of Nelson. My school, Slocan Elementary, had three classrooms: grades one and two, three and four, five and six. A block away stood a junior secondary school that housed grades seven through ten. After that, students had to bus to a larger secondary school at the southern end of the Slocan Valley.

Getting from Nelson to Slocan took forty-five minutes on bare roads, an hour in the snow. I wasn't eager to drive. I didn't mind the curvy roads, but I did mind the ice. Fortunately, I found colleagues to commute with: Tomo Naka, the principal of both the junior secondary and the elementary schools; Dick Hamakawa, who taught grade eight and nine social studies; and Martin Kitson, a delightful English fellow who was in Canada with his wife on a temporary teaching exchange and who taught the grade three-four class in the room next to mine.

Both Tomo and Dick, who were in their forties, had spent part of their childhood in Japanese Canadian internment camps during World War II, Tomo in the Okanagan and Dick in New Denver. This was the first time I had heard about these camps, or about Canada's treatment of citizens of Japanese origin during the war. (For that matter, I was also ignorant of the fact that the American government had done the same thing. It wasn't exactly covered in the American history curriculum when I was a kid.)

Tomo and Dick were a study in contrasts. Both were short and trim, with thick, straight black hair. Tomo had a thin, oval face, while Dick's was broad. But it was in their temperaments that they really differed. Tomo was genial, easy-going, a peacemaker. If he and his family had suffered during their internment—and no doubt they had—he never complained about it. He laughed easily, emitting a gentle chuckle when, for example, relating the bloopers of his weekend golf game.

The only word I could use for Dick was *bitter*. He rarely smiled. If he laughed, it was a sardonic croak. He railed about politics, cuts to education, and clear-cut logging, but his greatest vitriol was reserved for the degrading treatment he and his community had endured during the war.

"They treated us like animals," he'd say, scowling out the car window. "Stuffed into shacks like cattle in a rail car."

172   GALENA BAY ODYSSEY

"Now, Dick, it wasn't that bad," Tomo would say.

"Maybe not in your camp, Tomo. In ours, the walls were so thin that ice formed on the inside during the winter. My mother got pneumonia and nearly died."

"Well, yes, it's true that the cabins were poorly built, but—"

"Poorly built! They were substandard. And we had no school the first couple of years. The government wasn't going to spend money to educate 'Japanese brats.'" He practically spat the words.

"Yes, but that's ancient history, Dick," Tomo would interject. "We did get an education eventually, and here we are. We're doing fine. Life is pretty good, if you ask me."

Dick grunted.

These conversations stayed with me. Decades later, when I had become a children's author, I got the idea to write a book about the Japanese Canadian internment, no doubt partly inspired by memories of my colleagues. For research, I travelled to New Denver to visit the Nikkei Internment Memorial Centre located there. I stood inside one of the original shacks that had been built in 1942 for Japanese families arriving from the West Coast. As I looked around at the primitive conditions, the barren, uninsulated walls, the kerosene lamps, the lack of indoor plumbing, and the cramped spaces that would have been crowded with bodies, I understood Dick's bitterness.

The town of Slocan presented an interesting sociological divide. In the 1960s and '70s, when American draft dodgers and deserters and would-be homesteaders started moving north, and when Canadian young people began to leave cities to go back to the land, many of them ended up in rural British Columbia.

Nowhere was this more pronounced than in the Slocan Valley. Nearly every village up and down the valley boasted an enclave of hippie homesteaders living in tumble-down farmhouses or hand-built cabins or tipis. They grew gardens and pot, raised chickens and goats, wove and spun their own clothing, formed musical bands and theatre groups, opened artist's studios and yoga ashrams, and invaded the small rural towns they lived beside.

But the hippies didn't move into a vacuum. Long-established communities of working people were already in place. They were loggers and miners, small farmers and business owners, Women's Institute and Kiwanis Club members. They made their living from resource extraction. They drove big trucks and snowmobiles. They were church-goers.

Inevitably, there was a clash of values. And clash they did—in bars, at grocery stores, on logging roads, at town meetings.

"All you guys do is sit around and smoke pot," the rednecks would accuse the hippies.

"It's better than being drunk! Besides, you're just uptight and straight. Try it. You might open your mind," the hippies would reply.

The hippies would point to mountainsides denuded of trees through clear-cut logging. "All you guys do is rape the environment."

"Yeah, that's because we work for a living. Get a job!"

In the summer, people swam in the Slocan River. The hippies let their children run around nude—and sometimes even went nude themselves. "You guys have no morals," the rednecks would say.

"It's just skin, man. You're just blind to natural beauty."

(In a strange twist, the hippies tried to claim solidarity on the subject of nudity with the Doukhobors, a spiritual Christian group originally from Russia who had settled in the Slocan and Kettle valleys. The Doukhobors were pacifists who refused to pay taxes or send their children to school, and one of their forms of protest involved taking off their clothes at public gatherings and marching naked. However, the Doukhobors disavowed the hippies nearly as vehemently as the rednecks did.)

Whenever a community debated a development proposal, like putting a road into a recreational area or opening a new ski hill or allowing more businesses to operate, the hippies opposed it and the rednecks supported it. Town council meetings turned into shouting matches. In some cases, fistfights broke out in bars.

The town of Slocan, located at the southern end of Slocan Lake, where it channelled into the Slocan River, was a logging town. The main employer was a large sawmill, then operated by Canfor. But there was also a sizable back-to-the-land community on the outskirts of town, and I witnessed the divide between them in my classroom.

On parents' night, two groups sat on opposite sides of the room, one in checkered lumberjack shirts and baseball caps, the other in flowing garments in rainbow colours. On the playground, hippie kids and "townies" wrestled, calling each other the names they had heard their parents use.

People also disagreed about what kind of education they wanted for their children. A few years earlier, a group of Slocan Valley parents, dissatisfied with what they saw as the stultifying, conformist approach of the education system, had founded an alternative school. The Vallican Whole School emphasized creativity over traditional academics, letting children follow their own interests and learn at their own pace.

The contrast between the traditionalists and the free-schoolers was exemplified by two students in my class. Micah and John, both in grade two, were first cousins. Micah had attended the Vallican Whole for kindergarten and grade one, and then his parents had put him into public school for grade two. John, a town kid whose father worked at the sawmill, had gone straight into Slocan Elementary.

John was a quiet, obedient boy. When you told him to do something, he did it. He wasn't the brightest kid, but his printing was immaculate. He plugged away at his lessons and learned successfully.

Micah was a wild child. He couldn't, or wouldn't, sit still. He yelled out comments and answers without raising his hand. He came into grade two without the faintest idea of how to read, and not much interest in buckling down to learn.

One day, I set up easels around the classroom and put on a record of "Pictures at an Exhibition," one of my favourite classical pieces. I told the kids to paint whatever the music made them feel. John stood there with a dry brush in his hand, looking around as if hoping to spot the right answer somewhere in the room, while Micah immediately filled his easel with splotches and swirls of colour.

I was impressed with Micah's creativity, his lack of inhibition, his openness. I pitied John for his buttoned-up behaviour, his unquestioning willingness to follow the rules. But after a while Micah's lack of discipline began to wear on me. What was the use of having a "free," open-ended education if you couldn't sit, couldn't listen, couldn't follow instructions enough to learn? At times, I wanted to tie him to his chair and say, "Shut up and do the work!"

I decided that, if I ever had children, I would *not* send them to the Vallican Whole.

A wonderful thing happened that year in Nelson. I started dancing again.

As a child, my two passions were dancing and reading. I'd started taking dance classes at the age of eight, when a New York-based modern dancer named Kathleen Hinni, whom everyone called KT, offered classes in Linden.

I still remember the first class I attended. KT was a severe, scary-looking woman. She had frizzy, reddish-brown hair and wore huge, heavy hoop earrings that pulled her earlobes down toward her shoulders. Flat-chested, she wore a long black wrap-around skirt that resembled, in my mind, witches' garb. To count out the rhythm, she grabbed an empty metal wastebasket and pounded its bottom, sending out a chorus of terrifying thumps.

KT led us through a series of standing and sitting exercises. Once we were warmed up, she pulled out a long, wide, blue silk scarf and laid it on the floor.

"Imagine that this is a brook. You have to get across. You can get over the water any way you like—but don't get your feet wet!"

One by one, we ran up to the scarf and jumped or leaped or stepped over it. KT rustled the scarf to simulate waves, and the blue silk caught the lights of the gymnasium and made ripples of incandescence.

When it was my turn, I made a huge jump, tucking my legs under me to be sure my toes didn't touch the "water." I threw my arms up, reaching skyward.

I was hooked. When KT turned us loose to move as our imaginations dictated, I felt myself going someplace far away, disappearing into the dance the same way I disappeared into the pages of a book.

As a teenager, I declared that I was going to be a dancer when I grew up. By the time I was sixteen, though, I knew it wasn't going to happen. I might have been good enough to dance in a third-rate company, but not in one of those I aspired to, like the Martha Graham or Paul Taylor companies. And if I couldn't dance in one of the great companies, I wasn't going to be a professional.

I continued taking classes all through high school and college. But dancing ended when I got to the Farm. There were no studios nearby, and I was too busy working twelve-hour days in my first teaching job. And, certainly, there were no opportunities to dance in Galena Bay.

All that changed when Bill and I moved to Nelson in 1976. A young woman named Lynette Lightfoot—yes, that was her real name—had just arrived from Toronto, where she had been a member of the Danny Grossman Dance Company, a well-known modern dance troupe. Lynette opened a studio in Nelson, and her class was the highlight of my week.

Lynette taught a mixed technique combining modern, ballet, and jazz. We did a standing warm-up, then some barre work, then exercises on the floor. After that, we did combinations across the floor, and finished by learning some new choreography that Lynette taught us.

Almost as wonderful as dancing myself was watching Lynette dance. She was tiny, maybe five-foot-one, slender and fine-boned. She had fabulous technique, but what was most remarkable was her lightness. Embodying her name with every movement, whether a kick or a turn or a leap or a stretch, she seemed to float just above the earth.

Meanwhile, Bill was enjoying his professional year at Notre Dame University. He was elected president of the education students' association, serving as a liaison between the students and the faculty. Bill wasn't wild about his education courses, which were of the outdated "John Dewey revolutionized education in the early twentieth century by putting the focus on children" ilk. Nor did he enjoy writing lesson plans, which he found tedious, despite recognizing that they were necessary. But he loved his two practicums, one in a grade three-four class and the other teaching science to grades eight and nine. He got along well with his two sponsor teachers, was creative and energetic in the classroom, and received excellent reports on his teaching performance. He was awarded a BC teaching certificate at the end of the year.

Which precipitated the first crisis of our marriage.

That spring, as I was finishing my teaching year in Slocan and Bill was completing his teacher education, Lynette floated the idea of forming a dance company. It would be small, it would be semi-professional (meaning that the dancers might get paid a pittance), and it would perform only in the local area. But it would be a real company. Dancers would be expected to attend daily classes and rehearsals, chip in for costumes and studio time, and prepare pieces for performance.

From the moment Lynette uttered the words "dance company," I knew I wanted to be in it. I hadn't been good enough to make a truly professional company, but I would be good enough for this one. As well, I was twenty-seven now. Bill and I had talked about having kids. Once that happened, I wouldn't be able to devote myself to dance. This was my only chance.

Bill had other ideas. He wanted to teach. The problem was, whereas a few years earlier there had been plenty of teaching jobs in the Kootenays, now there were none. The only jobs available for new teachers were up north, around Prince George or even farther afield.

I wanted to stay in Nelson and dance. Bill wanted to apply for teaching jobs anywhere he could get one, to launch his teaching career.

We went around and around the subject:

ME: "It's only for a year. You can substitute-teach and then apply for next year. I'll go anywhere after that."

BILL: "That's no good. If I don't apply right out of school, it looks like I'm not really serious about teaching. I'll ruin my chances if I wait a year."

ME: "But it's my only chance. I've wanted this my whole life."

BILL: "I thought what you wanted was to be with me. The plan was that we would both teach. We'd make decent money and we'd be on the same schedule, have time off together to live in Galena Bay."

ME: "I know that's what we said, Bill. I just didn't expect this opportunity to come along."

BILL: "And what about security for our family? If we have kids, you'll be home and I'll have to support us. How am I going to do that if I don't teach?"

ME: "You're right. Everything you say is right. I know I'm screwing up your teaching career. I know I'm being selfish. But Bill, I've got to do this. Don't you see? I've got to."

We reached an impasse. Things were tense between us for weeks. Bill was hurt and angry, and I felt as guilty as hell. I had been raised to always think of others, to always put myself second. It felt uncomfortable to insist on what I wanted, especially when it was to Bill's detriment. But I wanted this year of dancing more than I'd wanted anything.

Finally, Bill gave in. Looking miserable, he said, "I don't want to go up north without you. I think this is a terrible decision, but I'll give up teaching to stay with you."

Crying, I hugged and kissed him. I was going to be a professional dancer.

11

Snow

The Canadian winter

When I was a kid growing up in New Jersey, a snowfall was a treat. My friends and I relished the three or four snow days that were called each year when blizzards hit and school was cancelled. We stayed outside all day. We built snowmen, had snowball fights, and made snow angels, coming inside only when our mittens were frozen stiff and our toes were numb.

But now, in winter 1973, "Holy shit!" was the only thing I could say as I stood at the cabin window and watched the snow fall for the eighteenth day in a row.

Bill joined me at the window. Silently the flakes fell. The world was hushed. No creatures stirred. Outside, the snowpack reached four feet, nearly up to the window frame.

"Beautiful, isn't it?" he said.

"Yeah, but . . . holy shit!"

To be sure, we had been warned. Back in Pennsylvania, when we were researching the Kootenays, we'd learned that Revelstoke and environs were considered a snow belt. When we arrived in Galena Bay, Walter and Bob told us that an accumulation of six feet was typical. We nodded, though we really couldn't imagine it.

Now we didn't have to imagine.

Snow had started falling in late November. It melted, snowed again, melted. By mid-December, it was on the ground to stay. Starting in January, it snowed for nearly six weeks straight, except for a glorious, bright, clear cold stretch in the middle two weeks, during which the sky was the deepest blue I had ever seen. At night, Bill and I heard the explosion of moisture in the trees freezing. By mid-February it had snowed some seventy inches. Of course, the snowpack wasn't that deep; the snow settled and compressed down to four or five feet. But when we exited the cabin, we had to take several steps *uphill* to reach the path. Every day, as we walked along our packed-down trails to the woodshed, the tool shed, and the outhouse, the trails seemed to sink lower as we walked between higher and higher walls of snow.

One night in early January, we heard a strange noise. Coming from above the cabin, it sounded like an airplane taking off right over our heads. Bill and I looked at each other in alarm. "What's that?" I said, thinking some powerful machine was about to crash into us.

A moment later, a wall of snow three feet deep slid past the window and landed on the ground with a loud *whump*.

We laughed in relief. That engine noise was the sound of snow sliding on our steep-pitched aluminum roof. Soon we got used to it, as we got used to shovelling the snow away from the windows so we could see out.

The first year I taught in Revelstoke, in 1973–74, the walls of snow created by snowplows at each intersection were so high that drivers and pedestrians alike had to inch out, peering around them, to see if any traffic was coming. Soon the walls were too high to be added to, so the plows scooped the snow into dump trucks, which emptied their loads into the Columbia River.

Amazingly, the continuous snow and the endless white didn't get me down. I didn't feel trapped or cabin-bound, even though we were. Bill and I loved the beauty of the winter in Galena Bay. Although sometimes we were incredulous at the ability of the sky to produce snow day after day after day, we appreciated the quiet. We were tickled by the fact that, when we skied or snowshoed in the woods, we passed trees at a much higher level than usual, ducking under boughs that were normally far above our heads. We enjoyed trying to identify animal tracks in the snow: the tiny prints of chickadees and the larger three-toed prints of ravens; the soft, rounded paw prints of martens and the deep, sharp-edged tracks of deer.

Granted, by March we were impatient for the snow to melt off the garden, and by April we were sick of every last flake, even the slushy piles in the woods. But living in a snow belt had its rewards.

When we put in our water line, in the early fall of 1972, we buried it eighteen inches deep all the way down from the intake, up near Bob's, to our cabin, a distance of fifteen-hundred feet. We had tremendous water pressure, and the water, fresh from its source in the Selkirk Mountains, was the most delicious I had ever tasted.

Our cabin had no basement, only a crawl space beneath. We placed cedar siding to cover the gap between the bottom of the cabin and the ground, all the way around. Still, where the water line emerged from the ground, it was exposed to the cold. An elbow made a right turn upward and entered the cabin through a hole cut in the floor. We wrapped that section of pipe in fibreglass insulation to keep it from freezing.

Squirrels, skunks, and martens found the insulation irresistible. Regularly they tore off shreds of it to line their nests or dens. Regularly Bill slid underneath the cabin to replace the insulation. Most years, snow arrived in early December, and there was enough to insulate the ground so that the water continued to flow. But in some years, cold weather preceded the snow, and the water line froze. On many a New Year's Eve, we watched the water flow from our kitchen tap gradually diminish to a trickle and then disappear. At the first signs of reduced flow, we filled up every available container with water, and for the next few weeks we were back to the old bucket-and-dipper-on-the-counter routine. Usually, in January, several feet of snow arrived. With this blanket, the ground beneath the cabin thawed, and running water returned.

While the water line was frozen, we hauled water from a spring about a quarter-mile away. Beavers had blocked the spring, creating a shallow pond. We had to snowshoe there, carrying three twenty-five-gallon buckets and our aluminum toboggan. Once we arrived, we took off our snowshoes and inched down the frozen bank, trying to get close enough to the water to lean over and dip in a bucket, but not close enough to slip in ourselves. (Bill was better at this than I was. I can still remember the shock of freezing water filling my boot after I took one step too many.) Once the buckets were full, we fastened lids on top and strapped them to the toboggan. Then, slowly, we dragged the tobog-gan back to the cabin. (Truth: Bill dragged the toboggan back to the cabin, while I called encouragement.)

Water fetched in this way was so precious that we saved it for drinking and cooking. That meant that we had to melt snow for wash water. We smushed as much snow as possible into a plastic pail and dumped it into an enamel canning kettle, which hissed on the woodstove.

What a revelation it was to learn that there were different kinds of snow, from slushy-wet-grainy, which coincided with temperatures near freezing, to dry-powdery-fluffy, produced by colder weather, and every gradation between. Although the dry, powdery stuff was the best kind for skiing and snowshoeing, the wet, slushy stuff was far superior for filling the kettle. On mild days, we could accomplish this task with three or four buckets full of wet snow, but on cold days it took ten scoops of insubstantial powder to yield the same amount of water. And even though the snow that fell on Galena Bay was as pure as snow could be, once melted, it had an odd, slightly metallic taste.

Who knew that something as prosaic as snow could be so varied and complex? And what joy when the massive snows of January came, and the water line unfroze.

Snowshoes

Bill and I had never snowshoed before coming to Galena Bay. As far as I knew, snowshoeing had died out with the early pioneers and fur traders. But we soon found that we needed to snowshoe if we wanted to get around in the winter. The snow was simply too deep to walk in, except for the short, packed-down trails we made from the cabin to the outbuildings. Our back roads, Ward and Dedosenco Roads, weren't plowed, and we had to park our truck a mile and a quarter away, where Ward Road met Hill Creek Road, which *was* plowed (and then shovel out the truck once we got there). Once we learned to cross-country ski, we could more quickly get to and from the truck on skis, but that was impractical when we were hauling dirty laundry out and carrying clean laundry and groceries in.

We visited Bob and asked, "What kind of snowshoes should we get?"

He pulled out a catalogue and showed us the options. At that time, there were no newfangled alloy frames and nylon laces. All snowshoes had wood frames with rawhide webbing, leather bindings that laced up over the forefoot, and a strap that went around the back of the boot and buckled at the front.

Sipping Bob's sludgy coffee, we looked at the different models. The Huron had a rounded footbed with a long wooden tail sticking out behind for balance. The Alaskan had the same general shape but was more oval. The Bear Paw was a rounded oval, without a tail. The Modified Bear Paw was a narrower oval.

"The Huron and the Alaskan are too round for our forest," Bob said, "and the tail will just get in the way. Besides, with our deep snow, you need all the webbed surface you can get. I'd go with the Modified Bear Paw. It has lots of surface area, but it's narrow enough to let you pass between trees."

So we bought Modified Bear Paw snowshoes, longer ones for Bill, shorter ones for me.

My first time out, in an effort to allow for the width of the snowshoes, I stood with my feet far apart, waddling from side to side on each step. That, I learned, was a waste of energy. I tried narrowing my stance. But I'd not take a long enough stride and end up stepping on my rear snowshoe with the back end of my front snowshoe. Then, when I attempted to lift my back foot, I'd pitch forward, face-first, into the snow.

Bill wasn't much better.

After several outings, though, we began to improve. We began to get a feel for how far apart to keep our feet and what length of stride would work. Bill and I learned to take turns breaking trail, especially in deep snow, which was exhausting because, even though you were mostly riding on top of the snow, you picked up an inch or two of fresh snow with each step, which accumulated and made the snowshoes heavy. When Bill went first, I carefully mirrored his snowshoe tracks, placing my right foot opposite his left, evening out the trail, taking pleasure in the webbed symmetry of our footsteps. Bill did the same when I led. In this way, the trail was much easier to follow on the way back.

Soon we were fairly adept. We could hike up to Bob's, a distance of half a mile, in about fifteen minutes, and to our truck in about forty-five. It was lovely to walk in the woods on top of the snow, brushing by snow-laden boughs and enjoying the silence of the winter forest. The only sounds were my own breathing, the swish of our snowshoes, the faint hum of a creek, and the occasional thump as a bough shed its load and then sprang back up, waving up and down like a vibrating diving board. The snow showered down with a hush so soft I wasn't sure if it made a sound or I only imagined it.

To maintain the condition of the snowshoes, we brushed the webbing with shellac every month or so. This protected the rawhide and maintained its suppleness. Shellacking the snowshoes wasn't my favourite job. The shellac had a sharp, resiny smell, and it was sticky while wet, hard to scrub off your hands. But, when they were treated, the snowshoes looked beautiful once more, the rawhide glowing golden-brown.

We wore leather mukluks for snowshoeing, supple ones that laced up to mid-calf. When we reached our destination and I slipped off my snowshoes, my feet felt so light that I felt as if I were floating.

In Galena Bay, mail was delivered twice a week, on Wednesdays and Saturdays. In the winter, when our truck was parked at the end of the back road, Bill and I had two ways of getting to the mail: snowshoe the half-mile up to Bob's and catch a ride with him, or snowshoe the mile to Walter and Margaret's and catch a ride with them. Although the hike up to Bob's was shorter, we usually went to Walter and Margaret's, partly because we knew we were going to see Bob afterward and partly because the elderly pair so appreciated the company. Also, if we got to Walter and Margaret's early, we could help them with any chores that needed doing: shovelling a path to their four-wheel-drive Scout or loading more firewood into the basement.

One Tuesday in January 1975, it started snowing in the afternoon, and it was still snowing heavily by the time Bill and I went to bed. By morning, about two feet of fresh snow had fallen, on top of the two feet that was already there, and it was still coming down.

I looked at Bill. "Should we bother going to the mail?" After all, if we didn't show up, our neighbours would figure out why. One of them would collect our mail, and we could get it from them later.

Bill shrugged. "Let's give it a try. We can always turn back if it's too hard."
We put on our snowshoes, leaving early to allow ourselves extra time.

"I'll break trail first," Bill said, starting down the driveway. I followed, stepping in the opposite spaces to balance his footprints.

By the time we got to the bottom of the driveway, a distance of one-hundred yards, we were breathing heavily. The snow was so deep and fresh that we sank about a foot with each stride. When we lifted our feet, we found ourselves carrying a good six inches of snow on top of our snowshoes—and this wasn't light powder, but heavy, wet stuff.

"I'll go," I said. I moved in front of Bill and turned left onto the back road. In this section, it went uphill. I could manage about twenty steps before I had to step aside and let Bill take over.

So we went, relinquishing the lead every few minutes. We continually had to kick our snowshoes to shake off the blanket of snow that rode on top. Soon we were panting. Our jeans were soaked from the knees down, adding to the weight. Even when we crested the hill and started on the downhill slope to Walter and Margaret's, the path was no easier, so exhausted were our legs.

By the time we arrived at the Nelsons', much later than the time we usually arrived, we expected to find them gone, having already driven up to the mailbox. Instead, Walter's Scout was in the driveway, and they were at home.

"We couldn't get up the road," Walter told us. "Anyway, they've cancelled the mail run today because of the weather."

Bill and I collapsed on the floor. Margaret revived us with tea and cookies.

Skiing

Neither Bill nor I had grown up skiing. In the 1950s and '60s, skiing was an activity for the wealthy. In my hometown, I had only one friend whose family skied, and they owned a chalet in Vermont. That friend left the rest of us after sixth grade to attend private school.

Also, as environmental consciousness grew in the 1960s, many people, including me, began to view skiing (I only knew about downhill at the time) as ecologically destructive. All that machinery! All that electricity! All those sheared-off mountainsides!

Besides, my family wasn't outdoorsy. We went to art museums, the ballet, classical concerts, good restaurants. The idea of my parents taking us skiing, or skiing themselves, was completely foreign.

But when Bill and I arrived in Galena Bay, we heard about cross-country skiing. It was environmentally benign. It was contemplative: you could whoosh through the woods and listen to the birds. It didn't require expensive equipment or fashionable clothes.

Then, too, it was a matter of practicality. Because our back road wasn't plowed in the winter, there were two ways to get around: snowshoeing and skiing. Snowshoeing was fine. But it was *slow*. Snowshoeing became the mode of travel we used out of necessity: when we needed to get to the truck to go into town, when we had to carry bags of groceries and laundry and needed free hands. Skiing was going to be our recreation.

Of course, we didn't know the first thing about cross-country skiing or what equipment to buy. Thankfully, in the late fall of 1972, Bill's friend Ray Chartrand, who had helped us build the cabin, came to Galena Bay for a visit with his girlfriend, Barbara Klassen. Both Ray and Barbara were knowledgeable about skiing. I drove with them down to Vancouver. Our trip had a dual purpose: to buy food supplies for the winter and to purchase cross-country skis for Bill and me.

After purchasing massive amounts of staples at Famous Foods, a natural foods store, then located on Hastings Street near Commercial Drive, we went to Sigge's, a venerable ski shop on West 4th Avenue in Kitsilano. I had brought a tracing of Bill's foot, so the helpful sales clerk was able to pick out a good pair of boots, skis, and bindings for him.

When it was time to outfit me, Ray beckoned me to the back of the store, where there was a rack of items on sale. "Fifty percent off on these boots," he said, motioning to a pair. "Why don't you try them on?"

The boots were on the snug side, but they *were* cheap.

Then Ray pointed to a pair of used skis. They were racing skis, thinner than regular cross-country skis, but they were the right length for my height.

"Do I want racing skis?" I asked anxiously.

"They'll be fine," Ray said.

For Bill's and my first ski outing, Ray and Barbara took us to Ferguson, an abandoned mining town up in the mountains about fifteen miles northeast of Galena Bay. We drove up the highway to Beaton, another abandoned town, located at the north arm of Arrow Lake, then headed up . . . and up. . . . As we climbed, the snow grew deeper, from about three feet at lake level to four, then five, then six. By the time we parked, having driven as far as the truck could go, the snowpack was so deep that, when we looked into an empty cabin, we peered down from the second storey.

From our parking spot, we faced a hill that rose about one-hundred feet in elevation. "Let's ski down that," Ray said.

My stomach dropped, but there was nothing to do but follow the others up the side of the hill. It was too steep to ski up, so we removed our skis and trudged through thigh-high snow. At the top, Barbara put her skis back on. "You probably don't want to ski straight down," she told Bill and me (*Oh, really?*), "so traverse back and forth across the slope. Like this."

She pointed her skis crosswise to the vertical plunge, pushed off, and zigzagged downhill, a picture of daring and grace.

Ray went next. Less graceful than Barbara, he was more of a daredevil. He went straight downhill in a spray of snow.

Bill and I exchanged a look. He was scarcely more eager than I was. "Here goes," he said. He traversed, fell down at the point where he needed to curve back in the other direction, and struggled back to his feet. He made another crosswise run. Because Bill didn't know how to turn, or stop, for that matter, he had to fall on purpose in order to stop and change direction. But, covered in snow—as I remember, we were wearing jeans and woollen jackets—he made it down.

I faced down the slope, heart hammering, almost paralyzed with fear.

When I came to Galena Bay, I had been afraid of many things. Of the physical work I would have to do. Of trying new things I had never done before, like gardening and building and raising animals. Of living in isolation. One by one, I had attempted these things, and I had survived. I had even mastered some of them. Those fears had fallen away.

This was different. I was not brave when it came to outdoor pursuits. Put me in a dance studio, and I could learn anything. Put me on a mountain, and I didn't know what to do. I was afraid I'd fall and get hurt. Afraid I'd look like a klutz. Most of all, afraid to fail. Cross-country skiing was one of those Kootenay skills that you had to master, or you weren't a good back-to-the-lander. What if I couldn't do it?

As I stood there, too scared to move, my skis decided for me. They started sliding, and I was going. For about six feet. Arms flailing, I toppled over, one foot bent backward, skis crossed, legs tangled. To stand up, I leaned forward, planted each ski, *stay there, goddamn it,* felt the upward momentum slip away, *oh shit,* slipped again, out of control, slide, yank ski out of snowbank, mitten off, fingers freezing, muscles rigid, *whoops,* crash.

"Plant your poles," Barbara called.

Whatever the hell that means, I thought.

Somehow, I got to my feet. I slid another short distance, then fell, my front ski outstretched, almost in a split. Again, it took me several ungraceful attempts to get back on my feet.

So it went all the way down the hill. By the time I got to the bottom, I was covered with snow and my feet were freezing in the too-small boots.

"I thought those racing skis might be a little fast for you," Barbara said sympathetically.

Now you tell me!

I was ready to quit, but Ray was already at the top again, windmilling his arms to urge us to come back up.

On Bill's second time down, he managed to stay upright more of the time, shifting his weight to keep his balance. *Showoff,* I thought.

I managed one more run, just as ungraceful and disastrous as the first. I couldn't control the skis and spent more time on the ground than upright. When I *was* upright, my poles stuck out on either side of me like the propellers of a helicopter. The only way I could stop was to fall, either accidentally or on purpose. By the time I got to the bottom, not only were my feet frozen, so were my hands.

Ray was all for continuing, but Bill, seeing the look on my face, said he thought we'd had enough. As we walked back to the truck, I growled to him in an undertone, "I never want to do that again."

Of course, I couldn't stick to that vow. Every day, Bill and I were travelling from Ebin's cabin to our own, where we were cutting up the trees that had been felled the previous fall. If we had snowshoed, it would have taken a couple of hours. Skiing there would take about forty-five minutes. I had to learn how.

My lack of proficiency wasn't the only thing I hated about cross-country skiing. Waxing was just as bad.

In those days, waxless skis hadn't yet been invented. Every time you skied, you had to wax the base of your skis to prepare them for the snow.

If the temperature was around freezing or above, that called for red wax. This was the gooiest, stickiest of the waxes. You dabbed it on the bottom of the ski and smoothed it out with a rectangular cork about the size and shape of a bar of soap. Naturally the wax got all over your fingers and clothes, creating sticky spots that in turn stuck to everything they came into contact with. Eventually we started using a propane torch to soften the wax, which made it easier to spread, but it was still a messy, sticky job.

If the weather was below freezing, you used violet wax, which was slightly harder than the red. Colder still, blue wax. Coldest, green wax, which was so hard that even my most vigorous rubbing with the cork failed to spread it; lumps of green sat on the bottom of my skis like pools of melted candle wax.

I hated waxing. Hated, hated, hated. Just the thought of having to do it put me in a bad mood. I bargained with Bill. "You wax my skis and I'll do all the dishes today." That didn't always work. "You wax my skis and I'll give you a backrub." That did.

In the winter of 1974, Bill and I took a day-long cross-country ski workshop in Revelstoke with a fellow named Soren Sorensen. A skiing pioneer and one of the people credited with introducing cross-country skiing to Canada, Soren was a tall, thin Swede with a deeply wrinkled face and a kind smile. He *loved* teaching people how to cross-country ski, even hopeless, fearful klutzes like me.

"Lengthen out your back leg so you get the longest stride possible," he said, and soon I was taking longer strides instead of short, choppy ones.

Soren taught us to keep our poles closer to our bodies so we could get more purchase on them to push off, instead of keeping them farther out for balance. He showed us how to herringbone up hills, angling the front ends of our skis out to the sides and the back ends slanted in together, forming the letter V; the diagonal edges bit into the snow and prevented you from slipping backward. This was a vast improvement on my previous technique, which had been to go up hills backwards on my bottom, pushing up one step at a time—the reverse of a toddler coming down the stairs. I left the workshop feeling marginally more confident.

After that ... somehow, slowly, I began to get it. Every so often, I felt myself glide—just for a few strides, but still. I stopped holding my poles in a death grip. I managed to keep my skis pointing forward instead of shooting out to the sides. Sometimes, when the snow was right, and the wax was right, and the sun made splotches of light on the snow, and the trees were clothed in white, and the sky was cobalt blue, and Bill and I were two figures in a postcard tableau, then I found the timing. I glided, I flew, I danced over the snow, and knew that I was really skiing.

To my amazement, I was even able to enjoy the beauty and quiet of the snow-laden woods as I swooshed along. Look, there's a raven flying overhead! Look at that shower of snow falling from the top of a fir. Listen to the gurgle of a spring underneath the white blanket.

It took several months, but by the end of that winter I was beginning to enjoy cross-country skiing. I wasn't very good, but I was getting better. I was ready to admit that this new activity might not be so bad—as long as Bill waxed my skis.

It was only several years later, when I bought new equipment, that things really changed. That was when I acquired my first pair of waxless skis.

These had only recently been invented. Unlike traditional wooden skis, with smooth bottoms, these had small, scallop-shaped pieces of fibreglass attached to their bases in an overlapping pattern like fish scales on the body of a salmon, giving rise to the nickname "fish scale skis." The top ends of the scallops slid over the snow, allowing forward glide, while the back ends provided friction and prevented you from slipping backward. *No matter the snow conditions.* Waxing was no longer required.

We had heard about fish scale skis from friends in Revelstoke, and Bill bought a pair in town. I was still stuck with my wooden skis.

Then two young couples moved into Ebin's cabin, where Bill and I had lived our first winter. When I mentioned to them that I was looking for waxless skis, one of the women said, "I've got a pair for sale." I immediately went over to the cabin and tried them on. The skis were the right length. They were barely used. Best of all, the boots fit, with room for my toes to wiggle.

"Sold," I said, and Bill and I went out that same day.

The fish scale skis didn't have as much glide as the wooden skis, and the scales made a slight whining sound, like an airplane taking off. But they had enough glide for me, and I didn't slide backward. *And I didn't have to wax them.*

Soon I was saying to Bill, "Want to go out for a little ski?" and we were skiing every day, even when we didn't have to get anywhere. I began to improve, to gain confidence. I began to love cross-country skiing.

I still do.

The West Kootenays were dotted with hot springs. Some were developed, like Nakusp or Ainsworth, which was northeast of Nelson and famous for its hot spring caves. Others were undeveloped, like the St. Leon and Halcyon hot springs, which were between Galena Bay and Nakusp.

Bill and I sometimes visited St. Leon and Halcyon, especially at the end of a hard day spent digging rocks out of the garden or burying the water line. The warm, sulphurous water soothed tired backs and aching muscles, and it was pleasant to soak in the open air, watching birds fly overhead, seeing the glint of Arrow Lake in the distance.

Halcyon was about eight miles south of Galena Bay, located beside an old logging road off the highway. A natural spring bubbled up from the ground, creating a small pool in the clay. Someone had lined the pool with a plastic tarp so you didn't have to sit on the ground. The plastic was slimy and slightly mildewed, but the water was grand. (Today, Halcyon is a fully developed resort, with comfortable cabins and chalets, three concrete pools of varying temperatures, a gourmet restaurant, and a spa. How things change.)

St. Leon was farther south, at the fifteen-mile mark, located a half-hour hike up a mountainside. It was a slog to get there, but worth the effort.

Years before, people had built a rock-lined basin to contain the natural hot spring, large enough for five or six people to soak in.

In the winter of 1976, our friends Paul and Eve came to visit us in Galena Bay for a few nights. They had grown up together as high-school sweethearts on Long Island. Paul, who had been Bill's college roommate at Penn State, was tall and muscular with a head of thick, curly hair and a strong New York accent. (I loved the way he said "culla" for "colour.") Eve, whose Portuguese father was originally from Tobago, showed her Mediterranean heritage in black hair and olive skin. Paul and Eve had immigrated to Canada a year after we did and had bought five acres of mountainside directly across Keen Creek from Michael and Vivianne.

The winter of Paul and Eve's visit to Galena Bay, we decided to go up to St. Leon for an afternoon. Because of the snow, we would have to either snowshoe or ski up to the pool; the snow was too deep to walk in. We decided to ski. Although we'd have to take off our skis in places where the trail was steep and rocky, there were also flat stretches where skis would allow us to move quickly.

We set off about midday, first skiing from our cabin to where our truck was parked at the end of the back road, a twenty-minute trip, then driving the fifteen miles south. At the base of the St. Leon hill, we put on our skis. At first, the trail rose gently. But soon we reached a steeper part. I tried to herringbone up the rise, and even stair-step—a technique where you point your skis perpendicular to the slope, lift your uphill ski and take a step, then bring your downhill ski up parallel to the first—but the terrain was too steep. We took off our skis and slogged through knee-deep snow.

Past the steep patch, we hit a flatter stretch. Back on with the skis, and whoosh-whoosh, for about five minutes. Then we came to another rise. And so it went. On and off with skis, slog and climb. In some places, boulders commanded the middle of the trail, and we had to toss our skis and poles up on top, then crawl up ourselves and retrieve them.

The result of all this bushwhacking was that it took a lot longer to get to the top than we'd expected. Finally, though, we sniffed the familiar sulphur smell, skied around one last bend, and there was the pool, steam rising from its still surface. No one was there. We had the place to ourselves. Gratefully we stripped naked (no bashful modesty among the hippies) and lowered ourselves into the water. Well, Bill lowered himself into the water. I always took longer to acclimate to hot water, submerging inch by inch.

Aahhh ... The water was glorious, the heat soothing, especially after our arduous climb. We soaked, tiny droplets of condensation settling on our hair. We washed with Dr. Bronner's peppermint castile soap (natural, organic, biodegradable, of course), rinsing off outside the pool.

We had been soaking for about an hour, thoroughly relaxed, when we heard voices. Two couples stepped out from the woods. Stopped. Stared, clearly disconcerted to find four naked hippies sitting in the pool.

Sensing their embarrassment, I said, "Give us five minutes and we'll clear out."

They withdrew behind the trees. We towelled off and quickly got dressed, shoving damp feet into damp socks and boots.

"It's all yours," I called.

The four people emerged. Eyes averted, they murmured thanks.

Now began the downward trek. Once again, it was skis on, skis off, stumble, glide, walk. Only now the shadows were lengthening, and it was harder to see the way. When we got back to the truck, it was dusk.

I began to worry. We had a twenty-minute drive back to our parking spot. By the time we started skiing back to the cabin, it would be dark. We had skied at dusk before, but never at night. How would we find the way? What if we missed a turn and skied off the road into the bush ... and got lost ... on a cold January night?

When we got out of the truck, Eve said nervously, "Can we do this? Should we just drive back to Nakusp and stay in town for the night?"

Paul said, "You do know the way, don't you?"

I was scared, too, but I said, "Sure we do. We'll be fine," and I set off in the lead.

There was a half moon that night, alternately obscured by clouds and then revealed. A million pinpricks of light spangled the sky. Within a few strides, my eyes had lost their light-blindness from the truck's headlights and adjusted to the dark. There was just enough light from the sky, reflecting on the snow, to make the road visible, a brighter blur than the darker shadows on either side.

The temperature had cooled down. The snow conditions were perfect: a skiff of fresh snow over packed tracks. My strides grew longer, more confident. I lengthened my back leg, using my poles to their full length. Soon I was gliding over the snow—no, not gliding, flying.

Fear fell away. Not just the fear of this run, in the dark, but the fear of skiing itself that had gripped me for so long. The fear of falling, of being clumsy. The fear of failure. Gone.

No one spoke. I could sense the others behind me, skiing just as effortlessly as I was. The only sound was the *shush-shush* of our strides. The moon came out, shining silver on the snow. We zoomed down the back road. The cabin came into view as we glided over the last stretch.

We stood on the driveway, our muscles warm, our faces light and shadow.

"Wow."

That nighttime run remains the most amazing, the most beautiful ski I have ever had.

Making a Living
PART FIVE: 1977-78

In the fall of 1977, I joined the dance company. We tossed around names and decided to call our company A Question of Balance Dance Theatre—because it really was. In addition to my teacher Lynette and me, there were four other women—Anita, Gail, Penny, and Sabbian—and one man, Michael.

Michael was a tall, lanky guy with a head full of long red curls. He wasn't a very good dancer. His movements were jerky, and he was often off the beat. But he was eager and, more important, strong enough to lift us when the choreography called for it.

Anita was a pal of Lynette's from Danny Grossman's company. Where Lynette was all ethereal grace, Anita was muscle and power. Her jumps exploded off the floor. I'd never seen anyone turn so well, her head whipping around on every spin, her body landing exactly 360 degrees from the previous turn.

Sabbian was by far the most flexible of us: sitting on the floor with her legs extended to either side, she could bend forward and place her entire chest on the floor. Penny had the best ballet technique. Gail was wiry and strong, the hardest worker in the group. My technique was middling, but I think it's fair to say that I had the most passion. I worked my butt off.

Lynette and Anita became our "dance mistresses." They took turns teaching class and collaborated on the choreography. Dancing every day, we actually improved. Our feet pointed more precisely, our legs lifted higher, our arms stayed in position longer.

Lynette choreographed a dance based on *Alice's Adventures in Wonderland*. Michael played the Mad Hatter in a tall black top hat, Sabbian was Alice in a blue pinafore, and I was the Cheshire Cat, moving sinuously across the stage.

Anita created a piece set to Aaron Copeland's "Rodeo." Dressed in overalls and gingham dresses, like pioneers of the American west, we kicked up our heels in an old-fashioned barn dance.

We rehearsed through the fall and winter. In the spring, we performed at several Nelson elementary schools, a few cultural festivals in the Slocan Valley, and small theatres in Castlegar and Kaslo. It was a thrill to put on makeup, to stand nervously in the wings and then leap or twirl or jazz-walk out in front of the spotlights. People actually applauded. We never made more than a few dollars, but I didn't care. I was dancing professionally.

After our last show in April of 1978, Lynette announced that she was shutting down the company for the summer. It would resume in the fall.

I knew I wouldn't go back. I'd loved every minute of it: the daily classes, the sore muscles, the sweat, the rehearsals, the costumes, the performances.

But I'd fulfilled my wish. I'd had my season of dance. Now I needed to devote myself to Bill and our plans together.

In the fall of 1977, when I joined A Question of Balance, Bill substitute-taught for a few months. He wasn't happy about it, but it gave him something to do and brought some money in. Then, in late October, he got a phone call. It was from Mike Jessen, a friend we'd made through our activism in the environmental movement. Mike was the director of SPEC, the Society Promoting Environmental Conservation.

"The feds are opening an energy conservation office in Nelson," Mike told Bill. "Would you like to work there?"

Let's back up a minute. In the early 1970s, members of the Organization of Petroleum Exporting Countries, the oil cartel, had deliberately withheld supplies from world markets in order to drive up prices. It worked. In addition to skyrocketing prices for oil and gas, there were shortages. In some North American cities, gasoline stations ran out of fuel while lines of cars stretched around the block, and some jurisdictions experienced brown-outs when their oil-fired generators ran low.

In response, governments increased their efforts to reduce reliance on Middle Eastern oil. The Canadian government focused on two areas: energy conservation and renewable energy such as solar, wind, biomass, and hydro. They opened a number of community energy conservation centres across the country. One of them was to be in Nelson, and Mike was to be its manager.

Bill eagerly accepted Mike's officer and became the assistant manager of the Nelson Community Conservation Centre (CCC).

The CCC brought together an eclectic group of people. Jim was a chain-smoking scientist whole sole focus was on remediating the emission of radon gas into people's homes. (Radon is a radioactive gas that is released when uranium in the soil breaks down. There were radon-producing uranium reserves in several areas of the West Kootenays.) Richard, a recent law school graduate who had been active in the West Coast Environmental Law Association, had decided he didn't want to practice law and was looking for a change. Lynne had been a teacher and was interested in environmental education. Wendy, an ardent feminist, was ready to hit the streets to protest anything; Mike had her work on getting a recycling program going in Nelson. Evelyn was the office manager.

Right away, Bill was in his element. He'd always had strong organizational skills and was good at planning and logistics. He was passionate about energy and environmental preservation. He and Mike soon had half a dozen projects going.

The CCC held open houses where people came to find out about programs to install everything from energy-efficient lighting to solar panels;

made presentations to encourage the City of Nelson to adopt more environmentally friendly policies; and produced information pamphlets. Bill and Lynne started developing an energy education curriculum for intermediate grades. Richard wrote articles for the local newspaper. Wendy started looking into the economics of recycling.

It was good to see Bill engaged and invigorated by this work. I sensed that he hadn't quite forgiven me for thwarting his teaching career, but he was getting closer. And, at least, in writing the curriculum, he was using his education training.

In the spring, when the dance company went on hiatus, Mike offered me a job at the CCC as well. I happily accepted and took on two roles: working with Bill and Lynne on the energy education curriculum, and working with Wendy on developing a recycling proposal for the City of Nelson.

Bill, Lynne, and I wrote lesson plans, devised science activities like building a solar cooker and a rudimentary water wheel, wrote educational stories, and got Evelyn, who had artistic talent, to illustrate and design our teacher's manual. One of Bill's former sponsor teachers agreed to pilot the program with her grade three-four class. She gave us feedback, and we made improvements.

Meanwhile, Wendy and I crunched the numbers on the recycling proposal, calculating the savings from waste avoidance versus the cost of picking up recyclables. We wrote a business case and made a formal presentation to Nelson City Council. When it was our turn to speak, the city councillor who introduced us said, "Now, let's hear what these two attractive young ladies have to tell us. I'm sure they'll be very entertaining." While the other councillors chuckled, I felt Wendy bristle beside me. She darted me a look, as if to say, *I'm not taking this. Let's go!* I squeezed her hand. She got the message: *Screw the male chauvinists. We're here. We've done all this work. Let's do it!*

So we did. We went through our proposal, showing graphs and charts. When we were finished, the councillors applauded, and their faces looked more impressed than they had when we came in.

The City of Nelson voted to adopt a recycling program the following year.

Working at the CCC was a wonderful experience for Bill and me. We got to work together, we collaborated with like-minded people, and, best of all, we felt that we made a difference.

But at the end of the summer of 1978, federal government funding for the energy conservation centres ran out. Bill and I headed back to Galena Bay, wondering what would come next.

Family

Learning to roar

For many years, when people asked me why I moved to British Columbia, I framed my answer in relation to Bill and the Farm: "I fell in love. He was moving to BC, so I went along; I joined a commune that was planning to leave the US and go back to the land in BC."

I also alluded to my own idealism and desire for adventure. "I was fed up with the US and wanted to make a difference; I was interested in trying a different lifestyle; I wanted to live in the mountains, grow my own food, and be kind to the environment."

All of those were true. But they didn't tell the whole story.

Bill had grown up in an unhappy household. When people asked him how he felt about moving so far away from his family, he joked, "If the continent were any wider, I would have gone farther."

I didn't feel the same way. I came from a happy family. My parents had a wonderful marriage. I was close not only with my immediate family, but also with my grandparents, aunt, uncles, and cousins, all of whom lived in Linden and whom I saw often. While I was excited about going to British Columbia, I wished I weren't moving so far away.

And yet ... in June 1972, as soon as Bill and I crossed the border into Canada and headed west, I felt what I can only describe as a sense of relief. It made me feel ashamed. I couldn't admit that I wanted to get away from my family. After all, I often raved about how wonderful they were, how close we were, what a happy childhood I had had. So where was this feeling of relief coming from?

It was only many years later that I admitted to myself that, in addition to being in love with Bill and seeking an idealistic adventure, I had also wanted to get away from my family. After much soul-searching, I figured out why.

One reason was the weight of expectation. As the oldest child in a successful, professional family, I knew from a young age that great things were expected of me. I was a bright girl and a conscientious student. Without my parents having said so, I knew that I was to earn straight A's in school. And I did. Mostly I did it without a great deal of effort. But I can remember an unspoken fear. *What if I don't? What if I can't?*

My parents didn't overtly put pressure on me. They always expressed pride and delight in my accomplishments, and never berated me for a less-than-stellar performance. "You'll achieve great things, Ellen," my father would say. While I glowed under the beam of his praise, I also felt pressured: *What does that mean? What does he expect of me? How successful is successful enough? To get a good job? To have a solid marriage? To be outstanding in my field, whatever that turns out to be?*

Perhaps that is the burden of every oldest child. Or perhaps it was just me. But it was real, and I felt it.

The other reason was the requirement to be good. In my family, we were polite. We didn't raise our voices. We didn't argue. We didn't shout, or swear, or say rude things.

When I got in trouble, in my teens, for smoking cigarettes, or staying out past my curfew, or sneaking out to date a non-Jewish boy, my parents didn't yell. Instead, they froze me out with an icy silence. "We'll see you in the kitchen," my father would say, and with heavy feet I would troop downstairs and wait for the lecture.

MY FATHER: "We are very disappointed in you, Ellen. We expected better of you."

ME (thinking: *But it was only [fill in the blank]. What's so terrible?*): "I'm sorry."

MY MOTHER (tearfully): "How could you do this to us?"

ME (guiltily): "I'm sorry."

MY FATHER: "These rules are in place to protect you, to teach you what's right and what's wrong. You've let us down."

ME: "I know."

MY MOTHER: "I can't take it."

ME (thinking: *For Christ's sake!*): "I'm sorry."

MY FATHER: "You're grounded."

ME (thinking: *Shit!*): . . .

As I sat there, seething, unable to speak out, I was furious. When my father scolded me, I never said, "Leave me alone! Your rules are stupid and I'm not going to follow them!" When my mother cried over my latest act of disobedience, I never yelled, "I can't stand it when you put that guilt on me!"

But I thought it. Of course, I thought it. I was human. I got frustrated and angry. I felt defiant and snarky. I wanted to be rude. To swear. To stamp my feet. To roar.

But I couldn't, because we didn't do that. Because, if I had, I would have made everybody even more upset, and then I would have felt even worse.

Bill came from a family of shouters. He said what he thought, and damn the consequences. I wasn't comfortable with that degree of candour, but, with him, at least, I didn't have to hold everything inside.

That was what the feeling of relief was about, I realized many years later. At last I was free. Free to say what I wanted. Free to be stupid and screw up and fail. Free to roar.

Visits

The enormous Winnebago camper jounced down the back road, plunging into potholes and tilting from side to side as the wheels slid into depressions on either side of the back road. It was the summer of 1973, and my family was visiting Galena Bay for the first time.

Bill was at the wheel, my father in the passenger seat. My mother, in the row behind, anxiously peered ahead between them, her knuckles white as she gripped the back of my father's seat. "Oh my God, oh my God ..." she murmured.

Audrey, her boyfriend Alan (whom she would later marry), David, and I crowded together in the remaining seats. "Wow," David said periodically. "Look at that boulder. Did you see how tall that tree is? Wow."

Bill parked at the bottom of the driveway, where the ground was level.

"Here we are," I said brightly, and everyone climbed out.

Several days before, my family had flown into Calgary. Bill and I had taken the train from Revelstoke and met them there. My parents, reasoning that they would need someplace to stay once they got to Galena Bay, had rented the Winnebago. The seven of us had spent a few days in Banff National Park, camping—if you can call sleeping in a hotel on wheels, complete with a chemical toilet, propane stove, shower, and fold-out beds "camping." Still, for my city-bred family, this was truly roughing it.

Now they were about to see my home for the first time. Finally, instead of trying to convey in letters or over the telephone what my life was like, I could show them.

Before Bill and I left for Calgary, I had scrubbed the cabin floor, washed the windows, polished the woodstove, and made the cabin as tidy as a sixteen-foot by sixteen-foot rough frame house can be. Now, I opened the cabin door and gestured with my arm. "Welcome."

My mother stepped over a muddy patch in front of the cabin. My father held her hand, helping her up the three steps onto the landing. I watched their faces as they came inside.

My father's remained impassive. He looked around, nodded. I couldn't tell if that nod meant *good* or *appalling*.

My mother's eyes flickered with shock and dismay as she took in the cable-spool table, the rough-cut walls, the stained enamel sink, the open kitchen shelves crammed with jars of lentils, rice, oats, beans, honey, and powdered milk. "Very nice," she squeezed out through clenched teeth.

At that moment, I realized that I had actually been expecting them to like it, to smile and say, "Oh, Ell! It's wonderful. And you and Bill did it all by yourselves. We're so proud." And I realized how utterly foolish that was. How could I have expected my mother to make the leap from French provincial to stump-and-plank design? How could I have expected my father to rejoice at my rejection of his lifestyle?

Still, it hurt.

Trying for a cheerful tone, I said, "Want to see the loft?"

My mother glanced at the ladder. "Uh, no thanks."

My father, Audrey, Alan, and David said yes, so I led the way up the rungs. "Watch your head," I said as each person approached the opening at the top.

We stood, hunched over beneath the steeply sloping eaves. I saw my father glance at the boxes crammed into the corners, labelled WINTER CLOTHES, HAMMOCK, BOOKS.

"That's where Bill and I sleep," I said, indicating our mattress on the floor.

"At least you get your exercise climbing up and down," my father said in a lame attempt at a joke.

"But Ell, what happens when you have to go to the bathroom at night?" David asked.

"We use chamber pots."

"Gross!"

David, Audrey, and Alan salvaged the visit. David, fifteen years old, with long, wavy hair and the shadow of a moustache on his upper lip, shot questions at me as he tore from one corner of the homestead to another.

In front of the cabin: "You and Bill built it all by yourselves?"

"Well, we had lots of help, but yeah, pretty much."

"Wow. How did you know what to do?"

"Well, that's the amazing thing, Dave. You learn. It's not that hard. I mean, it's hard work, but it's not impossible to figure out."

He grinned. "My sister, the carpenter."

At the outhouse: "A two-seater! Do you and Bill ever come out here together?"

"Actually, no. It turned out to be not such a great idea. But it's a pretty spot, don't you think?"

David turned and looked at the dappled sunlight filtering through the trees, at the mobile of translucent fish I had hung from a nearby branch. He put his skinny arm around me. "Yeah, it is. I'm proud of you, Ell."

I squeezed him back. I was twenty-three, and it was weird to accept praise from my kid brother. But I appreciated it just the same.

I could see Galena Bay making an impression on my sister. Audrey was nineteen and had just finished her first year at the University of Maryland. We had grown up sharing a strong interest in the arts, especially dance, but the four-and-a-half-year age difference meant that we were out of sync when it came to political and social causes. When I was a sixteen-year-old, haranguing my parents about Vietnam and civil rights, Audrey was not quite twelve, too young to join the discussion.

But now she was a young woman, and had spent a year away from home. She was aware of the anti-war movement, the Watergate scandal, the flow of hippies leaving the cities to go back to the land. Audrey and I had discussed these things before I left for Canada. Although she wasn't as passionate as I was, or interested in making as radical a statement, I knew that she was intrigued.

"Don't you miss electricity?" she asked as we walked out of the cabin.

"Yeah," I admitted. "It would be nice to have a refrigerator and electric lights. But the propane lights are pretty good. We keep cheese and stuff in a crock buried in the ground. Besides, it's better than having half the mountain raped to make way for transmission lines." I indicated pristine Mount Murray behind us, covered with green.

Audrey looked consideringly at the slope. I could tell she was picturing transmission towers, and, maybe for the first time, making the connection between electricity and the environment. "Well, yeah, but you don't want to do without all conveniences, do you?"

"No." I led her toward the garden. "Maybe someday we'll have a Pelton wheel." I showed off the new vocabulary that Walter had taught us. "That's a small water wheel you put in a creek, and it generates electricity."

"Cool."

I nodded. "But in the meantime, I don't mind. It's actually fun to cook on a woodstove. And Bill and I are learning how to do all kinds of new things."

Audrey looked around. "It's awfully far from civilization. Don't you miss people?"

"No," I said emphatically, and I meant it. I was thrilled to be here alone with Bill. Even Paul, as much as I loved him, felt like too much company at times.

"Like Dad," she said, and we chuckled. Our father was an extreme introvert, and we both took after him. David, social and outgoing, was at ease with people, like our mother.

"Maybe not quite that bad," I said.

Audrey and I stood at the bottom of the driveway, near the Winnebago, and looked back up at the cabin.

"I get what you're doing now," she said in a quiet voice. "It's not for me. I could never live like this, never work so hard or do without. But I can see what you guys are aiming at. And it's really cool."

"Thanks, Audge."

She jerked her finger at the Winnebago. "But I'm sticking with the heated shower. If you think I'm bathing under the hose, forget it."

We both laughed.

It was Audrey's boyfriend, Alan, who seemed to get it the most. This was the first time I had met him. He and Audrey had met midway through their freshman year of college and were already living together (although my parents didn't know that). Alan was six-foot-two and skinny, with a long, curly, black ponytail.

I saw right away, on meeting Alan, that Audrey loved him, and that was enough to make me like him. But what cemented it was Alan's and my discovery, on the long ride from Calgary, that we were both Bob Dylan fanatics. All the way to Galena Bay, we debated which were his best songs.

"'Tombstone Blues,'" I said.

Alan waved his hand. "'Sad-eyed Lady of the Lowlands.' Can you imagine having a song like that written about you?"

He had a point. "Yeah, but if you're talking about the best lyrics ever, it's 'A Hard Rain's a-Gonna Fall.' End of story. Period. In fact, *Freewheelin'* is my favourite album."

"Are you crazy? *Blonde on Blonde* is a masterpiece!"

And so on.

Alan was an American Studies major. When I asked what that meant, he explained that it looked at all aspects of American culture: art, music, film, literature, politics, sociology. From that perspective, he was interested in what Bill and I were doing as a social phenomenon.

"Why'd you want to leave the States?" he asked one day when he was helping me weed the garden. "You could do this in California, or Oregon, or Colorado. In fact, from what I hear, lots of people are."

"Well, Nixon ... Watergate ... Vietnam ..."

"But Bill's not a draft dodger, is he? You didn't have to leave?"

"No, he got a deferment," I said, and told him about Bill's meeting with the sympathetic Quaker psychiatrist who had furnished him with a letter saying that he was unfit for service, based on highly exaggerated drug use.

"But it's the whole war machine, the militaristic attitude that we have the right to invade your country and tell you how to live."

Alan nodded. "Okay, I get that. But how's this—" he swept his hand outward, as if to indicate the entire homestead, "—going to change anything?"

I looked past him at the cabin, and the forest beyond. "To be honest, I don't know. Maybe it won't. But if more and more people refuse to go along with the status quo, refuse to be consumers, refuse to contribute to pollution, it's got to have an effect on society. It's got to get people thinking, maybe change their values. At least I hope so."

Alan shrugged. "You guys have a more positive idea of human nature than I do. I don't think there's a hope in hell."

"It can't hurt."

"No, it can't. And in the meantime, you're having a pretty amazing experience." He leaned close. "Must be pretty easy to grow your own dope out here."

I laughed. "It is. We've got a dozen plants down the back road. Normally Bill would be watering them every day. But we thought we'd better put that on hold while the parents are here."

"Think Bill could take me on a little jaunt to see them?"

"Sure."

Bill and Alan came back with a smug smile ... and slightly bloodshot eyes.

My family stayed in Galena Bay for four days. Each night, the five of them trooped down the driveway to the Winnebago. They exclusively used the toilet on board, avoiding the outhouse, and took turns showering in a tiny stall rather than undergo the thrill of seeing whether there was enough warm water in the hose to last through a shower. (Usually there wasn't, and, like in a low-rent apartment, you felt the water gradually get cooler ... and cooler ... until you finished under an ice-cold spray.)

I have to give my parents credit. They put up with my lentil soup and heavy whole wheat bread ("It's *grainy*," David remarked), my homemade granola, and, since it was one of the few garden crops that was flourishing, zucchini everything: zucchini pancakes, zucchini muffins, zucchini casserole.

Even more impressively, they put up with Bill's and my self-righteousness.

When Alan lifted a forkful of vegetarian lasagna and said, "Don't you miss the meat layer?" I replied, "No! The meat industry is responsible for polluting hundreds of rivers and streams with fertilizers, and turning the prairies into a monoculture desert."

When my mother, touring the garden, said, 'You two have sure put a lot of work into this," I said, "Yeah, and you and Dad should dig up the back yard and plant a garden. Grass is a waste of space."

When I mentioned that Bill and I went into town only once a week, and my father said, "Gee, your gas bills must be low," I said, "Yeah. You guys should keep your car in the garage and take the bus."

"I don't think I could get to the hospital to make my rounds on the bus," my father said quietly.

I was undaunted. So charged with excitement about what we were doing, so filled with information from all the books we were reading and the conversations we were having with our neighbour Bob, I couldn't—or wouldn't—restrain myself. Bill and I, I believed, were doing the right thing, and everybody should follow our example.

When I look back, I cringe at how obnoxious I must have been, and I'm amazed at my visitors' forbearance.

After a few days in Galena Bay, we all travelled down to Kaslo to visit Michael and Vivianne. Michael met us at the bottom of their hill in an old pickup truck they had bought, and we all piled in, my parents in the front seat, the rest of us in the bed. I could see my parents bounce up and down, their heads nearly hitting the ceiling of the cab as the truck jolted over potholes and swerved around boulders.

Michael and Vivianne's cabin, a one-storey, twelve-foot by sixteen-foot structure built of salvaged lumber, made our cabin look palatial. We all squished in, my parents on two chairs that Vivianne had scrounged from somewhere, the rest of us on stumps or on the floor. Vivianne served tea and cookies, and we chatted about Michael and Vivianne's plans to get jobs in town to earn enough to buy a horse (a lifelong dream of Vivianne's), about our gardens and how they were coming along, and about our grandiose aspirations to have self-sufficient homesteads within five years.

"So, Ruth and Bernie, what do you think of Bill and Ellen's place?" Michael asked.

There was a moment of silence. "Very nice," my mother said.

"They've put a lot of work into it," my father said.

Another silence.

As the conversation went on, I could see my mother looking more and more uncomfortable, although I couldn't tell if it was the topics we were discussing or a physical ailment that was bothering her. Finally, she stood up. Looking embarrassed, she said, "Uh ... I have to go ... is there ...?" Her voice trailed off.

Michael rose. Without a word, he handed her a shovel. He pointed out the window. "That way."

It took a moment for the truth to dawn on my mother's face. It would have been bad enough to go in an outhouse, but Michael and Vivianne hadn't even built one yet.

My mother's shoulders slumped. She headed out the door and across the logged-over clearing beside the cabin, past bracken and fallen branches, to the shelter of the trees.

My father snapped a picture, and it is in the family scrapbook—my mother, Ruthie Rosenberg, doctor's wife, arts patron, Saks Fifth Avenue shopper—trudging through the woods on a godforsaken mountainside to dig a hole, squat, and do her business.

Later, we all laughed about it, even my mother. But at the moment, all I could think of as I watched her small round figure walk away was *Poor Mom.*

My parents visited several more times. Once they even slept in the cabin. Bill and I camped in a tent while they gamely, if slowly, climbed up the ladder to the loft and lowered themselves onto the mattress. My father split a few pieces of wood. My mother helped me cook oatmeal on the woodstove. They even used the outhouse.

"The garden's doing better, isn't it?" my mother said on that visit. We were picking peas, pushing our way through chest-high vines tied to stakes, pulling off the plump pods and tossing them into a basket.

"Here, eat some," I said, splitting open a pod and handing it to her.

"Raw?"

"Yeah. Just try it."

She stripped the pod and popped the peas in her mouth. A look of wonder came over her face. "I've never eaten anything so sweet."

A warm feeling went through me. "Amazing, aren't they? Here, try a fresh bean."

On later visits, my parents commented on the beautiful scenery that surrounded us and complimented us on the work we had done: clearing the upper field, planting a buckwheat cover crop, putting in a second garden. But in spite of their growing appreciation of what homesteading involved and of the new skills Bill and I had acquired, I don't think they ever truly understood why we wanted to live there. Why, I could see them wondering, were we content to live such a difficult life, one in which we had to cut down trees and split logs to heat our house? Why would we want to make do with propane lights and live without refrigeration and indoor plumbing and running hot water? Why would we choose to live so far away from town, neighbours, friends, parties, movies, museums?

I can't fault them. Born in 1923, they were children of the Great Depression. In their world, financial security was a cherished ideal, along with working in a respected profession, having status in your community, and, if all went well, enjoying luxury: a beautiful home, the ability to go on vacations, eat in good restaurants, wear nice clothes, and drive a powerful car.

Bill and I, part of the first wave of baby boomers, were in the privileged position of having enough education, enough wealth, and enough leisure to be able to criticize our parents' lifestyle. We were well-off enough to be able to turn our backs on materialism. We were prosperous enough to indulge in idealism and, idealistically, to define an entire new set of values. (At the time, I didn't appreciate the irony.)

So it's not surprising that my parents, while supportive, remained baffled by my choice.

But I wanted more than just support. More than acceptance. I wanted them to get it, to get *me*. That they didn't remained a source of sadness.

Still, I'm grateful for the support and acceptance they did muster. From Linden, New Jersey, to Galena Bay, British Columbia; from a large, modern, split-level house to a rough-hewn cabin; from New York symphony halls to the melodious chorus of Swainson's thrushes at dusk—what an incredible and, in some ways, unbridgeable distance.

When you're twenty-three, and madly in love, and filled with idealism, and eager for adventure, you don't think about the long-term implications of a decision to move three-thousand miles away from your family. If you had asked me, in 1972, "Do you plan to stay in British Columbia permanently?" I would have answered, "Sure, why not?"

It was only later that I came to understand how that decision affected *me*—how I was losing out.

I missed teasing my mother about going to the beauty parlour every Friday. "God forbid you should skip a week and have one hair out of place," I used to say, sending her into peals of laughter.

I missed seeing David grow up.

I missed family dinners where every single one of us had to compliment my grandmother on her pot roast or her potato latkes or her pound cake, before she would believe it was good.

I even missed the interminable Passover seders with my grandfather droning over the *Hagaddah*.

These feelings of loss didn't hit me right away. At first, I was too excited about my new life. After a few years, though, when we went back east, I began to notice that I was no longer in the thick of family conversations. I saw how my relatives had common experiences that I no longer shared. They had new gossip and new memories to laugh about. They spoke the shorthand of familial understanding.

"Wasn't that funny when Dad saw a patient at the opera and buried his head in his program so he wouldn't be seen?"

"Didn't Mom do an amazing job of organizing that Hadassah conference?"

"Weren't Grandma's matzo balls lighter than air?"

I didn't know. I wasn't there.

It was my own doing. It was my choice. But I still felt like I was missing out.

This sense of loss became more acute when our first child, Merri, was born. I was anxious for my daughter to experience the joy of close family contact, to know her grandparents and aunts and uncles and cousins. I made sure to visit at least once a year. My parents, to their credit, came once a year as well, and Bill's mom made the trek almost as often. I pinned family photos to a bulletin board on the cabin wall and told Merri stories about the people in the pictures. "That's Papa. He's a doctor. Remember when he let you play with his stethoscope?" "That's Nana. Remember Jamie, her little white dog?"

It took dedication, on both sides, to make all those trips. In the end, Merri and Amy established close, loving ties with their extended families. But it always hurt my heart when we were back east and their cousins played more easily with one another than they did with my children. It was only to be expected. After all, they lived nearer each other and saw each other more often and shared more family dinners and celebrated more holidays together. Still, I couldn't help regret that I had forced on Merri and Amy the separation that I had chosen for myself.

Over the five decades that have passed since Bill and I moved to British Columbia, we often discuss what we have gained and what we have lost.

"Aren't you glad we live in Canada rather than the US?" he'll ask.

"Yes, of course I am."

"And don't you think we've had a better quality of life here?"

"Absolutely."

"And don't you appreciate the fact that we're surrounded by a beautiful environment?"

"Mmm-hmm."

"And don't you think this was a better place to raise our kids?"

"No question."

If Merri and Amy are present, they will chime in. "We're happy we grew up here," Merri will say. "It's beautiful and peaceful."

"And relatively clean and green," Amy will add.

"And not warlike."

"And a more mutually supportive society."

"Sure, we didn't get to be as close with the grandparents as the cousins did," Merri will acknowledge. "And sure, we didn't get to spend as much time with the cousins as we would have liked. But we're still close with them."

"And we—the four of us—got to do things our way, and pull together as a family," Amy will say.

All true. On balance, I agree that our move to Canada, and our lives in Canada, have been positive. We have gained more than we have lost—much more.

But there *has* been loss. For me, that is indisputable. It is the price that my eager, idealistic twenty-three-year-old self did not foresee.

One day in about 2010, my mother and I were sitting at the kitchen table in Linden. My father was upstairs, reading; Bill was in the basement, watching TV.

My mother and I were reminiscing about my parents' first visit to Galena Bay.

"I'll never forget walking into the cabin," my mother said. "I thought, 'My Ellen, living like this?'"

"I was really hurt," I told her. "Bill and I had built it with our own hands."

My mother nodded. "I know. I felt bad. But I had never seen anything so primitive. I didn't know how to react."

"It *was* pretty cramped," I said.

"But I could see you were happy."

"You could?" I felt a lift.

"Sure. I couldn't imagine why you would want to live like that, but it was obvious that you and Bill were excited about it."

I wished she had told me that back then. It would have made me feel better.

I felt a gathering in my chest—a question that I had been carrying all these years. A question I had always been too afraid to ask.

I forced it out. "Can you forgive me for moving away?"

My mother looked at me like I was crazy. "Of course! Did you think we were angry at you all this time?"

"I don't know. Angry. Hurt. Upset."

My mother took my hand. "It's true that we weren't happy when you left. It was so far away, such a foreign idea. We missed you. But we were never angry."

"But ... but I hurt you," I said.

"We loved you. How could we be hurt when you were doing what you loved?"

"You weren't mad?" I said to my lap.

My mother lifted my chin with her finger. "*Mommie-shainie*, listen to me. You were entitled. Entitled to live your life. To do things your way."

"But—"

"No. Listen. You were always independent, always rebellious. Dad and I knew we had to let you go. We didn't say it out loud, but we knew we were smothering you. That's why, when you told us you were going to BC, we weren't entirely surprised. Deep down, we knew you needed to get away."

"You did?"

"Well, we didn't exactly expect you to live in the suburbs and shop at Saks."

I managed a strangled laugh.

"Now, don't get me wrong, we didn't expect you to go off to the middle of nowhere. We weren't wild about that idea. But you had to do it. You were entitled."

That broke the dam. I lay my head on the kitchen table and sobbed. My mother put her arms around my shoulders. "Ellen ... *mommie-shainie* ..."

My father must have heard my weeping, because he came downstairs. My mother recounted our conversation. He put his hand on my shoulder. "We love you so much, Ell, you could never hurt us," he said. "There's nothing to forgive."

I'd like to say that I shed all my feelings of guilt on that day. I didn't. I suppose I will always have them.

But those words—"You were entitled. There's nothing to forgive"— relieved a large part of my burden.

That wasn't all. I realized that, although my parents didn't understand my choice of lifestyle, they understood *me*. They let me go.

That, I realized as I finally dried my eyes, was love.

Misadventures

In the pines

In the fall of 1974, Bill and I noticed an influx of people wandering the woods of Galena Bay. (The increase totalled only eight or ten, but, considering that that more than doubled the full-time population, it could justifiably be considered an influx.) We spotted them bent over with small spades in their hands and wicker baskets slung over their shoulders. After making inquiries, we learned that the strangers were searching for pine mushrooms.

Walter told us that the foragers sold their haul to buyers in Revelstoke, who in turn sold them to dealers in Japan. Apparently, the mushrooms were highly prized there, where they not only featured in seasonal recipes but also were believed to hold medicinal value and to increase vigour and longevity.

"I've heard that the buyers in Revelstoke are paying more than twenty dollars a pound," he said.

"Twenty dollars a pound!" I repeated, looking at Bill. Regular white mushrooms cost about three dollars a pound in the grocery store, and thus, for us, were a rare treat.

Later, Bill said to me, "That's a lot of money for wild mushrooms. Are you thinking what I'm thinking?"

"You bet. I mean, we wouldn't make a living at it ..."

"No, of course not. But a little extra cash would come in handy."

"We don't know any buyers in Revelstoke," I pointed out.

"True. But if the demand is as high as Walter says it is, it shouldn't be too hard to find one."

"Okay! Let's do it."

Neither Bill nor I had ever foraged for mushrooms before, and naturally we didn't want to pick poisonous varieties by mistake. We consulted the

Field Guide to Mushrooms of British Columbia and found out that pine mushrooms, *Tricholoma magnivelare,* grew at the base of lodgepole pine, Douglas fir, and hemlock trees. They were often submerged under the soil and leaf litter of the forest, though sometimes you could spot a pointy white top poking above the ground. The mushrooms ranged in size from that of a plum to that of a grapefruit, and were shaped like portabellas, but with a more pointed cap. Dense and meaty, they had a strong aroma and a resinous flavour.

The guide said that no poisonous mushrooms closely resembled the pine mushroom. That was a relief, but, just to be sure, we checked out some of the bad ones. The false chanterelles were orange on the cap and the gills. The scarily-named death cap had a much longer stem and a thinner cap. The blue-staining boletes were similar in shape, but turned blue when bruised or broken.

"We'll break off a piece and make sure it doesn't turn blue," Bill said, and I nodded.

Reasonably reassured, one cool, cloudy October day, we tucked the *Field Guide* into a rucksack, grabbed a couple of burlap sacks and hand spades, and set off to earn some easy money.

The **bay** part of Galena Bay is a west-facing, scooped-out curve in Upper Arrow Lake, which is part of the Columbia River. The ferry dock is located a few miles south of the lower end of the curve. A peninsula of land delineates the upper part of the bay, and locals call that area Galena Point.

Bill and I had seen mushroom pickers in the woods along the dirt roads that threaded through Galena Bay. We figured that few of those people would have ventured out onto Galena Point, so we decided to focus our search there.

We drove as far as the road reached, at the eastern end of Galena Point. By this time, it was about two in the afternoon. We followed a faint trail into the woods. The trail shortly disappeared, and we walked in the forest, pausing at each tree, looking for telltale white mounds on the ground.

I spotted a rounded hump at the base of a fir tree. "Here's one ... I think," I said. I dug underneath, loosening the soil, then carefully pried the mushroom up. Bill came over and broke off a small piece of the cap. We waited. Nothing happened. The cap and the piece stayed white.

"Whew," I said, and put the mushroom in my sack.

A moment later, Bill found one. We repeated the bolete test. Nothing turned blue. After a few more tests, when no colours changed, we grew more confident, first, that we could correctly identify pine mushrooms, and second, that we weren't going to find any blue-staining boletes in these woods.

We separated, walking from tree to tree. The mushrooms seemed to favour dry, sandy soil with a great deal of leaf litter. That made them hard to find, and sometimes we had to pry them out from beneath rocks or between roots. But there were plenty of them, and after an hour or so, we had each filled half of our sacks.

"They're heavy," I said, slinging my sack over my shoulder.

Bill nodded. "Maybe we should head home."

"Okay. This is a good haul, huh? How many pounds do you think we've got?"

Bill held both bags out in front of him. "Maybe twenty in mine, fifteen in yours."

"Thirty-five pounds!" I did the math. "That's seven hundred bucks!"

We grinned at each other.

We hefted our sacks and looked around. We were in the middle of the woods. There were no trails, just the trunks of hemlocks, pines, firs, and cedars rising all around us.

"Well, we know the lake is to the south. So once we spot water, we can walk east and hit the road," I said.

But, peering through the trees, we could see no sign of the lake, no shine or reflection of water.

"It must be about four o'clock, right?" Bill said. "So if we can see the sun, we'll know which way is west."

But the sky was completely obscured by clouds.

"Which way do you think we came from?" I said.

Bill shrugged, pointing. "Let's try that way."

We did, scrambling over hummocks and down depressions and around rocks.

"I think that stump looks familiar," I said.

Fifteen minutes later, we were still in the middle of the forest, and nothing looked familiar. Or, rather, everything did.

My sack of mushrooms was heavy on my shoulder.

"Here, let me take some of those," Bill said.

I let him dump a third of my mushrooms into his sack and gratefully hefted my lighter load.

We tried another direction, then another. Late afternoon shadows deepened.

"If we have to spend the night …" I began.

"We won't have to spend the night," Bill said.

"I was just going to say it's not that cold. And maybe the sky'll be clear in the morning and we can figure out where we are." Though I dreaded the thought of sleeping on the forest floor in nothing more than a flannel shirt and jeans.

We wandered, peering through the thickening gloom. We looked for spots where the leaf litter at the base of trees had been disturbed, indicating that we had harvested mushrooms there. But the piles of dead needles and ferns and leaves all looked the same.

After another half hour of fruitless wandering, Bill said, "There's no sense schlepping all these mushrooms around. They're probably bruised and not worth much anyway."

"You mean dump them?"

"Well, not all of them. We can keep some to eat, or try to sell."

We went through our bags, tossing out the most bruised and mangled specimens until we had emptied most of our harvest on the ground.

"There goes our fortune," I sighed.

"Yeah, too bad. But there are plenty more. We can come back tomorrow."

"No thanks!"

With lighter loads, we set forth with new energy. Finally, at about five-thirty, when we could hardly see where to place each step, we stumbled on a faint path on the ground.

"Do you think that's the trail?" I said.

"I sure hope so."

We followed the barely visible path. The way ahead looked less dense, though it was hard to be sure in the gathering dark.

The trees thinned, and we emerged into the clearing. There was our truck.

"Yay!" I shouted.

"I knew we'd find our way," Bill said. I looked at him and we both laughed.

At home, after taking off our filthy clothes and washing, and after I had scrubbed a couple of the mushrooms we had salvaged, I sliced and sautéed them, added eggs and cheese, and we sat down to our first pine mushroom omelette.

The mushrooms had a strong, resinous, almost tarry taste.

"I don't like them," I said.

"I don't either," Bill said.

We dumped the omelette in the compost and ate toast and peanut butter for dinner.

"Should I save the rest?" I asked, looking at the twenty or so mushrooms sitting on the counter.

"They're not in very good shape," Bill said. "Probably no one will buy them."

We tossed those mushrooms in the compost, too. And that was the end of our pine mushroom money-making venture.

Chainsaw massacre

In the winter of 1975, Bill and I started clearing a large swath of land, about an acre and a half. We planned to put in a hayfield and pasture for dairy goats, plant a larger garden plot, and build a log house.

This time we were using a chainsaw. We felt sheepish and slightly ashamed, because of the noise and the pollution, but we had learned our lesson the first winter, when we had bucked all the logs from the lower clearing with a Swede saw. Aesthetically pleasing and environmentally benign, yes, the only sound the rasp of the saw blade as it bit through the fragrant wood. Efficient, no. It took forever. We succumbed and purchased a noisy, smelly Stihl saw.

Every day, except for "town days," we headed outside to work on the clearing. Bill felled the trees with the chainsaw, I hacked off the limbs with an axe, Bill bucked the logs into eight- or twelve-foot lengths, and we piled them in stacks around the ever-growing clearing: hemlocks and firs and birches for firewood, cedars for fence posts and building logs for our future home. Every day we stood at the back of the new clearing and looked at the expanding view to the west, toward Mounts Odin, Thor, and Freya. Every day we could see a little more of their peaks.

One day, while we were snowshoeing to where our truck was parked on Hill Creek Road, we heard a loud racket in the bush about a quarter-mile down the back road. When we came closer, we saw a huge yellow snow Caterpillar in the woods. A man wielding a chainsaw tackled a tall hemlock. The tree fell. Another man bucked the branches with a smaller gasoline-powered saw. A third man, driving the Cat, pushed the log over to where a pile was growing.

"Loggers," I said disdainfully to Bill.

"Wonder whose property that is," he answered. "Hope they don't make too big a mess."

I snorted. "They always do."

A thought prickled. What we were doing on our land wasn't all that different. We were cutting trees. They were cutting trees.

But we're doing it with love and care, I told myself. *They're doing it for a quick buck.*

As we passed, the fellow driving the Cat raised his hand. Bill and I half-heartedly raised ours. After that, we saw the loggers every time we passed down the back road. We exchanged curt nods but didn't speak.

One day in February, after we had been working for about four hours, Bill abruptly turned off the chainsaw. The silence of the snow-covered forest returned. "I'm going inside for a minute," he said. "Be right back."

I nodded and continued chopping branches off fallen trees. It wasn't uncommon for Bill to halt work to fill the saw's tank with gas and oil, or to sharpen the chain. This was nothing out of the ordinary.

By the time I had I finished limbing the latest batch of felled trees, though, Bill still had not returned. For a moment I was annoyed: *What's he doing, taking a nap?* Then I got concerned. I put down the axe and went into the cabin.

That was when I saw Bill holding his right thigh, just above the knee, his jeans torn, blood seeping down his leg.

"What happened?" I gasped.

"I was stupid," he said. "Was getting tired but didn't want to stop. The saw slipped and I cut myself. I've been trying to get it to stop bleeding, but it won't."

I froze. We had no electricity, no phone. Our truck was parked a mile and a quarter away, at the end of the unplowed back road. Clearly Bill had to get to a hospital—but how? He couldn't snowshoe all the way out. He'd lose too much blood.

Then I remembered: the loggers. Ordinarily we considered them the enemy. Right now, they were my best friends.

"Stay here," I said to Bill, quickly explaining my plan. Pale-faced, he nodded. I threw on my snowshoes and *ran* down the back road, breathing hard, sweating, occasionally tripping over my feet and hauling myself up, to where they were working. I waved my arms and yelled. "Help!"

The guy with the large chainsaw spotted me. He shut off the saw and came over. Panting, I explained.

Without a word, the three loggers sprang into action. They started up the snow Cat, I climbed aboard, and we rumbled back over the three-foot-deep snowpack toward the cabin. While they turned the Cat around at the foot of the driveway, I ran up to the cabin to get Bill. He had wrapped a clean cloth around his thigh. The wound was still seeping, though not, I hoped, at a life-threatening rate.

One of the guys helped Bill climb onto the snow Cat and settled him in the cab. The loggers drove us all the way down the back road to where our truck was parked. Every time the Cat lurched over a bump, Bill grimaced, but he didn't say anything. I kept my eyes on the road ahead. *Come on, come on*, I thought, willing the truck to come into view.

Finally, we got there. One of the loggers helped Bill down and into the truck. "Good luck," he said, banging the bed by way of goodbye. They all waved.

I was so choked up I could barely speak. "Thank you. Thank you so much."

I headed toward Nakusp. Revelstoke had a bigger hospital, while Nakusp had only a small clinic, but to go to Revelstoke we'd have had to wait for the ferry, and the trip would have taken over an hour longer. Even so, the ride seemed to take forever. The first fifteen miles were on a gravel road, and the packed-down snow made humps and ridges. The truck bounced even though I went over them carefully.

"You okay?" I asked, darting a glance at Bill.

He nodded, though his jaw looked grim.

"In pain?"

"Not too much."

"How's the bleeding?"

"Not too bad."

I risked a glance at the cloth around his leg. It looked redder, I thought.

By now we had reached the paved part of the road. I sped up. Fifty ... sixty ... seventy ...

"Take it easy," Bill said. "It would be a huge bummer to die on the way to the hospital."

I managed a laugh. The fact that he could joke comforted me.

Finally, forty-five minutes after we'd reached the truck, we arrived in Nakusp. I dropped Bill off at the hospital and went to park. By the time I dashed inside, he was getting stitched up.

"He's lucky," the doctor told me. "A few inches higher and he would have cut an artery."

I collapsed onto a chair.

"The cut is wide but not too deep," the doctor went on. "There's some tissue damage but nothing that'll cause problems in the future."

I grabbed Bill's hand and squeezed.

The next day I took a batch of home-baked muffins to the loggers. They were embarrassed to be thanked, glad that Bill was okay. We had a conversation, about the perils of working in the woods, about gory accidents they had heard about—or experienced themselves.

After that, when Bill and I went back out to work on our clearing, I kept my eye on him. Every couple of hours, I said, "Let's take a break." Bill shot me a look, as if to say *I don't need one*, but he shut off the saw and came inside with me. We both knew what could happen when you got over-tired.

Bill still has the scar, about three inches long by half an inch wide, on his right thigh. Amazingly, that was the only serious medical emergency we had in our eight years in Galena Bay.

And I learned something about loggers.

Around the bay

On a sparkling, cold January afternoon in 1976, Bill and I set out, with our friends Ray and Barbara, to snowshoe on Galena Point.

Ray and Barbara, the people who had introduced us to cross-country skiing, were spending the winter in Nakusp, where Barbara worked as a nurse. Once every few weeks, they came up to Galena Bay and we skied or snowshoed and had a meal together.

We parked the truck near the starting point of Bill's and my ill-fated pine mushroom expedition. A snowpack of about three feet covered the ground. It had barely snowed for several days, and the nights had been frigid, in the teens Fahrenheit, so the snow had packed down with a nice crust. The night before, a light skiff had fallen.

While we put our snowshoes on, I noticed a trail of large paw prints in the snow. They measured a good four inches across. I knew they weren't from a bear, or a dog.

"Is that ... a cougar?" I asked.

Barbara, who had grown up in Jasper, Alberta, and knew wildlife better than the rest of us, came over to examine it.

"Yup."

"I'm sure it's long gone," Ray said.

The tracks looked fresh to me. I knew that cougars were unlikely to hunt during the day, and even less likely to attack a group of adult humans. Still, I shuddered.

We set out westward. Our plan was to walk to the western edge of the Point, enjoy the view, eat lunch, then turn around and retrace our steps to the truck. I had invited Ray and Barbara to join us for dinner.

The snowshoeing was easy, and we chatted as we walked. Initially, we went two abreast, then, once we entered the woods, went single-file, taking turns breaking trail. About an hour later, we stood on a high bluff overlooking the lake. To the south, on our left, jutted out the spit of land that formed the upper end of Galena Bay. To the north, Arrow Lake narrowed and extended toward the abandoned mining town of Beaton, out of sight around a curve. Westward, directly in front of us, the Monashee Mountains glittered white against a cobalt sky.

We sat on the cliff, snowshoes dangling, sharing homemade bread, cheese, and apples. By this time, it was about three in the afternoon, and shadows were lengthening. I shivered as my sweat evaporated in the cold air.

When we packed up to return, Ray said, "Let's not go back the same way. That's boring. Let's go down to the lake and walk along the bay."

"It'll take longer," Bill said.

Ray shook his head. "Not really. It's the same distance back, we'll just be doing it at lake level instead of up here. And it'll be pretty by the lake."

Bill looked at me. I shrugged. "As long as we get there before dark."

We snowshoed diagonally down the slope, zigzagging around trees and rocks. Sliding down the last steep bit, we arrived at the lakeshore, at the north end of the bay.

Ray was right. It *was* pretty. Along the shore, the lake was frozen for about three feet out. Beyond that, the water gleamed dark grey. Because of undulations in the bay, we couldn't see clear across to the eastern shore, where we had started out, but we could see trees rising on the slope and knew that our cabin was tucked into the woods back there. In the distance, to the south, we could see the ferry crossing to Shelter Bay.

Barbara looked at her watch. "That must be the 3:30 sailing."

I nodded, calculating. If it took us a little longer to get back to the truck than it had taken us to get here, say, an hour and a half, we'd reach it by about 5:00. Forty-five minutes from our parking spot on Hill Creek Road to the cabin ... I could have dinner on the table by 6:30, and Ray and Barbara could head back to Nakusp at a reasonable hour.

The beach was flat, the snow shallow and hard-packed, so we took off our snowshoes and tucked them under our arms. After about ten minutes of easy walking, though, the beach ended in a jumble of boulders that jutted out into the lake. Ice sparkled on the stones' surfaces.

"Do we have to climb over them?" I asked.

Ray shook his head. "We can walk around them on the ice."

We ventured carefully onto the frozen lake. Close in, the ice was thick and opaque, but as soon as we moved out far enough to skirt the boulders, it creaked beneath our feet.

"That doesn't mean anything," Ray said. "Ice always makes noise."

We edged farther out. Clicks popped underfoot. A crack appeared, and we scrambled back to shore.

"Guess it wasn't thick enough," Ray muttered.

Our choices now were to climb over the boulders or climb back up the slope and walk in the woods.

"I vote for the woods," I said, and although I could tell that Ray was all for icy rock-scaling, the others agreed.

We climbed on an angle, carefully placing our feet between rocks and tree roots. It was a slog, but eventually we reached a level bench overlooking the lake. Here, though, the snow was deep, so we put our snowshoes back on and again took turns breaking trail.

When we had covered a few hundred yards, Ray pointed down toward the lake. "Look. We've gone past the boulders, and the beach is open again."

"It *would* be easier to walk down there," Barbara said.

Again, we snowshoed down the slope, reached the beach, and removed our snowshoes.

By now, it was nearly dusk. We still couldn't see straight across to our destination because a curve in the bay blocked the view. But I was sure that once we hiked around that curve we'd be able to see our ending point. I wasn't even concerned about the growing dark. We knew where we were. We were close.

But when we came around the curve, instead of seeing the open bay, we were greeted by another curve of land.

I exchanged looks with Bill.

"After this one, surely," he said in a low voice.

No such luck. Not only was there yet another curve to walk around, but at the apex of the curve a jumbled pile of driftwood logs prevented our passage.

"Guess we're going up again," Ray said with a sigh.

Again, we trekked uphill, sinking into the snow. Again, at the top, we put our snowshoes back on. A half moon had risen, and the snow and ice at the lakeshore gleamed in its wintry light. But up here, in the woods, it was dark. The trees cast shadows, and it was hard to discern where was a safe place to step, what was a depression, what was a half-buried rock. The tip of my snowshoe jammed under a tree root, and I sank to my knees, soaking my jeans. Behind me, I could hear Bill breathing heavily.

After a short distance we emerged from the woods and headed back down to the lake. The walking was easier, and the lake and shore shone silver in the moonlight. But there was another curve, and another. And then another obstacle on the beach, and we had to climb back up to get around it.

"Are we going to have to spend the night up here?" I whispered to Bill.

"I don't think so."

But it looked like we would never get there. And of course we had come out unprepared. There was plenty of snow for water, but we were out of food and had no matches for starting a fire.

Then I remembered the cougar tracks. I looked around, imagining a sleek, furry body hidden on a tree branch, a pair of yellow eyes trained on me in the dark, waiting to pounce. I shivered.

For another hour, we scrambled up the slope, walked in the woods, traversed down, walked along the beach, came to another obstacle. Snowshoes on, snowshoes off. Ice, snow, sand, rocks. Full dark. Another curve. Another.

The temperature fell. My sweat evaporated, and I felt chilled. And afraid. What if we *did* have to spend the night in the woods? We could huddle together, but it would still be frigid. It was January: the night would be long.

What idiots we were for coming out unprepared. What idiots we were for following Ray's suggestion. What idiots we were for underestimating the circumference of the bay, with all its curves and twists.

Finally, we came around the last curve, and there, spread before us, was the open bay. It was too dark to see our destination, or the truck, but they were *there*, within reach.

We quickened our steps. Thankfully we encountered no more obstacles on the beach.

Next to the truck, the cougar tracks had iced over. The prints made shadowy depressions, and their edges sparkled in the moonlight.

By the time we got back to the cabin, it was eight o'clock. We had been trekking for six hours.

I threw together a quick dinner of scrambled eggs and toast. We drank strong cups of tea with lots of milk and sugar. We fell on our food as if we hadn't eaten in a week. We didn't speak, just ate, listening to the melodious crackle of the woodstove.

Ray and Barbara stayed over on Paul's mattress on the floor. After I got them settled, it was all I could do to drag myself up the ladder to the loft. As Bill and I snuggled under our quilt, I heard a high-pitched, ululating cry. It sounded like a woman wailing.

A cougar.

Epilogue

We learned our lesson. After Bill cut his leg, we took a St. John's Ambulance course and put together a first aid kit. After our snowy trek on Galena Point, we started carrying a compass and matches.

The precautions took some of the romance out of our adventures. But at least we survived to have more of them.

14

Paul

"I choose Galena Bay."

When Paul chose Galena Bay, on the night in August 1972 when Bill, Paul, Michael, Vivianne, and I wrestled with the choice between Galena Bay and South Fork, I was surprised. Not that he would favour Galena Bay. I could tell that the gentleness of the land, with its promise of year-round sunshine and the potential for a good growing season, appealed to him. And I knew that he was turned off by the logged-over mess on the Kaslo land, as were Bill and I.

What did surprise me was that Paul would choose to join Bill rather than Michael. Paul and Michael had formed a close bond out in Oregon, and their closeness continued in Pennsylvania. Michael was an upbeat, gregarious person, and his optimism meshed with Paul's quiet, sensitive character. Bill, on the other hand, was assertive and strong-willed. He believed in the project so strongly that his dedication sometimes came across as combativeness: *Are you in or out? If you're not sure, get lost.* I sensed that, although Bill and Paul liked each other, Bill secretly doubted Paul's commitment, while Paul sometimes found Bill's brashness off-putting.

But Paul chose Galena Bay. And so, we started our experiment in homesteading as a threesome.

That fall, we worked hard. We cleared a quarter-acre of land, built the cabin, dug the water line, prepared a garden spot, and built an outhouse. Of all those jobs, the water line and the garden were the hardest. No, not just hard. Brutal.

Paul, Bill, and I started each day full of energy. We shoved our spades into rock-packed earth. We heaved pickaxes and chopped at tree roots. Sometimes it took forty-five minutes to dig up a single root or boulder.

As the days went on, I noticed that Paul took longer and more frequent breaks—when he went into the cabin for a drink of water, when he went to the outhouse, when he paused to wipe his face or push his hair out of his eyes or examine a mosquito bite. I couldn't blame him. I hated the work, too. But somehow, maybe because I had Bill, I knew that I could get through it. I wondered if the difficulty and drudgery of this job would change Paul's zest for the very idea of homesteading.

Paul was a fit young man. He was of average height, about five-foot-ten, with a slim build, and had been a very good basketball and tennis player. He wasn't terribly muscular, though, and he tired after a few hours of work.

Bill, on the other hand, was a workhorse. About five-foot-nine, he had a classic mesomorph body: deep chest, broad shoulders, muscular torso and legs. He had been an outstanding athlete in junior high and high school, excelling in football (his first love), basketball, baseball, and track.

Bill's remarkable strength gave him the capacity to work for hours a day. As well, he was so passionate about our homesteading project that I don't think he *allowed* himself to get tired. He could dig the water line for three or four hours, take a break for lunch, go back out for another few hours, then come back to the cabin and split a wheelbarrow full of firewood and haul rocks out of the garden, all before dinner. And do it the next day, and the next.

Paul didn't have that kind of stamina. He worked as hard as anyone could reasonably expect, but he needed to rest. He needed downtime. I sensed an undercurrent of tension between him and Bill, Bill resenting Paul for not working harder, Paul resenting Bill right back for making him feel guilty.

The tension was slight. It was unspoken. But it was there.

Perhaps that was why, one morning in November 1972, as we sat over breakfast, Paul said, "I've been thinking. We've spent a lot on building materials, not to mention the land. We could use some cash, right?"

"Right," I said, wondering where this was going.

Paul nodded. "Michael and Vivianne are going back east for the winter, to substitute-teach and save money. I think I'll go with them. I can live with them at Michael's parents' place and save on rent. I'll be back in the spring with a pile of money. Sound good?"

"Sure, if that's what you want to do," Bill said.

"I think it's for the best," Paul said. "We can't do any building projects over the winter anyway. And this way we'll have an infusion of cash when spring rolls around."

And Bill and I will have some privacy, I thought, secretly glad.

Another thought niggled. *I wonder if Paul just wants to get away from Galena Bay. Away from Bill and his bossiness. Away from the snow and the trees. The solitude. The loneliness.*

Spirituality

For as long as I had known him, Paul had been interested in spirituality. This wasn't unusual in our generation. During the sixties and seventies, many young people had turned away from traditional religions (in our commune, for example, all of us except Vivianne were Jewish, but not one of us was observant) and turned instead toward Eastern spirituality and mysticism. Partly this was the influence of the Beats, some of whom, like Allen Ginsberg, championed Buddhism. Partly it was dissatisfaction with the materialism we saw around us, a search for something more meaning-ful. (Ironically, the post-war affluence that we baby boomers enjoyed gave us the leisure to reject it.) Partly it was the fact that many young people, me included, equated organized religion with the establishment: the govern-ment, the military, all the institutions we were rebelling against.

In college, I dabbled in yoga and meditation, but only sporadically. Stilling the mind was a lot more arduous than getting high and letting the mind trip out. Besides, sitting in the lotus position made my legs fall asleep.

Paul was much more serious. Our second summer in Galena Bay, he became interested in transcendental meditation (TM). This practice had been popularized by The Beatles, who had travelled to India to study under Maharishi Mahesh Yogi, a well-known TM guru. Paul heard about a TM group in Revelstoke and persuaded Bill and me to join him in becoming initiated.

I was skeptical. I didn't enjoy meditation and didn't think, or didn't want to admit, that I needed it. But Bill was interested, and it was uncool to reject anything spiritual, so I agreed to go.

A group of fifteen people gathered in the home of one of the devotees. I was pissed off when I learned that we had to pay $35 apiece to receive our mantras (if meditation was so liberating, shouldn't it be free?), but I kept my mouth shut.

A South Asian man of about fifty, in a white robe and a long beard, sat barefoot on the floor at the front of the room. We all sat before him. He clasped his hands together in the *namaste* position. "Welcome, my dear ones," he said, smiling. "I'm about to impart to you the secrets of transcen-dental meditation, which will lead you to peace and enlightenment."

He beamed from one side of the room to the other. "In a moment, I will give each of you a mantra. This is a unique word, fashioned just for you, that vibrates with the energy of the universe. You are to sit in meditation twice a day for twenty minutes and repeat your mantra in your mind, over and over. If your thoughts wander, do not fret. Just come back to your mantra. You will soon see remarkable effects of calmness and joy in your life."

He called us up one at a time. When it was my turn, he leaned over, cupped his hands around my ear and whispered, "Shireen."

Shireen? I thought. *What kind of strange word is that? Does it mean anything?*

Back in Galena Bay, Bill, Paul, and I faithfully practised our TM. I sat on a pillow on the floor, closed my eyes and thought, "Shireen ... shireen ... shireen ..." My leg itched. I scratched it. *Oops.* "Shireen ... shireen ..." I opened one eye and peeked at our wind-up alarm clock. *Only four minutes gone?* "Shireen ..."

I stuck it out for about a month, then gave it up. Bill was more diligent than I. He carried on meditating for several months. Paul was the most dedicated of all. He sat every morning before breakfast and every evening before dinner. And he did seem more calm and joyful. When he rose from his meditation, he looked refreshed.

I felt like a failure. *What's wrong with me? Why can't I get into it, like Paul?*

Paul's next spiritual exploration was "the Fourth Way," a path of consciousness raising created by a Russian mystic and philosopher named George Gurdjieff, and further developed by his disciple, P.D. Ouspensky. Paul bought Gurdjieff's *All and Everything* and Ouspensky's *In Search of the Miraculous* and read them obsessively. At mealtimes, he explained the philosophy to Bill and me.

"See, we're all spiritually asleep. We don't have a unified body-mind consciousness. We function as automatons, thinking that our narrow perceptions are the whole truth. But we're wrong. What's real is the god inside us. We can transcend to a higher state of consciousness and achieve our full human potential."

"Really? How?" I said dryly.

Paul didn't pick up on the sarcasm. "By doing what Gurdjieff calls the Work. It unites the body, the mind, and the emotions to promote balanced inner development. We have to stop daydreaming and start paying attention to the inner voice."

Is the inner voice saying "Shireen"? I thought rebelliously.

I never figured out exactly what the Work entailed. Paul read and underlined, thought and meditated, wrote in a journal. He seemed like the same old Paul to me, although he was certainly energized with these new ideas.

Bill read *In Search of the Miraculous* but wasn't inspired to follow the Fourth Way. I opened the book. The first page was impenetrable. It put me to sleep—literally.

A couple of years later, Paul met a couple from the Slocan Valley, Pam and Sandy Stevenson, and through them was introduced to yet another spiritual movement, Self-Realization Fellowship (SRF). Paul immediately became interested and persuaded Bill and me to come down to Winlaw, about sixty-five miles south of Galena Bay, to meet Pam and Sandy and hear about SRF.

Pam was a tall, skinny redhead with earnest brown eyes and impossibly long limbs. Born in Hawaii, she had been interested in the mystical lore of the islands from an early age and had a particular affinity for dragons, which she worshipped as ancient spiritual beings. Pam was a talented ceramic artist. At the time I met her, she was experimenting with blue glazes, and her plates and bowls glowed in jewel tones of cobalt, turquoise, and teal. Her cups and urns sprouted twisted, curlicued handles, evoking the wings of Antoni Gaudi's fantastical buildings.

Sandy, who had grown up in the Okanagan, had thick, wavy blond hair and the clearest, Icelandic-blue eyes I had ever seen. He was a metal sculptor, creating wall pieces that depicted mountains, eagles, rivers, gardens, and skies. Many of his sculptures were whimsical, with roly-poly gnomes or mischievous-looking mice hidden behind swirls of bronze.

Bill, Paul, and I sat on stools in Pam and Sandy's tiny kitchen and sipped herbal tea from hand-thrown turquoise mugs. We talked gardening and building, art and music, bears and astrology. Right away, I felt I knew them, felt we spoke the same hippie language. Because I liked them, I agreed to give SRF a try.

SRF had been founded in 1920 by Paramahansa Yogananda. When he was an infant, in India, his parents' guru foretold that he would be a yogi, carrying "many souls to God's kingdom." Later, Yogananda founded Self-Realization Fellowship (SRF) to spread the teachings of *kriya* yoga, a sacred spiritual science originating millennia ago in India.

SRF was an inclusive, non-sectarian philosophy, honouring the saints and prophets of all religions, from Moses, Allah, and Jesus to the holy men and women of Buddhism and Hinduism. As a practice, it incorporated both the physical and the spiritual. Each day, you started with a series of exercises to wake up the body, then sat in meditation for about half an hour. You sang Sanskrit chants. Every week, the SRF Center, in Los Angeles, sent out a package of lessons, including stories and parables told by Yogananda and lessons on such topics as how to weave god into your daily life, yoga methods of diet, healing and rejuvenation, and karma and reincarnation.

I tried; I really did. But within a few months, I knew that I didn't enjoy it. I found the written material opaque. What did "The godhead within is a signifier of deeper connection" even mean? I had no idea, nor did I want to find out. I felt increasingly irritated at the obligation to sit, and to pretend that I was into it.

Bill, to my surprise, took to SRF quite readily. He hadn't expressed the need for a spiritual practice in his life, but he sat, palms up on his knees, thumb and index finger pressed together, not moving a muscle. Behind his closed eyelids, I could see his eyes turned upward toward his "third eye." I was full of admiration. I was jealous.

Paul, of course, melted into SRF as if he had been searching for it all his life—and I suppose he had. He did the exercises, chanted, meditated, read the weekly lessons over and over. He looked lighter, happier, as if he truly found joy in the practice.

I was truly glad for him. I just didn't want to have to do it myself. I kept up with SRF for about eight months. Then one morning, when I came down the ladder from the loft, Bill and Paul were standing with their arms raised, ready to start the exercises. Paul motioned, as if to say, *Join us.*

I shook my head. "I'm sorry. I feel like a shit, but I can't do it anymore. I don't *want* to do it anymore."

Paul gave me a pitying look. "Are you sure? Everybody struggles—"

"You don't," I blurted.

He laughed. "Sure, I do. But I know the only thing to do is keep at it. Just keep trying."

I shook my head again. "I'm done."

Bill and Paul exchanged a look, then started their exercises.

Admitting that I had flaked out on yet another spiritual path was difficult. In our hippie crowd, practising Eastern spirituality was *de rigueur*, akin to growing your own organic food or making your own granola. To be skeptical about peace, love, and your inner god was seen as shallow. I kept telling myself that I should try harder, push aside my doubts, and just go with the flow. But every time I did, I felt like a fraud, as if I was going through the motions. Not only that, but I also felt resentful, because time was precious, and chanting and meditating wasn't how I wanted to spend my time.

What I wanted was to do what I did right then: I settled into our easy chair with a cup of coffee and *A Tale of Two Cities*. I wanted to read, to sink into my imagination. To feel caffeine (frowned on by the SRF crowd) jolt through my bloodstream. To be free to think my snarky thoughts and not have to exude a joy I didn't feel. I took a sip, opened the book, and disappeared into the story.

Bill continued with SRF after I quit. He and Paul, along with Pam and Sandy and other SRF friends from the Kootenays, attended annual meditation retreats in Los Angeles, and came back refreshed and inspired. Later, when Bill and I moved to Vancouver, our children attended an SRF Sunday school. That was fine with me. The teachings were inclusive and positive. They didn't proselytize for any one religion. I liked the local SRF-ers. I respected Bill's dedication. I just didn't want to practice it myself.

After a dozen or so years, Bill quietly let his SRF practice go. Work, children, coaching, life, crowded it out of his days. I felt slightly guilty. If I had stayed with it, he probably would have, too. But it just wasn't in me. To Bill's credit, he didn't use my non-involvement as an excuse; nor did he, in all the years he meditated, put pressure on me to come back to the SRF fold. Perhaps that willingness to let each other go our separate ways when it came to matters of faith was one of the contributors to our long, happy marriage.

Paul eventually left SRF behind and explored other—many other— new-age practices. He is still searching.

Years later, when I began to write fiction, I realized that *this* was my spirituality: to live in the world of stories, to receive them like a gift from the cosmos, to struggle with them and craft them and give them to the world. This was my self-realization. And I finally forgave myself for not being willing, or able, to stick with the paths of Eastern spirituality that everyone else seemed so easily to espouse.

Finding love

For as long as I had known him, Paul had never had a romantic relationship. At the University of Wisconsin, where I met him, I thought he had a crush on my housemate Deedee, an adorable, freckled Wisconsin farm girl. He used to come over whenever Deedee was off work and chat with her. But he never made a move, and a relationship never developed.

At the Farm in Pennsylvania, Paul remained resolutely single. I often saw him talking to one of our single women friends, having what looked like an enjoyable conversation, but I never saw him put an arm around anyone, or kiss anyone, or slip away with anyone. Briefly I wondered if he was gay. At that time, being homosexual was seen as not quite normal, even by our liberal crowd, so it wouldn't have been an easy thing to admit. But I had a gut feeling that he wasn't gay, and he certainly showed no signs of attraction to men.

Still, gay or straight, I knew he must be lonely. He had the rest of us for companionship, but that couldn't have been fulfilling. He seemed to pour all his love into his guitar.

I worried about Paul. He was a kind, sensitive, funny guy. Yet something held him back. I didn't want him to go through life alone. One of the songs he liked to play was "Desperado" by the Eagles, which tells of a loner who resists loving and being loved. I wondered if, when he sang "Desperado," he knew he was singing about himself.

In the fall of 1978, Paul moved to Nelson to take a job as a newspaper reporter. The next time he came to Galena Bay, he smiled shyly. "I met someone."

"Who? Who?" I said.

"Her name is Glenda. She's a kindergarten teacher. She's ... she's wonderful."

And she was. Glenda Miller was a roundish woman with granny glasses, like Paul's, and short, wispy brown hair. The first time she came to Galena Bay, she put on a bandana and work boots and dug beets and potatoes with us for hours. She was unpretentious and down-to-earth, with a chest-rumbling laugh. Outgoing where Paul was shy, practical where Paul was dreamy, she was warm and easy to talk to.

Within six months, Paul told us that he was moving in with Glenda. Now I was worried for the opposite reason. "Are you sure you're not rushing?" I asked him.

He patted me on the shoulder. "I'm sure. She's the one."

Paul and Glenda were married a year later. He was a desperado no more.

As it turned out, Paul never spent a winter in Galena Bay, other than a few weeks during Christmas vacations. He was usually away teaching, coming back in the summers. When he was with us, he worked in the garden, helped build whatever outbuildings were under construction, played the guitar, joined Bill and me for afternoon dips in the lake, gathered eggs, harvested honey, and, not very happily, helped slaughter chickens when they had reached the end of their laying days.

Although he never articulated it, I think Paul realized early on that homesteading wasn't for him. He still believed in the lifestyle, but he preferred to contribute financially rather than live on the land.

This arrangement was fine with Bill and me. We were glad to have Paul's company when he was there. His support meant that Bill and I could stay in Galena Bay longer without having to leave and go to work, while our efforts on the homestead enabled him to fulfill the goal he still, on some level, felt part of.

One day, not long after he had moved in with Glenda, Paul came up to Galena Bay and sat Bill and me down at the kitchen table.

"Let's face it," he said. "I've loved being partners with you guys in this land. But I'm never going to live here again. I'd like you two to buy me out."

Bill and I gulped. Our equity in the land was in the work we had put in, not in cash. We didn't have that much money.

Before we could say anything, Paul smiled. "For one dollar."

"One dollar?" I gasped.

"That'll do just fine. Consider it my gift to you for all the zucchinis you've provided me with."

We laughed, handed over a dollar bill, and shook hands. And that was the end of our three-way partnership. Galena Bay now belonged to Bill and me.

I don't know why the back-to-the-land lifestyle never clicked for Paul. Although Bill's pushiness irked him, there never was a rupture between them. Maybe it was the loneliness. Maybe it was the cramped quarters of the cabin, or the bugs, or the gruelling work. Maybe, for him, the dream was more attractive in the abstract than in reality.

Still, I'm glad to have shared the experience with Paul. I will always love his virtuosic guitar-playing and his excruciating puns. And, of course, I will always be grateful that he invited me to the Farm, where I met Bill. More than five decades on, Paul is still a dear friend.

Back in Galena Bay in the late summer of 1978, Bill and I wondered how we would support ourselves, now that the Community Conservation Centre had closed. We didn't have to wonder long. In the early fall we received a letter from Mike Jessen: "The feds are launching a new program called the Energy Van. They're looking for a couple to travel around BC doing energy education. Interested?"

Interested? The job sounded tailor-made for us. A couple. Passionate about energy conservation. Both with a background in teaching.

We applied and got the job.

In September, the feds flew us to Ottawa. Until then, I'd always thought of government employees as civil service spongers, in it only for the cushy job and the pension. Our clients in the Office of Energy Conservation changed my mind.

Sandra Kritsch ran the Energy Van program across Canada; at that time there were also vans in Ontario and New Brunswick. She was about thirty-five, a tall, solidly built woman with a dry sense of humour. Her boss, Wally Raepple, was a long-time energy advocate. He'd been championing energy conservation for years, garnering no interest, until the oil embargo hit, when suddenly his ideas came into vogue.

Sandra explained how the Energy Van program would work. "We'll set up a route and schedule for you. You'll pick up the van in Vancouver, and we'll ship you out teaching materials. We've got lesson plans, environmental videos, and beautiful puppets that the little kids love."

"I love the idea of doing a puppet show," I said.

"How much travelling will we do?" Bill asked. "BC's a huge province."

Sandra laughed. "Don't worry, we don't expect you to cover the whole thing. The contract runs for six months, so you'll get to as many places as you can in that time. You'll generally stay in each town for a week. Mostly you'll be doing school presentations, plus some radio interviews and talks to local community groups."

"Basically," Wally added, "your job is to promote energy conservation and renewable energy to anyone who'll listen, from little kids to grandparents."

Bill and I were thrilled. We looked forward to seeing the province, getting together with friends from the environmental movement, meeting new people, and spreading the gospel.

There was only one complication. I was pregnant.

I was thrilled. I'd previously had reproductive complications and wasn't sure if I'd be able to have kids. As it turned out, I'd got pregnant easily.

Now, I felt I had to inform our clients. Sandra's forehead furrowed. "Are you okay? Will you be able to do the job?"

"I'm fine," I told her, and it was true. I was youngish (twenty-nine) and healthy. I was feeling well, full of energy. The baby wasn't due until mid-April, when our contract would be drawing to a close. My doctor in Nakusp had arranged for me to visit consulting physicians along the way for my monthly checkups. Our last few weeks of presentations were in the West Kootenays, so I'd be near the Nakusp hospital when the time came.

"All right then," Sandra said, hugging me. "Congratulations! And good luck."

In early November, Bill and I flew to Vancouver, picked up a white van, applied a huge CANADA ENERGY VAN decal to its side, loaded it up with materials the feds had shipped, and set out on our trip. Our itinerary would start in Prince Rupert. Travelling east, we'd make our way to Prince George by mid-December. We'd spend Christmas in Galena Bay, then tour Vancouver Island in the new year. In early spring, we'd do presentations through the West Kootenays, finishing in Nelson. Then, in April, I'd have the baby in Nakusp.

We took the overnight ferry from Port Hardy to Prince Rupert, stopping in Bella Coola, where Bill and I stood on the deck, shivering in the damp wind, gazing in awe at the massive glacier that loomed behind the town. In Prince Rupert, we settled into an efficiency hotel (I'd asked Sandra to book us into hotels or motels with kitchens so I could cook us dinner; I didn't want to eat in restaurants all the time) and started our school visits.

Here's how it went:

If we were talking to primary-grade kids, we did a short presentation on how fossil fuels came from decayed plant and animal remains from the time of the dinosaurs. This always entranced the little kids. "You mean my car is burning dead dinosaurs? Gross! Cool!" Then we talked about solar energy. I got the kids to pretend to be seeds, and they "danced" from a scrunched-up crouch to full unfolded glory as I, the sun, shone on them and gave them energy.

With intermediate kids we showed a cut-away diagram of a house and had them point out all the examples of energy waste they could spot. Sometimes we led them in building a solar cooker out of cardboard and aluminum foil, or a simple water wheel simulating hydroelectric generation. At other times, we showed the film *The Lorax*, based on the Dr. Seuss story, and discussed environmental conservation.

A real treat was when we brought out the puppets. Someone in Ottawa had created gorgeous puppets with papier-mâché heads and cloth bodies, and had adapted *Star Wars* to give it an energy conservation theme. In the new play, called *Energy Wars*, the Princess Leia and Han Solo characters, now called Princess Energlow and Solar, had been recast as valiant energy conservers, while the Darth Vader character was a dastardly energy waster called Darklander. There was even a little silver R2D2 robot named R Factor 12 Factor Robot. Usually, Bill and I dragooned the principal of the school into playing Darklander, and the kids howled and booed at his energy-wasting antics.

After finishing our classroom presentations for the day, we met with the teachers to hand out information and educational materials. Often, at the start of the day, they had seemed more interested in having guest presenters as a diversion than in learning about energy conservation. But when they saw how enthusiastically their kids responded, and how easy it was to fit energy activities into the science and social studies curricula, they were eager to get their hands on more materials. Our after-school sessions sometimes stretched for over an hour.

"We can really tell you guys have classroom experience," teachers sometimes said. "You're so good with the kids. How'd you like to work here?"

Bill and I laughed. As much as we loved travelling and doing our presentations, Galena Bay was home.

Another bonus was that Bill and I were making piles of money. Our contract paid us a weekly salary, plus a per diem for meals and accommodation. If we stayed with friends, the accommodation allowance was reduced, but there was an extra payment so we could buy our hosts a gift or take them out to dinner. Since we usually ate in, we saved money on the food per diem. We had no expenses, other than incidentals, so were able to save almost all of our salaries.

And I felt great. Every month I visited another doctor and had the usual prenatal check-up. Each doctor pronounced me fine. It was in Fraser Lake in early December that I felt the baby move for the first time. It was so faint that I wasn't sure if I'd imagined it, but then there it was again, like a butterfly's wings brushing against my insides. Tears came to my eyes when I told Bill.

So we made our way, week by week through the fall of 1978, making stops in Terrace, Smithers, Hazelton, and Fraser Lake. We hit Prince George in mid-December, then headed home and had a wonderful, restful Christmas vacation in Galena Bay. I baked, we read, Bill played the guitar, and we did some gentle cross-country skiing. By now I was in my fifth month and my belly was prominent. The baby kicked day and night.

In early January, we took the ferry to Vancouver Island for a week of school visits in Victoria. One night, we decided to go out to a club to see live music. The James Cotton blues band was playing. Blues was—and still is—my favourite style of music, and we were eager to take advantage of being in the "big city." The club was crowded, the music was rocking, and Bill and I danced to every song. At one point, I felt a tap on my shoulder, and a male voice shouted, "Dance?" The fellow clearly hadn't seen that I was dancing with someone else. As I turned around to explain, my belly slowly came into view. I was wearing a bright red maternity top, which made it look even bigger. I'll never forget the look on that young man's face. Shock. Embarrassment. "Sorry!" he yelled and melted into the crowd.

After Victoria, we did presentations in Nanaimo, Parksville, and Qualicum. In early February, we arrived in Courtenay. The federal government had just designated a large tract of land, on the west coast of Vancouver Island, a national park. The area was a magnificent expanse of beaches, coves, islands, and old-growth forests, and everyone we talked to said we had to go out there and see it. So the weekend before we were to start our school visits in Courtenay, Bill and I drove to Tofino and booked a cabin at the Pacific Sands Resort. The resort was built right on its own cove, and each small rustic cabin had a fireplace with a stack of firewood and an ocean view.

The west coast was just as wonderful as everyone said. Bill and I strolled on the beach, snuggled in front of the fire, and slept to the soothing sound of waves rolling in and out.

On the Saturday, we set out for a hike that was supposed to take an hour, about what I could manage at that point. It was spectacular. We gawked at cedars that were fifteen feet around, felt the spray from rushing waterfalls, and marvelled at the series of boardwalks that hardy people had built decades earlier. But somehow, we got lost and ended up walking for two-and-a-half hours. By the time we got back to the cabin, I was bone-tired. I had to lie down for a while, something I rarely did, even during the pregnancy. I felt an ache deep in my pubic area and thought I had to move my bowels. But when I sat on the toilet, nothing came. The feeling passed. Half an hour later it came back. Again, I tried to go to the bathroom. Again, nothing.

Then it hit me. What if this was labour? But it couldn't be. I was only thirty-one weeks' pregnant. Hiding in the bathroom so Bill couldn't see, I grabbed my pre-natal book and read about contractions. *Whew.* This must be Braxton-Hicks contractions, also called false labour. I decided not to say anything to Bill.

But during the night the sensation came back. It was mild, a low ache that I felt more in my lower back than in my uterus. It came and went in waves. I couldn't deny it any longer. I woke Bill. "Bill, I think I'm going into labour."

"You can't be," he said, alarmed.

"I know. But something is happening. I think I should see a doctor."

"Okay," Bill said. "We're heading back tomorrow. We'll call a doctor as soon as we get to Courtenay."

I slept fitfully the rest of the night. In the morning, we drove back across the island and checked into our motel in Courtenay.

Stupidly, I didn't go straight to the hospital. I still wasn't sure if this was the real thing or just false labour, and, remembering how annoyed my father used to get when patients bothered him "for nothing," I didn't want to make a fuss. Plus, I didn't want to disrupt our Energy Van schedule if it wasn't necessary.

I waited until Monday morning and then called a doctor. He couldn't see me for a few hours, so I made an appointment for later in the morning. Bill and I had a radio interview scheduled for 9:00 AM. Like a trouper, I went to it. I remember deep-breathing through contractions while the interviewer asked a question, then answering in a rush while I waited to take the next breath.

Finally, I saw the doctor. After examining me, he said, "You, young lady, are going straight to the hospital."

"You mean, it's really labour?"

"Yes, it's real. We'll put you in bed and give you a drug to stop the contractions. With any luck, you won't have this baby just yet."

"But ..." My mind was full of worries. What if the baby did come? Would it live? Would it be healthy? And what about the Energy Van, our contract, our schedule? We had weeks of school visits arranged, here on Vancouver Island and then in the Kootenays. What about my promise to Sandra that everything would be okay?

There was no time for buts. At St. Joseph's Hospital in Comox, I was put on vasodilan, a muscle relaxant. It worked. The contractions went away. But I had to stay in bed. I wasn't even allowed to get up to go to the bathroom.

Bill and I decided we had to tell our clients what was happening. In the best case, if the drug continued to work, I was probably going to have to stay in bed for the rest of the pregnancy. If it didn't work and the baby came, I wasn't going to be able to do the Energy Van work anymore. Either way, our commitments were going to have to change. Secretly I was relieved that it was Bill, not I, who had to call Sandra and Wally.

They could not have been nicer. They expressed concern for me. Together with Bill, they decided that he would do this week's presentations in Courtenay and the following week's visits in Campbell River on his own. After that, when we were scheduled to head back to the Kootenays, we would see.

I lasted a week. Around four in the morning on February 12, 1979, the vasodilan stopped working and I went into labour for real. When my favourite nurse, Pat, came to wheel me down to the delivery room, she winked at me and said, "Full moon tonight. There's always lots of babies born during the full moon."

One good thing about giving birth prematurely is that labour is generally short because the baby is so small. I was in labour for about two hours, pushed for about half an hour, and Elora Merri Schwartz was born at 8:30 in the morning, eight weeks early, weighing four pounds, one ounce. She was immediately put in an incubator in the special-care wing of the nursery.

I was terrified. Even though the nurses assured me that four pounds was a good weight for a preemie, the baby looked so tiny and helpless lying in the incubator. What if she didn't make it? What if she had some terrible illness or debilitating condition? Was it my fault she had been born so early? *If only I hadn't lifted all those heavy boxes of school materials*, I thought. *If only I had rested more.* Should I have realized that the Energy Van job was too much for a pregnant woman and talked Bill into turning it down? And now my poor baby had to be separated from me, and I couldn't even hold her, and what was that doing to her psychological development?

There was nothing to do but take it day by day. And, fortunately for us, Merri (we started calling her by her middle name, and it stuck) was healthy, just small. She had a mild case of jaundice, which the nurses assured me was common, even in full-term babies, and had to go under special lights that emitted light from the blue-green part of the spectrum. She wore a tiny mask and looked like a raccoon.

Merri was too weak to nurse from the breast, so at first she had to be fed by gavage—that is, by a tube down her throat. But it was important she get breast milk.

"How will she, if I can't nurse her?" I asked Pat, the nurse.

"Simple. You'll express breast milk."

"Huh?"

I'd never heard of such a thing. Pat showed me how to squeeze my breast to push out the milk. I collected it in tiny sterile bottles, and the nurses fed the milk through Merri's gavage tube. At first, I was awkward and could manage only a few squirts, but after a while I became quite adept at it. Bill joked that my forearms looked like Popeye's from all the squeezing. Eventually we rented an electric breast pump. It was a heavy, clunky thing that made me feel like a cow hooked up to a milking machine, but it was more efficient than pumping by hand.

We began a waiting game. The nurses weighed Merri before and after each feeding, as well as every morning. Some days she gained a couple of ounces. Other days she lost a couple. She couldn't be released from the hospital until she weighed five pounds and had been established on the bottle or the breast. I thought she'd never grow big enough.

Once again, our clients were incredibly kind and understanding. They even sent a gift, and Sandra joked that we should have named the baby Vanessa. At that point we didn't know how long we would be stuck in the area, so Sandra contacted the local schools and arranged for Bill to do three weeks of presentations in Campbell River instead of just one. We agreed that once Merri came out of the hospital, we would terminate the contract, skipping the visits in the Kootenays.

I felt blue coming home without my baby—and "home" was our motel in Courtenay. The owners went out of their way to be kind, asking about the baby every time we saw them. But I was still down in the dumps. For the first week after I got home, I was too weak to go with Bill on school visits. I had nothing to do but sit in the motel room, pump breast milk, and worry. When Bill got home, we went to the hospital and visited Merri, stroking her through the ports in the incubator wall.

"Do you think she looks a little bigger?" I would say.

"I think so," Bill would reply.

After a week or so, I started feeling stronger. Realizing that I was better off keeping busy than moping in the motel room, I began going with Bill on school visits, lugging the breast pump and finding a private place in which to pump a few times a day. Everyone was very accommodating: "Oh, you're the young couple who had the premature baby. How's the little one doing? What can we do for you?" It was good to be back in the classroom again.

Merri graduated from gavage to a bottle. (I learned that it takes less energy and strength for a baby to suck from a bottle than from a breast, which is why preemies are put on the bottle first.) Now I could hold her and feed her once or twice a day. The nursery continued with the daily weigh-ins. Slowly, slowly, she gained weight. She moved from the bottle to the breast.

Finally, at one month, Merri reached the five-pound threshold. "She's ready to go home," Pat said.

Now I was terrified for the opposite reason. The hospital had done everything for Merri. What did I know about taking care of a little baby?

"But . . . but . . . where will I put her? We don't have a crib," I said, making the first excuse that came into my mind.

"She doesn't need a crib. Wrap her up nice and tight and put her in an open dresser drawer. Preemies like small spaces. She'll feel cozy."

Our friends from the Kootenays sent a box of baby hand-me-downs: sleepers, blankets, hats, even a Snugli baby carrier. We brought Merri to the motel. The owners fussed over her. She slept in the dresser drawer.

A few weeks later, we flew to Ottawa with two-month-old Merri to give our clients a final report on our Energy Van experience. Sandra and Wally were very pleased with Bill's and my work on the program. The entire Office of Energy Conservation congregated to see Merri and pass her from hand to hand. Only one grouchy woman, a senior official, disapproved of my nursing Merri in the departmental boardroom. Fortunately, I was unaware of it at the time and blithely opened my blouse.

We bade them a fond farewell, then flew home. Our Energy Van contract was over. Back in the cabin, we were entering a new phase, parenthood—and once again wondering how we would make a living.

15

Raising a Child

Making room for Merri

"You're not taking that little baby to live in the wilderness, are you?" my mother asked in horror when I told her on the phone that we were returning to the cabin with Merri. "Without electricity, without hot running water, without a toilet or a bathtub?"

I laughed. "What do you think will happen to her, she'll get eaten by a bear?"

"No, but it's so cold there," my father said.

"No, it's not. The cabin is nice and warm. And we'll put her in a snowsuit when we take her outside."

"What if you get snowed in?" my mother asked.

"It'll be the same as every other winter," I said. "We'll put her on our backs and snowshoe out."

"Is that safe?" my father asked.

"Dad! Safer than driving in New York traffic, that's for sure."

"The thing that really bothers me," my mother said, "is that you're so far from a hospital. What if she gets sick? Babies' temperatures can rise really fast. By the time you get to your car and drive to town—"

"Don't worry," I said, more gently than before, because this was something that concerned me, too, though I wasn't about to admit it to them. "First of all, Bill and I both know first aid. Second of all, we'll be taking her to the doctor for checkups once a month. Third of all, there's a public health nurse in Trout Lake, and she's got a radio phone, so we can reach her from Walter's. And if Merri starts to get sick, we'll head for town, just in case."

"Don't wait. At the first sign, go," my father said. Something in his voice made me realize that Merri was not only my blood, but his as well.

"I have one more question," my mother said. "Where are you going to put her?"

She had me there. For the time being, Merri was sleeping in a wicker basket. It was oval-shaped, about three-feet long and two feet wide. There was no room in the cabin for it, nor for all the paraphernalia—diapers, blankets, sleepers, snowsuits, washcloths, booties—that accompanied her. And the basket was only a temporary solution. Soon she would need an even larger crib.

On our first day back, I held her while Bill tried, in vain, to find a spot on the floor for the basket.

"I guess we could put her upstairs, on the floor of the loft," I said.

Bill and I went over to the ladder. "You'll have to climb up and down every time she cries or needs to be fed or have her diaper changed," he pointed out.

"And I'll have to do it one-handed while holding a squirming baby in the other," I added.

We looked at each other and said, "No."

I laughed. "We'll just have to put her on the ceiling."

Bill looked up. "Hey, wait a minute." He stood on a chair and reached up to one of the sills that supported the loft floor. "We could hang her basket by ropes hooked to a couple of sills."

I considered the basket. It had four raffia handles, two on either side. They looked strong. The sills were thick enough to hold stout nails. It might work.

"The hanging basket," I said. "Sounds like a house plant."

So we suspended Merri's basket over the kitchen table. It rested just high enough that it cleared our heads when we sat to eat. I became adept at stepping onto a chair and transferring her to the basket all in one fluid motion, without waking her up. The hanging basket had the advantage of being suspended by ropes, which meant that when I gave it a push, it swung back and forth like a cradle, soothing her when she was fussy.

I knew that soon Merri would be too big and too active to safely sleep in a hanging basket. I also knew that my mother and Bill's mother would have a fit if they saw what we had done. Bill and I were careful not to send them any incriminating pictures.

But just look at how cute she was, lifting her head to peek out over the edge of the basket, looking around with her big bright eyes and breaking into a smile when she saw us!

By the middle of June, when she was four months old, Merri started rolling over. I stretched a bungie cord over the top of the basket so she couldn't fall out. Every time she turned over, the basket swung back and forth on its ropes. I added a second bungie cord. My mantra morphed: If my mother could see this, she would *slaughter* me.

Merri grew quickly, and that was good because she had a lot of catching up to do. But it presented problems, too. The cabin was cramped with just Bill and me. With Merri, it was stuffed. We revived the old idea of building a log house at the top of the rise, near the root cellar. But when we calculated the cost, it exceeded our savings. Besides, the space problem was immediate.

We decided to build an addition onto the cabin, something we could do fairly quickly. Bill became excited about using his newly acquired knowledge of energy-conserving construction, and sketched out several possible plans. We decided to add on a space measuring sixteen by twelve feet, on both levels.

The main debate centred on what to do about the roof. The A-frame roof on the original cabin was ideal for shedding snow. But its steep slope meant that you could stand up straight only in the centre of the loft, and it severely limited the usable space. The diagonal area under the eaves was filled with awkward-to-reach boxes of spare clothes, books, and shoes, now even more jammed with Merri's things.

In a home construction book, Bill came upon a design for a gambrel, or barn-style roof, in which the roof sloped downward in two gentle pitches. We were both attracted to the graceful gambrel shape, for both aesthetic and practical reasons.

"But how do we join an A-frame to a gambrel?" I asked.

"I have no idea," Bill said, his brow furrowed. He delved back into the book. After many sessions with a tape measure, protractor, and T-square, he came up with an ingenious geometric scheme that would connect the two differently shaped roofs. The two peaks would be the same height. The steep walls would butt against the more gently sloping walls, meeting at the peak. The sections of wall that extended past the outline of the A-frame would be insulated and finished like exterior walls.

"Would there be room to stand up a night table next to our mattress?" I asked.

"Sure. A dresser, even."

"Wow!"

Paul, who was living in Nelson with Glenda at the time, came up on weekends to help pour concrete pads for the foundation. Michael also came up for several days from Kaslo to help with the framing.

The greatest assistance came from Bill's old college roommate, Paul Cowan, who lived in South Fork, across the valley from Michael and Vivianne. Paul helped Bill construct the tricky roof join. He was an excellent, if self-taught, carpenter, and was also fearless working at height, a trait that Bill did not share. Paul stayed with us for a couple of weeks, and I remember two things from that visit. One was his tall figure straddling the second-story floor joists while Bill handed him up sheets of plywood, Paul's corona of curly hair backlit by the sun.

The other was music. By the late 1970s Bill and I had a small cassette player, which we ran off a car battery. It was great to be able to play our small supply of tapes—Bob Dylan, Dave Van Ronk, Joni Mitchell, James Taylor, Motown—but we were woefully out of date when it came to current sounds. The only time we heard anything new was when we went back east, and our friends turned us on to groups we hadn't heard before: Ry Cooder, Dire Straits, Jackson Browne.

Paul Cowan came with reggae. We had heard of reggae but never really listened to it before. Now, we were swept away by Bob Marley, Jimmy Cliff, and Toots and the Maytals. I can picture Bill and Paul hammering the framing studs to the beat of "The Harder They Come," "By the Waters of Babylon," and "Pressure Drop." I've loved those songs ever since.

While Bill and Paul worked on the addition, I was on parent duty. I was smitten with my child and gazed at her in wonder. I had never imagined this kind of love. Surely, she was the most adorable, the most alert, the most intelligent, the sweetest baby who ever lived.

At the same time, I was a nervous wreck. *What if I make a mistake? What if I handle her wrong? Has the separation caused by her premature birth wrecked our bonding and scarred her for life?* I was so worried about doing a good job, about being the perfect mother, that I hovered, reacting to every bleat and rushing to hold, rock, and soothe her. Every time she squawked, I stuck my breast in her mouth. Because Merri had been born early, her digestive system was immature, and this overfeeding only made things worse. Merri cried and fretted, and my anxiety grew.

I remember one evening in early June. Merri had been fussing for an hour, taking a few gulps of milk and then turning away and crying. It was about 6:00 PM; the days were long and it was still light out. I put her in the Snugli and took her for a walk down the back road. As usually happened, she miraculously calmed down as soon as we started moving, and was soon dozing on my chest.

About a quarter of a mile along, I came to a large mound of fresh-looking bear shit in the middle of the road. I knew I should turn back, but Merri was finally asleep, and if I took her out of the Snugli after so short a time, she'd wake up. I carried on. A couple of minutes later, I heard a crashing sound in the woods. There was a bear cub. The mama emerged onto the road and stood there, head turned my way, sniffing.

"Uh ... I was just leaving," I said, and turned around. Every few minutes, all the way back—a walk that I completed in record time—I looked over my shoulder. Mama and baby had disappeared.

So had this mama and baby.

What saved me from being overwhelmed by motherhood were the demands of the homestead. While Bill was busy with the addition, I had to keep things going. It was spring. The soil needed to be turned over and the seeds planted.

I was happy to get outside and do physical labour again. Normally, over the winter, I would have stayed in shape by splitting and hauling wood, cross-country skiing, and snowshoeing. But the previous winter, I had been pregnant, travelling around in a vehicle. As I started digging, I could feel flabby muscles protesting, and at first I could work for only an hour or so at a stretch, much less than my previous "Energy Queen" level.

What to do with Merri while I was working in the garden? I couldn't leave her in the cabin. We didn't have a portable playpen. I tried putting her in the Snugli, but it was awkward to dig with her on my chest, and I was afraid I'd clonk her with the spade. Finally, I came upon a solution. I opened up a hard-body suitcase, placed it on the ground, and lay Merri in one of the open halves. I covered her with screening to keep the mosquitoes off. Merri napped in the suitcase, and then, when she woke up, I took her inside and nursed her. The suitcase joined the basket on the growing list of "if my mother could see this, she would kill me" items.

There was no way Bill and I were going to use disposable diapers. We were environmentalists, after all, critical of the impacts involved in producing and disposing of them. The harvest of wood for making pulp, mainly from tropical forests in South America. The energy required and the pollution generated to manufacture them. The accumulation of tons of dirty diapers in landfills. No. We would not be party to that. Sure, we would use disposables when we were travelling. But for everyday use we would stick to tried-and-true, ecologically pure cloth diapers.

I purchased a supply of flannel diapers, diaper pins, and plastic (yeah, I know) liners. But then the question arose: What was I going to do with the dirty diapers? Of course we didn't have a washing machine; we either washed our clothes by hand or took them into town to a laundromat. I pictured Pat Harrington, standing over the woodstove, stirring a boiling pot of diapers. I may have been an environmentalist, but I wasn't going to work *that* hard.

I figured out a system. Pee-soaked diapers went into a ten-gallon bucket filled with soapy water. Poopy diapers I rinsed under a hose and then put in the bucket. On town days, we dumped out the water, wrung out the diapers, wrapped them in a triple layer of plastic bags, and took them into town with the rest of our laundry.

This system was easy to follow during the summer and fall, when the hose was running outside and we could park the truck in the driveway. In the winter, though, the outside hose was turned off and the truck was parked a mile and a quarter away at the end of the unplowed road.

No problem for the intrepid Schwartzes! When Merri pooped, we filled a pot with water at the sink, carried it outside, and poured it over the dirty diaper. This didn't remove as much of the shit as the hose did, but it was good enough. Then we packed up the diapers as usual, put them in a backpack along with the rest of the laundry, and snowshoed them out to the truck, one of us carrying the pack and the other carrying Merri. At least, on the reverse trip, the dry diapers were lighter than the wet ones.

When I look back, I'm amazed that I went to this much trouble to stick to my environmental principles. What harm would have befallen the planet if I had used disposable diapers, even if only in the winter? The answer is: too much harm. I never considered switching. It just wasn't in Bill's and my environmental code. Besides, we were young and fit, and adding the diapers to the other supplies we had to pack in and out was a negligible burden. Fussing with the buckets was a hassle, but the pleasure of wrapping Merri's bum in a soft cotton diaper, and the satisfaction we gained from doing the ecologically positive thing, made it all worthwhile.

On a cool day in October 1979, Bill removed the east-facing window and, with the chainsaw, cut out a six-foot-wide, floor-to-ceiling section of wall. When the smoke cleared, there was a passageway from the old part to the new. And not a moment too soon—Merri was practically rolling out of the basket, in spite of the bungie cords.

The new space was magnificent, at least by the standards of the original cabin. The walls were made of planed, varnished cedar rather than rough-cut lumber. We carpeted the downstairs section, partly for insulation and partly to cushion Merri's knees. We built in a floor-to-ceiling bookcase and put a desk under the north-facing window. We installed a baby gate across the opening between the old part and the new, so that Merri could have the run of what we now called "the living room," yet not be able to get near the woodstove or the wood heater.

Upstairs, we set up a crib in the old loft and moved our mattress to the new bedroom. There was no door between the two rooms; rather, the opening stretched across the complete width of the cabin, rising to an A-shaped peak on one side and a gambrel-shaped slope on the other. This way, I could easily hear Merri at night and could look across the opening to see her in her crib. Bill made a closet pole out of a thick dowel, and, for the first time since coming to Galena Bay, we were able to hang up our clothes.

We stood in the living room, while Merri crawled around, exploring the new corners and removing everything she could reach from the lowest bookshelves. I put my arm around Bill's waist. "This isn't a cabin anymore. It's a house. Two up and two down."

"Well ..." he said, blushing.

"It's gorgeous. It's wonderful. It's comfortable."

"It's built a lot better than the original cabin, that's for sure," Bill said, allowing himself a bit of self-praise.

"Now all we need is a bathroom," I said, and we both laughed. After seven years, the outhouse no longer represented adventure and ruggedness. The little room in the front corner of the cabin was originally meant to be a bathroom, but it was so full of stuff—firewood, canned goods, first aid supplies, work gloves, gumboots, toothbrushes, shampoo, the rifle, hand tools—that if we emptied it to make it a bathroom we'd have to build another little room in which to store all the junk.

"Next house," Bill said.

"You're on."

Have I mentioned that Merri was a fussy baby? She wasn't a very good sleeper, either. Eventually I managed to get her to take a couple of naps a day, but they were typically short, half an hour or forty-five minutes. At night, she woke up every two hours. This, the nurses had told me, was normal for preemies: they needed to feed often in order to catch up. By about five months, though, she began to go for longer stretches at night, sleeping for three hours, then four, five, six. By the end of July, she was sleeping through the night. Heaven.

At that time, my sister Audrey, her husband Alan, and my niece Sara were living in Lawrence, Kansas, where Alan was attending grad school. I wanted to visit Audrey, and I wanted Merri to meet her cousin. Bill and I planned a trip. We would drive to Spokane, Washington, about five hours from Galena Bay, where the nearest large airport was located. He would fly to California for the annual SRF meditation retreat, and I would fly to Kansas. A week later, we would meet back in Spokane and drive home together.

A few days before our departure, when Merri had been sleeping through the night for about a week, she woke up crying at about 3:00 AM. Thinking that this was just an aberration, I got up and fed her. The next night, she woke up twice. The night after that, three times.

I felt trapped. Clearly Merri was regressing, and clearly she didn't *need* to nurse that often. I knew I should let her cry so she would get back to her previous schedule. But I didn't know how long it would take to break this new habit. In a day or so I would be at Audrey's. My sister had a fourteen-month-old baby. Alan had to get up early to go to school. I couldn't take the chance that Merri would disrupt their nights. So, even though I knew it was a bad idea, I gave in and nursed her when she woke up. By the time I arrived in Kansas, she was back to feeding every two hours, and I was ragged.

Audrey and I had a wonderful visit. When I arrived, Sara was sitting in her highchair, eating Cheerios. She looked at me with her enormous dark eyes, her face framed by black curls, and smiled. I was smitten. Audrey fussed over Merri, exclaiming at how adorable she was, and Merri produced a gummy grin. At night, I grabbed her as soon as she squawked, trying not to let her wake up the household.

When Bill and I got back to Galena Bay, Merri was firmly re-established in her every-two-hours feeding schedule. I knew that the time had come to break this new habit. I dreaded it.

The first night, Merri went down at ten, as usual. Bill and I got into our own bed and hoped for the best. She started crying at midnight.

"Don't go," Bill whispered. "Let her cry."

I nodded.

Merri's crying got louder. From the pitch of her wails, I could tell that she was on her hands and knees, peering into our room and directing her cries at me. *Why, oh why hadn't we put a door between the two rooms?*

I couldn't stand it. Sure, Merri was manipulating me, and sure, she wasn't starving, but she was only a baby. What if my failure to appear felt like abandonment and scarred her forever?

I made a move to get up. Bill held me down. Literally. He pushed down on my shoulders and didn't let me up.

Merri howled.

She fell asleep.

At two o'clock, she woke again. This time I fed her. After all, I couldn't expect her to switch immediately from every-two-hour feedings to none.

The next night, she slept through the midnight feeding and woke at two. Bill held me down.

In the morning, Merri and I did our regular 6:00 AM feeding. She burped and gave me a big smile.

"You rascal," I said.

Within three nights, she was once again sleeping through the night.

Health and food

Needless to say, I was obsessively health-conscious when it came to feeding Merri. I even gave up coffee while I was pregnant and nursing, a major sacrifice, and suffered instead with horrible drinks made from Inka (a coffee substitute made from roasted barley, rye, chicory, and beet roots) and carob powder. (I made no such sacrifice when I was pregnant with our second daughter, Amy, arguing that if caffeine was going to hurt her, so be it. It didn't hurt her, and I kept my sanity.)

When Merri was ready to eat solid food, I didn't consider buying commercial baby food. I bought a food grinder and prepared my own mashed squash, carrots, peas, apples, pears, eggs, and beans—organic, of course. For a sweet treat, I gave her a carob pod to suck on. Merri was a good eater, and thrived on this healthy diet.

We did allow her one indulgence. As a wedding gift, Bill and I had received a White Mountain hand-crank ice cream maker. Inside a beautiful oak barrel nestled a cylindrical stainless-steel container. You packed salt and ice (or, in our case, snow) around the container, poured in the ice cream mixture (which I made with honey, not sugar), and turned the handle. Half an hour later you had delicious, fresh, homemade ice cream. We made vanilla, coffee (flavoured with Inka, but the honey and cream masked the chicory taste), and fruit varieties with our home-canned peaches, apricots, and strawberries.

Watching Merri eat ice cream was hilarious. She loved the taste but was perplexed by the coldness. Sitting in the highchair, she eagerly opened her mouth like a little sparrow. When the spoonful went in, she pursed her lips, and the melted ice cream dribbled down her chin. She smacked her lips and opened her mouth for the next bite.

When Merri was just over a year old, Bill and I took her back east for the first time. My family gathered in Linden to celebrate our new arrival. Audrey, who was not nearly as fanatical about health food with Sara as I was with Merri, was horrified to learn about the lack of sweets in Merri's diet. "Never eaten chocolate!" she said in dismay.

"You've deprived my granddaughter!" said my father, a noted chocoholic.

With my reluctant permission, Audrey gave Merri a miniature piece of Hershey's chocolate. While everybody watched, Merri carefully unwrapped it and stuck it in her mouth. I waited, hoping she would spit it out, proving that my health-food approach had triumphed.

A smile slowly spread across her face. She sucked and drooled over that piece of chocolate, licking her fingers and even licking the last traces of chocolate off the wrapping.

My family teased me mercilessly. I was unmoved. Back in Galena Bay, I stuck to my health-food principles. When our second daughter, Amy, came along, I inflicted carob pods on both of them. They have never let me forget it.

Perhaps not surprisingly, Merri developed a keen interest in food. She became a pastry chef—and a chocolatier.

When Bill and I first brought Merri to Galena Bay, and Bill's and my parents asked, "What if she gets sick or injured?" I brushed off their fears. But that concern stayed in the back of my mind. Bill's leg injury with the chainsaw reminded me that accidents could happen, and that our isolation could make it difficult to get help.

We did what we could to keep Merri safe. We put up barriers so she couldn't get near the woodstoves and kept an eye on her when we were outside. I watched closely for signs of illness and infection.

Bill and I had a wonderful family doctor in Nakusp, Dr. McNeill, and we took Merri in every month or so for checkups. Although at first Merri was under-size and underweight for her age because of her premature birth, she was gaining and growing appropriately. Dr. McNeill pronounced her healthy and said she would soon catch up to full-term babies.

We were even more fortunate to have a public health nurse living in Trout Lake, a tiny village about twenty miles northeast of Galena Bay. Irene was Scottish, with a beautiful, rich brogue; I loved visiting with her just to hear her talk. She was kind enough to come to the cabin to give Merri her vaccinations—talk about a house call!—so we didn't have to make an extra trip to town. She brought a portable scale and weighed and measured Merri, echoing Dr. McNeill's opinion that she was growing as she should.

Irene was about ten years older than I was, with a round, kind face and warm brown eyes. As we sat over cups of tea, Merri cradled on Irene's lap, I found it easy to ask questions. *Am I nursing right? What if I don't get a burp? What do I do for this diaper rash?* Her answers reassured me. Her matter-of-fact manner reminded me that what I had told my mother and mother-in-law, with false confidence, was true: that generations of women had raised babies in similar conditions, that caring for a child was largely a matter of common sense rather than expertise, that we were doing fine.

Bill and I were lucky. Merri was a healthy baby, and, aside from the usual colds and an occasional fever, she never had a serious illness. She ate a goodly amount of dirt, got stung by a few bumblebees, ingested wildflowers and huckleberry leaves, fell down, got up, and thrived. I didn't take any of this for granted. If Merri had been a less sturdy child, we might not have been able to stay in Galena Bay with her for as long as we did.

There's no denying that raising a child in a place like Galena Bay had its drawbacks. There were no other children to play with. There were dangers. It would have been much easier to live in a place with a washing machine instead of having to *schlep* our dirty diapers into town. Even with the addition, the cabin was cramped, and there was no private corner where Bill or I could get away from Merri and have some quiet time of our own.

Still, I look back at the time we had with Merri in Galena Bay with profound gratitude. Bill and I got to raise our baby in the place, and in the lifestyle, we loved. We were able to share the parenting during that first year and a half. Merri ate healthy, organic food straight from the garden. She was introduced to the forest and quiet and snow, to the smell of wood smoke and the sound of birdsong, to the coziness of the cabin and the expanse of stars in the winter sky.

You could argue that these things are immaterial. After all, it doesn't matter what environment babies are raised in, as long as they are cared for and loved. And Merri was too young to actually remember her time in Galena Bay, so what difference did it make?

A great deal, I think. Galena Bay marked Merri. It's in her bones. She has always had a keen interest in natural food, gardening, the outdoors, adventure. In a sense, she has always been "going back to the land."

And she now lives in the Kootenays.

Making a Living

When Bill and I got back to Galena Bay in the spring of 1979 with Merri, we weren't hurting for money. We had saved a lot from the Energy Van contract. In fact, we'd made more during those five months than we'd ever made before.

Still, I could see that Bill was worried. "I'm thirty-two," he fretted. "I'm a dad. What am I going to do when I grow up? How am I going to support this family?"

I tried to reassure him, saying that we would figure it out when the time came. This was a neat reversal of roles, since it was usually Bill who was more relaxed, and I who was the worrier. But I could tell he was stewing about it.

Then, in early 1980, we received a letter from Sandra Kritsch, our old Energy Van client. The Office of Energy Conservation was so pleased with Bill's and my work on the van that they wanted us to write a training manual and make a video for other Energy Van teams. Were we interested? Did we think we could do it with a little baby around?

Yes, and yes. Bill and I talked over the structure of the manual: an introduction, lesson plans for school audiences of different age levels, general tips for managing the travel, teaching tips, advice on handling media interviews and public presentations, and keeping in touch with the managers back in Ottawa. Then, because I was the better writer of the two of us, I set to work to write the thing.

The difficulty, of course, was how to get any work done with an eleven-month-old baby. The cabin, upstairs and downstairs, was one open living space; there were no doors or private places. Merri still wasn't much of a napper, though I managed to grab half an hour here, half an hour there during her catnaps, and a little more time while Bill played with her. (Her favourite game at the time was when you built a tower of blocks and she knocked it down. "Boom!" Hysterical laughter. Repeat. Repeat.)

Most afternoons, to allow me to concentrate, Bill put Merri in the baby backpack and took her out snowshoeing or cross-country skiing. One time, he was skiing in the woods between our place and Bob's. "I was zooming along, Merri chirping away in the backpack," Bill told me later. "The front tips of my skis slid under a log, and I fell forward onto my knees. Merri shot out of the backpack and landed face-first in the snow. I ran to her, expecting her to start shrieking. Instead she gave me a big grin and licked the snow that was melting on her face."

I had written energy education material before but never a manual aimed at my peers. I felt daunted at first. But once I got going, I found the process enjoyable. It was fun to go back over our experience and think about what had worked and could work for others. I enjoyed trying to find the right words to say what needed to be said simply, clearly, and concisely.

Bill reviewed my draft and made suggestions. (At first, I was sure that none of his changes were needed. Reluctantly, I admitted that my text could use a few improvements.) I revised the manual, and we mailed it to Sandra.

A few weeks later we got a letter: "It's wonderful! Thank you so much. We're making arrangements to bring you here to shoot the accompanying video."

In the spring of 1980, we flew to Ottawa. Merri, now a year old, toddling in her little white shoes and talking precociously, charmed everyone. Sandra Kritsch carried her around the office: "This is the baby who was born on the Energy Van!" Merri gave her adorable smile, drinking up the attention.

This time my parents and Bill's mom came up from the States, so we had lots of Merri-minders while Bill and I were busy in the studio. That sounds very "Hollywood," but it wasn't all that glamorous. A video operator shot us greeting future Energy Van teams, explaining what the program was about, and going over the highlights of the manual. It was done in an afternoon.

When that job was finished, we once again said goodbye to Sandra and Wally, and flew back to Galena Bay.

Writing the training manual had given me a taste of writing. I liked it. I was in no way thinking of *becoming a writer* (in my eyes, writers were geniuses who were either dead or lived in garrets in New York), but I wanted to keep doing it.

I thought about the lesson plans we had written and presented on our school visits. They were good lessons. But if the kids we were trying to reach were anything like me, they would rather learn about something through a story than through facts. It occurred to me that perhaps the best way to convey energy information was by telling an educational story.

So I set out to write one.

I made up a fictional world called Entropia, where people wasted energy. Their slogan was: "For a life of comfort, joy and delight, use energy all day and all night!" As a result, almost every river was dammed to produce hydroelectricity, killing fish. Oil and coal plants ran overtime, polluting the air. People consumed too much stuff, and litter was strewn across the landscape. The king and queen were worried about the environmental future of Entropia, but they didn't know what to do about it.

Then three children from our world magically arrived in Entropia. They taught the king and queen to save energy, rely on renewable energy sources, consume only what they needed, and recycle their waste. Just in time! The king and queen proclaimed that energy conservation would henceforth be the way of the land, the people of Entropia eagerly adopted the new practices, and the environment was saved. And everyone lived happily ever after.

The challenge, once again, was to find a way to concentrate on writing. Merri was a walking, talking (non-stop) toddler, curious about her world and eager to play. She loved books and soon learned to "read" them by herself. She'd sit on the floor, a book open on her lap, and point to a picture. "Bird. Mommy. Bird." If I didn't respond right away with "Yes, that's a bird," she would repeat "Bird ... bird ... bird ..." until I did. Then she'd turn the page. "Dog ... dog ... dog ..."

Somehow, snatching time when Merri napped or when Bill took her outside, I finished the story. I had a ball writing *Adventure in Entropia*. I didn't know the first thing about writing fiction, but three decades of avid reading had unconsciously taught me narrative structure. Somehow, I knew to write in scenes, and to put in plenty of action and dialogue.

I sold the story to the provincial department of Conservation and Renewable Energy for $1,500, a considerable sum at the time. The government decided to print it as a combination storybook and colouring book. Bill and I talked our clients into hiring our artist friends Pam and Sandy Stevenson to draw black and white illustrations to accompany the story. *Adventure in Entropia* was released in the spring of 1980. The provincial government distributed 75,000 copies to schools across the province.

Those early attempts at writing turned out to be the foundation of a long, satisfying career. Trying to write with a baby around taught me to value my writing time. In later years, when I dropped off my kids at a babysitter's so I could have a morning to write, I truly appreciated the luxury of that two-and-a-half-hour expanse. Later still, when I periodically left the kids home with Bill and went off to a borrowed cabin for a three-day writing retreat, I knew that I was giving myself the gift that I had learned to treasure at my desk in Galena Bay.

Bill and Merri and I spent an enjoyable summer in Galena Bay. Merri was a rampaging toddler, and we had our hands full keeping her out of the gardens.

In midsummer we received a surprising letter from Wally Raepple. He had just moved to Vancouver from Ottawa. The provincial government was starting an Energy Van program of its own. Wally knew that Bill and I could not embark on another tour, not with a little child. But the province was looking for someone to run the program: to hire and train a couple, plan their trip, and administer the program's budget and logistics. Would Bill be interested in doing this? The government intended to hire the manager on a one-year contract. The only catch was that it would mean relocating to Vancouver.

Bill and I debated the pros and cons. We weren't on opposite sides of the issue, like we had been over the dancing/teaching debate a few years earlier. We just weren't sure what was the best thing to do.

"It's only for a year."

"But we've been away so much recently. It's time to settle down."

"It would be interesting to run the program. And our experience would really help the new team."

"We don't know anybody in Vancouver. It'll be lonely."

"It would be good money. And then we could come back with savings."

"We've finally got the cabin in shape. It's comfortable. It's a home."

"It might be fun to be in the city for a change. We could go to movies, plays, music, dance: all the culture we haven't been able to indulge in for so many years."

"But Vancouver! Crowds, pollution, traffic, noise, concrete!"

We vacillated daily. One minute, Bill would say "Let's do it," and I would raise all the objections. Then we would switch sides. But we didn't have any other ideas. There were no job prospects in Galena Bay. I couldn't go back to teaching with a baby. Bill, I could tell, felt a strong need to support our family, and he was up for the challenge of running the program.

In the end, we decided to give it a try. This wasn't a permanent solution, but it would give us a short-term boost. What it came down to was: *It's only for a year. How bad can it be?*

Bill's contract started in early September. He moved to Vancouver to start work and find us a place to live. Merri and I stayed in Galena Bay until the beginning of October. In a reversal of our roles from when Bill stayed behind to finish up the garden while I moved to Revelstoke to teach, I now harvested the garden and got the cabin ready to be shut down for the winter.

Bill came home every second weekend. One Thursday evening, when he was expected the next day, I said to Merri, "Guess who's coming tomorrow. Daddy!"

Merri immediately ran to the screen door and peered out. "Daddy! Daddy!" she said, her arms outstretched.

"No, sweetie, he's not coming today. He's coming *tomorrow*," I said, but it was no use. Merri became inconsolable when Bill didn't show up.

That was a lesson in a toddler's sense of time—or, rather, the lack of it. I learned to speak more carefully.

Finally, at the beginning of October, Bill came back to pick us up. We loaded up the car (the truck was long-gone and we now had a Toyota Corolla station wagon) with clothes for Merri and me, cookware, books, and toys.

As we rolled down the driveway, I turned to look back at the cabin. Little did I know that we would never live there again.

Leaving

Vancouver 1980

Bill and I found a roomy, two-bedroom apartment near Victoria and 49th. We didn't know anybody in the city, and I hated it. I didn't know the streets and continually got lost as I drove around. I didn't know the shops. I didn't even know the neighbours, who seemed to walk past Merri and me, eyes down, with purposeful steps. From our apartment, we could hear the traffic at the intersection. Some nights I lay in bed, listening to the squeal of brakes and the beep of horns, and missed the silence, the birdsong, the sigh of tree boughs.

Bill settled into his job. He enjoyed meeting colleagues who were as passionate about energy conservation as he was, and enjoyed even more the view over Coal Harbour from his twenty-sixth-floor office in a downtown tower. He discovered that he had a knack for administration, and the Energy Van program was soon flourishing under his direction. For me, it was disconcerting to see him head out every morning in a sport coat and tie ("bull in a china shop" was the phrase that came to mind), but he looked handsome, and I was proud.

But I missed Bill. So far, we had raised Merri together. Now I was left alone with her all day. I felt lonely. I found a local playgroup and met other moms and toddlers. (At that point, all the participants were women.) I began to swap babysitting with some of the moms, and made friends. Best of all, the leader of our playgroup, a lovely young woman named Berny, offered to babysit in her home. I started dropping Merri off a couple of mornings a week so I could concentrate on my new vocation, writing.

After having sold *Adventure in Entropia* to the provincial government, I started work on another educational story. This one was called "A Bottle of Sunshine." It featured a miniature fairy-like creature named Sunny, who represented energy from the sun. In the story, Sunny emerges from a dusty old bottle, like a genie from a lamp, when it is accidentally rubbed by sister and brother Peggy and Andy. Sunny magically transports Peggy and Andy inside the bottle to meet all the different forms of energy (an eagle for wind energy, a beaver for wood, a dinosaur for energy from oil, coal, and natural gas, and so on). On their journey, Andy and Peggy learn that all forms of energy (except nuclear) originate from the sun and that it is important to conserve. Then Sunny slips back into the bottle, and the children go forth to tell everyone to use less energy.

Eventually, I sold "A Bottle of Sunshine" to the National Film Board of Canada, which adapted it into an animated film as part of an educational package on energy. But in the fall of 1980, I was just feeling my way into the story, and I was tremendously grateful to Berny, who took off my hands an active, non-stop-talking toddler who wasn't much interested in napping.

Because Bill and I were going to be in Vancouver for only a year, we decided to take advantage of our time in the big city. We subscribed to the Vancouver Symphony Orchestra. I went to see Ballet BC, and Bill went to BC Lions and Vancouver Canucks games. We went to clubs like the Town Pump and the Railway Club to hear folk music, blues, rock, and jazz. We went to exhibits at the Vancouver Art Gallery and plays at the Vancouver Playhouse. We had never gone out so much in all our years together. We had a blast.

All that going out helped me learn my way around. I discovered parks and playgrounds and cafés. I got to know the local shopkeepers. I exchanged babysitting with new friends. I started to appreciate Vancouver as a beautiful, vibrant city.

In the fall of 1980, I got pregnant again. The baby was due in August 1981. I felt queasy but basically fine, and, besides, I didn't have time to be ill with a nearly two-year-old underfoot.

In the third week of May, when I was in my twenty-eighth week, my water broke. I went into the hospital, where I was put on vasodilan, the same medication I had been given with Merri, to try to stop the contractions. Initially it worked. And now Bill and I faced a terrible dilemma. I was going to have to stay in bed for the rest of the pregnancy, or at least for several weeks, until I stabilized. Bill had to work. What were we going to do with Merri?

"Can you take a leave of absence?" I asked Bill as he sat beside my hospital bed.

"Maybe for a little while, but not indefinitely. Not for the next twelve weeks." Bill paused. "I talked to my mom. She suggested we send Merri out to her."

"To Pennsylvania?" I said, alarmed.

"I'd fly out with her. We could leave her there as long as necessary."

"But Bill, she's only two! I don't want her to be separated from me for such a long time."

"I don't either. But what else can we do?"

We looked at each other bleakly.

In the end, nature solved the problem. After a couple of days, the baby's heartbeat, measured by a fetal monitor, started speeding up, and I developed a fever. Both were signs of a uterine infection, an extremely dangerous situation for both the baby and me. I was taken off vasodilan and put on oxytocin to induce labour. Amy Jill Schwartz was born on May 24 at twenty-eight weeks' gestation, weighing two pounds, eleven ounces. Bill later confessed that, after the birth, he cried on the shoulder of the pediatrician, a diminutive Chinese woman.

Amy was in considerably more danger than Merri had been. Although underweight, Merri had been big enough to survive with minimal support. Amy relied on technology and cutting-edge care to stay alive. She was hooked up to heart and breathing monitors, and fed intravenously (at first on donated breast milk; mine was unsuitable for a few days because I had been on antibiotics) through a tube inserted in her scalp. Every few days the nurses shaved off another square inch of hair so they could move the tube. Within a week, Amy had lost all her beautiful, thick brown hair and was bald except for a fringe around the bottom, like a little old man. Her arms and legs were as thick as Bill's thumb. Her skinny body lay in the incubator, dwarfed by even the tiniest diaper. Every time I visited her, I didn't see how such a tiny, helpless being could survive, let alone thrive. *Make it,* I whispered through the incubator. *Come on. You've got to make it.*

This was a stressful time. I went to the hospital most days, either taking Merri with me (siblings were allowed to visit twice a week) or dropping her off at Berny's and then rushing across town. Bill raced from work to the hospital. We were exhausted. Plus, I was pumping and delivering breast milk, and recovering from the birth. And we were consumed with worry. Would Amy live? Would she have permanent disabilities? How long would she be in the hospital?

No one would tell us. "So far so good," the nurses would say, "but it's too soon to know anything definitively."

Amy's progress was agonizingly slow. She'd gain an ounce, lose half an ounce, gain two, lose one. She needed a couple of blood transfusions. Because of her immature brain, she had apnea and, every so often, forgot to breathe. Bill and I were in the nursery one time when she had an apnea episode: an alarm in her monitor went off, and nurses hurried over to stimulate her to get her breathing again. It was terrifying.

But she did gain. She did grow. Her skinny limbs filled out. She graduated from being fed intravenously to being fed by gavage, through a tube down her throat, then by bottle, and finally by breast. She appeared to be healthy and alert, without any physical or mental deficits. On a rainy July afternoon, after two months in the hospital, she came home. She still wasn't due for a month.

My new friends came forward with generosity and kindness. They brought casseroles and soups. They brought baby gifts. They took Merri for a morning or an afternoon. They offered a shoulder in case I needed to cry.

I was grateful that Bill and I had been living in Vancouver when Amy was born. If we had still been in the Kootenays when I went into labour, I would have been flown to Vancouver, and I would have had to leave Merri behind. Amy had received the best of care. There was something to be said for living in the city.

Crossroads

In the summer of 1981, when Bill's one-year contract was up, the province offered him a regular full-time job as a communications officer in the Conservation and Renewable Energy Branch. This was unexpected, and it posed a dilemma.

We had planned to be in Vancouver for only a year. We wanted to return to the Kootenays to resume our lifestyle. To raise our children.

But there were strong reasons to stay.

Amy was only a few months old, still a fragile newborn. We were reasonably sure that she was healthy, but I wanted the security of doctors and hospitals nearby in case she needed medical attention.

I had finished "A Bottle of Sunshine" and sold it to the NFB. I was beginning to think seriously about writing as a career and wanted to take courses.

Then there was the perennial question of work. I couldn't go back to teaching with a two-year-old and a baby, and I had sabotaged Bill's teaching career when I pressured him not to go up north right after he earned his BC teaching certificate. Besides, there were few teaching jobs available and a downturn in the Interior economy. This job in Vancouver had benefits and a good salary.

We ran through all the familiar arguments. It's a good job. But if we don't try to find work in the Kootenays, we'll never know if it's possible. In the meantime, how would we live? What about my writing? What's best for the kids? I miss Galena Bay!

"Tell you what," Bill said, "let's give it another year or so. Maybe by then the economy'll be better in the Interior, and we'll be able to figure out how to make a living there."

"Okay." I felt terrible. But it made sense.

And, in any case, we hadn't abandoned Galena Bay. We went back whenever Bill had time off. When we pulled up the driveway, my heart leaped to see the cabin, so small and sturdy, sitting at the edge of the woods. Inside, I sniffed deeply, taking in the smell of the fir walls, the stacked firewood, the dust. I hurried to build a fire in the woodstove to take off the chill of the empty cabin, listening for the snap and crackle of the kindling, holding my hands over its warmth.

On each trip, we visited Bob Harrington, and Walter and Margaret Nelson. In answer to the question "When are you coming back?" we said, "Soon. We don't know exactly. Soon."

In discussions with Bob, I was surprised to find myself defending city life. When he railed about pollution, about the unnaturalness of so many people living so close together, about the fact that city people were disconnected from the wild world, I said, "It's not so bad. We have a little garden in the yard behind our apartment. And we don't need to use our car so much. We can walk or take the bus. So we're actually polluting less."

Bob did not look convinced.

We loved our vacations in Galena Bay. Bill played the guitar. I read and wrote. The kids played elaborate dress-up games in the living room and felt important when they carried in a stick or two of wood. They loved tromping around in the snow and digging in the resurrected sandbox.

And then, each time, we packed up the car and headed home. Home to Vancouver.

A year went by.

Another.

We stayed ... and stayed ...

In 1984, the provincial government announced a sweeping set of cutbacks. The Conservation and Renewable Energy Branch was chopped, and Bill's job disappeared.

So we came to another crossroads. Bill's layoff looked like a message: it was time to go back to the Kootenays.

Still, we hesitated.

I had started taking creative writing courses. My first trade book, *Dusty*, had been published in 1983. I applied for and, in the summer of 1984, was accepted into the master's degree program in creative writing at the University of British Columbia. I longed to go, to study writing seriously, to learn in a community of peers.

The kids had been attending preschools. In the fall of 1984, Merri was about to start kindergarten. She was a highly verbal child, and we were intrigued by the idea of enrolling her in a French Immersion program.

The economy in the Interior was still in the pits.

So we entered the familiar debate. Stay or go. Pros and cons. Work, school, money, old friends, new friends, opportunities for kids, pristine nature, risk, familiarity.

We decided to stay. Bill, filled with entrepreneurial spirit, started a company called Polestar Communications and quickly garnered contracts to do the same kind of writing, editing, and organizing on energy conservation that he had been doing for the Ministry.

We moved into family housing at the University of British Columbia, and I, terrified and elated, started grad school. Merri entered kindergarten in French Immersion. Amy attended a preschool on campus.

We continued to visit Galena Bay as often as we could. The kids loved being there. Bill and I loved being there. But more and more, Galena Bay felt like a vacation place, not like home.

After a few years, Bill argued that we should sell the land. "Let's face it, we're never going to live there again."

"But we might."

"Be realistic. There're no jobs. Merri's in school, and Amy will be soon. Where would they go to school?"

"But we can't just give up."

"It's not fair to the land. Someone should own it who will use it."

I knew Bill was right. Secretly, I felt guilty that the land was sitting idle. We weren't there for long enough stretches to grow a garden. We could no longer raise chickens or bees. When we were there, we tinkered rather than undertook real projects. But I refused to countenance giving up on our dream.

We held out for a couple more years. Finally, I agreed.

When we told Bob Harrington of our decision, he offered to buy back the twenty acres from us. "I don't want it to fall into the hands of someone who will log it or destroy it," he said.

For Bill and me, this was the perfect solution. We knew Bob cared about the land. We knew our little homestead would be preserved.

We negotiated a price, based on inflation and the improvements we had made. Over the next several visits, we packed up tools and canning supplies, burned trash, got rid of junk, gave away books and furniture.

In the summer of 1986, we loaded the car with the last of the cabin's contents. The price had been paid, the paperwork done, the title transferred.

Bill and I walked over the land. The cabin. The outhouse. The tool shed. The "Charcoal Hilton." The lower garden and the upper garden, sandbox still at its side. The woodshed. The field, with the concrete foundation of our abandoned log house. The root cellar, site of the late, great sauna. The new sauna. The view of Mounts Odin, Thor, and Freya from the clearing.

"I feel like we sold out," I said to Bill. "What about our dreams? What about changing the world?"

"Maybe there are other ways to change the world," he said.

"Maybe. But—oh, Bill, part of our moving here was to get away from it all, and now look at us, living in the city. Traffic and pollution, crowds and noise. All the things we've always hated."

"We had to make a living."

"I know, but—"

"And we had to educate our kids. Would you have wanted them to go to the one-room school in Trout Lake?"

"No," I admitted.

"I love this place," Bill said, "but in a way it was a foolish choice."

"What do you mean?"

"The isolation, the lack of electricity and telephones, the snow, the fact that there were no jobs anywhere nearby—we were never going to be able to support ourselves here."

I sighed. "It's true. All the things we love about Galena Bay meant that we were going to have to leave."

Bill paused. "Do you regret coming here?"

"No! Do you?"

"Not for one minute."

We threw our arms around one another. I wept on Bill's shoulder. Even Bill's eyes grew moist. Merri and Amy pressed near us, sensing that we were distressed but not knowing why.

We got in the car and drove away.

Every so often, over the years, I have cast my mind back. If, in 1978, I hadn't insisted on joining A Question of Balance Dance Theatre and had agreed to move up north so Bill could get a teaching job, would he have been able to establish a teaching career, enabling us to stay in the Kootenays? (Yes, but then Bill wouldn't have ended up founding our company, Polestar Communications, and having a career as a business owner and communications specialist, which probably suited him better than teaching would have.)

Or if, in 1984, when Bill got laid off from the Ministry of Energy, Mines and Petroleum Resources, we had taken our courage in our hands and moved back to the Kootenays in spite of the lack of jobs, would we have figured something out and managed to survive there? (Yes, probably, but then I wouldn't have gone to grad school and become a writer, and Merri and Amy wouldn't have been able to play ringette and softball and take dance classes and go to school in French Immersion.)

Rationalizations? Practical assessments of reality? Wishful thinking? All of those, I suppose. I know that it is fruitless to speculate, and even more useless to feel guilty. We chose. We made a good life. We have enjoyed every aspect of our lives in Vancouver.

Looking back

I didn't love everything about Galena Bay. I hated the mosquitoes. I hated every boulder we had to dig out of the lower garden. I hated working outside on cold, sleety fall days, chilled and wet, rushing to finish a project before winter set in. I hated having to haul water when our water line froze, dragging heavy buckets on a toboggan from a spring, and I didn't much like getting stung by honeybees either. I missed my family and keenly felt the loss of closeness with them.

And yet . . .

The epigraph to this book is a quote from an American soldier who volunteered to fight with the Republicans in the Spanish Civil War: "We were naïve . . . but it was the kind of naïveté the world needs."

That quote perfectly sums up Bill's and my adventure in Galena Bay. Naïve is too mild a word for what we were. We chose a rocky, forested, mosquito-ridden piece of land because it was pristine, never mind that its very pristine isolation made it impossible to stay there. We moved into the middle of bear country, and then grieved when we had to shoot some of the magnificent beasts. We placed a chicken coop at the edge of the woods and then were annoyed when hens disappeared into the jaws of martens and skunks. We took crazy risks as we tackled logging and building projects, and were incredibly lucky to have escaped with only a few injuries. Time and again, we wandered into the wilderness without compass or provisions, and were fortunate to find our way out again.

But oh, what we learned! Canning and building, growing a garden, cooking on a woodstove, splitting firewood and shakes and kindling and learning which species of wood to use for which purpose, snowshoeing and cross-country skiing, shooting a rifle, drying food, learning about ecology, backpacking, raising animals, recognizing trees and birds, learning the difference between a Swede saw and a crosscut saw and when to use each one, cleaning a chimney, replacing a mantle in a propane light, planting by the phases of the moon.

That was the least of it. Galena Bay was the cradle of Bill's and my relationship. As we developed the homestead, as we lurched from accomplishment to mistake and back again, we fell more deeply in love. We became true companions. We learned to take risks, to say, "Well, we don't know how, but we'll figure it out." We worked hard, to the point of exhaustion, and then basked in well-deserved rest. We worked side by side, and discovered that we liked it. (In fact, we have spent most of our adulthood working together. Frequently, people's reaction is, "How can you do that? I couldn't stand to work with my husband/wife/partner all day." We just shrug. We do better together than apart.) We conceived of projects and carried them through. We grew up.

And it's not as if we abandoned our values when we decided to stay in the city. After I earned my master's degree in creative writing, I started working with Bill in Polestar Communications, and almost all of our work has focused on socially positive themes: energy conservation, environmental awareness, sustainable forestry, heart health, financial literacy. Bill has spent years volunteering at the civic level. I write books for children, to make them think and feel, to give them hope.

Merri and Amy are grown now. Perhaps not surprisingly, they both inherited a strong dose of idealism. For many years, Amy was part of an anarchist collective, and now works to support and seek justice for prisoners of conscience. Merri founded a non-profit organization that teaches inner-city school kids how to grow urban gardens and to cook what they have grown. Recently, she moved back to the Kootenays, drawn by roots that were planted in childhood.

Naïveté—the kind the world needs.

Bill and I lived in Galena Bay for eight years. I look back on that time with the most profound gratitude—for the beauty of the place, for all it taught us, for the fun we had. May the place, and the land, and our homestead live on in pristine beauty, and may they inspire some new young hippie couple to stop and look, to breathe in the cedar-scented air, to take a chance.

To dream.

Acknowledgements

I would like to thank the following people:

For outstanding and sensitive editing: Jesse Marchand.

For encouraging me to write the book in the first place: Robert Harlow, late professor of Creative Writing at the University of British Columbia: "You learn how to write a book by writing it."

For reviewing the manuscript and providing invaluable feedback: William Schwartz; Merri Schwartz; Chris Petty; Aaron Rabinowitz; Morna McLeod; Heather Duff; Graham Bibby; Lori Thicke; Vivianne Ellington.

Ellen Schwartz is the author of eighteen award-winning books for children, as well as one non-fiction book for adults, a collection of profiles of women singer-songwriters. In addition to writing books, Ellen works as a corporate writer and editor and as a freelance magazine writer who has published hundreds of magazine articles. Ellen has taught creative writing classes for many years at the college and university levels. Her passions include reading, jazz dancing, baking, and hiking. Ellen and her husband now live in Burnaby, BC.